Status in Law and Morality

OXFORD LEGAL PHILOSOPHY

Series Editors
Timothy Endicott, Irit Samet, and Nicolaos Stavropoulos

Oxford Legal Philosophy publishes the best new work in philosophically oriented legal theory. It commissions and solicits monographs in all branches of the subject, including works on philosophical issues in all areas of public and private law, and in the national, transnational, and international realms; studies of the nature of law, legal institutions, and legal reasoning; treatments of problems in political morality as they bear on law; and explorations in the nature and development of legal philosophy itself. The series represents diverse traditions of thought but always with an emphasis on rigour and originality. It sets the standard in contemporary jurisprudence.

also available in the series

From a Realist Point of View
Brian Leiter

The Principle of Legality
A Moral Theory
Conor Crummey

Value and Circumstance
Justice, Consent, Equality, and Law
Timothy Macklem

Elucidating Law
Julie Dickson

The Right of Redress
Andrew S. Gold

Faces of Inequality
A Theory of Wrongful Discrimination
Sophia Moreau

Coercion and the Nature of Law
Kenneth Einar Himma

Property Rights
A Re-Examination
J. E. Penner

A Theory of Legal Personhood
Visa AJ Kurki

Imposing Risk
A Normative Framework
John Oberdiek

Law and Morality at War
Adil Ahmad Haque

Ignorance of Law
A Philosophical Inquiry
Douglas Husak

Reason and Restitution
A Theory of Unjust Enrichment
Charlie Webb

Status in Law and Morality

GEORGE LETSAS
Professor of the Philosophy of the Law, University College London, UK

OXFORD
UNIVERSITY PRESS

OXFORD
UNIVERSITY PRESS

Great Clarendon Street, Oxford, OX2 6DP,
United Kingdom

Oxford University Press is a department of the University of Oxford.
It furthers the University's objective of excellence in research, scholarship,
and education by publishing worldwide. Oxford is a registered trade mark of
Oxford University Press in the UK and in certain other countries.

Published in the United States of America by Oxford University Press
198 Madison Avenue, New York, NY 10016, United States of America.

British Library Cataloguing in Publication Data
Data available

Library of Congress Control Number: 2026934380

ISBN 9780198936695

DOI: 10.1093/9780198936725.001.0001

Printed and bound by
CPI Group (UK) Ltd., Croydon, CR0 4YY

MIX
Paper | Supporting
responsible forestry
FSC® C013604
FSC
www.fsc.org

The manufacturer's authorized representative in the EU for product safety is
Oxford University Press España S.A. of Parque Empresarial San Fernando de Henares,
Avenida de Castilla, 2 – 28830 Madrid (www.oup.es/en or product.safety@oup.com).
OUP España S.A. also acts as importer into Spain of products made by the manufacturer.

To Virginia, Ross, and Nina

Series Editors' Preface

Status can open doors for you. Equally, it can exclude you from things you want or to which you aspire. Status in that sense is a comparative notion. It turns on what one gets relative to others. It designates one's place in the pecking order, and can be associated with esteem, privilege, advantage, or inclusion, as much as with indifference, contempt, disadvantage, or exclusion.

Sorting people according to status so understood seems morally objectionable. It assigns persons their social rank, fixes one's place in a social hierarchy, and entrenches relations of inferiority. We may illustrate this kind of objectionable sorting with examples from medieval Europe or the caste systems that persist in many parts of the world. But milder or at least less egregious versions of this social arrangement can be seen all around us today. Perhaps they always will be, the only question being whether their toxic aspects can be mitigated.

In this intriguing, wholly original study, George Letsas shows that there is another sense of status, role status, where asymmetries of power and authority need not entail objectionable inferiority. Role status is familiar to lawyers. It refers to a set of rights and responsibilities that attach to persons in virtue of certain distinctive, morally significant circumstances or relations, such as being a refugee, a parent, or an employee. These rights and responsibilities inhere in relations where at least one party is in a position of vulnerability. Status so understood assigns to the stronger party role obligations owed to the weaker, and to the weaker rights against the stronger.

Once a subject of intense philosophical interest, status so understood came to be neglected in moral theory. We moved on, thought Henry Maine, from status to contract. Our rights and responsibilities in our interactions with others are now a matter of contingent free agreement. Not so, says Letsas. Rights and duties that derive from parties' moral status may not be negotiated away. Such rights and duties limit and partly shape the parties' relations, to protect the weaker ones and maintain the parties' standing as moral equals.

Letsas finds materials for his account in a rich legal and philosophical tradition, ranging from Roman law to the work of Samuel von Pufendorf, Immanuel Kant, Jeremy Bentham, and F.H. Bradley, through to contemporary moral philosophers.

The book brings theoretical novelty and philosophical sophistication to a neglected, underexplored topic of great moral and legal importance.

Timothy Endicott
Irit Samet
Nicolaos Stavropoulos

Acknowledgements

The idea for this book came about in a somewhat serendipitous way in early 2020, just as the pandemic was unfolding. I heard that someone was assigned a status without having any of its functions and began to reflect on what, if anything, might be morally wrong with that. By that time, I was already working on a paper on the idea of role obligations, seeking to provide a deontological defence of it, as a neglected but significant domain of morality. The initial trigger for my interest in role obligations was Ronald Dworkin's claim that legal obligation is associative or one 'of role'. After some research on status, I stumbled across John Austin's bizarre claim that status is the most difficult problem in jurisprudence. This took me to Bentham, then Kant, and eventually Pufendorf. Slowly, I started to discover the long philosophical pedigree of the idea of status and its close connection to that of obligations of role. It felt like everything clicked and a book-length project on a general theory of status was appropriate.

Maintaining my enthusiasm for the project during the crazy times of the lockdowns, let alone making a bit of progress, was not easy. But many people supported me. Scott Shapiro was so keen to keep himself busy during the lockdowns that, on top of doing his legendary podcasts, he generously offered to read a draft. During a three-hour Zoom call, he gave me incredible feedback, shared my enthusiasm for the project, and strongly encouraged me to pursue it. I might well had given up without his encouragement. In 2021, I presented a draft, online, at the Toronto Legal Theory workshop. Chris Essert, Arthur Ripstein, Malcolm Thorburn, and Sabine Tsuruda gave me enormously helpful comments that were pivotal in shaping the main argument of the book. I cannot thank Arthur Ripstein enough for subsequently making time to discuss and correspond on status in the last few years. I know that, just by disagreeing with his account of status, I reduce the chances of getting it right to a tiny percentage.

Leslie Green and Timothy Endicott, the series editors for legal philosophy since I approached OUP and up until the time when I signed the contract, were extremely supportive, making suggestions and helping me to navigate the reviewing process. I am deeply grateful to both. This book aside, they have taken great care of the field of legal philosophy, making sure it's both 'philosophy' and 'legal'. I have learned so much from their work and our interactions over the years. I would also like to thank the anonymous reviewers for the press, for all the detailed comments and suggestions. They were so right about what the focus of the book should be and what to avoid. I would also like to thank OUP's Brian Stone for handling everything so expertly, Rizwaan Ahmad Mirza for his patience until submission, and Jacqueline Ridberg Larabee for her efficient and professional handling of production.

Conversations with Massimo Renzo have, as always, been invaluable. He has given me comments, acted as a respondent, and taken long walks, and coffees, with me to discuss ideas in this book. I do not know anyone else who is so keen to discuss other people's work at such a great length and detail. Seana Shiffrin and Jonathan Wolff made time in their busy schedules to read the chapter on role obligations and send me written comments, helping me to see mistakes and revise it substantially. That chapter has also benefited substantially from an extensive written response by Tom Adams, which is forthcoming in a volume on interpretivism. This was all thanks to Nicos Stavropoulos, who organised a series of online seminars on interpretivism during the lockdowns that culminated in a major conference at Magdalen College, Oxford in summer 2024. During these sessions I received very helpful feedback from Scott Hershovitz, Dimitris Kyritsis, Larry Sager, and Laura Valentini, among many others. Nicos's influence on my work over the years has been enormous. He has been a mentor, a teacher, a friend, and a collaborator. His insistence on clinical precision to philosophical questions is unmatched and I can never come close to it, no matter how hard I try.

Niko Kolodny was very generous with his time during the UCL workshop on his book *The Pecking Order*. It is a book I truly admire and, as they say, I wish I had written (and were able to write). I am very grateful to him for engaging with my theory of status, as a different way to look at social equality. Though the main ideas in this book were formed before I read his book, his account became a source of inspiration and, at a fundamental level, there is little with which I disagree. His emphasis on social hierarchy, as a way to understand equality, is a very important turn in political philosophy.

I have been fortunate to have amazing colleagues at UCL from whom I constantly learn. Jeff King acted as a respondent, giving me as always very thoughtful and wise feedback, when I presented Chapter 8 at the UCL Dworkin colloquium. Ian Williams, who I hope will never read the chapter on Roman law, gave me great comments on the non-historical Chapters 4 and 5, before moving to Oxford. Philip Schofield guided me through Bentham's work and pointed me in the right direction. Many other colleagues read drafts and gave comments. Isra Black, Robin Jacob, Emily McTernan, Jonathan Montgomery, and Philippe Sands provided feedback on Chapter 8, saving me from many errors. Jeff Howard, Saladin Meckled-Garcia, and Robert Simpson, all gave me incredibly helpful feedback on the very first draft of Chapter 7, on role obligations. My former PhD students, Conor Crummey and Jeevan Hariharan, read various chapters and sent me fantastic comments. I am very grateful to them for doing so—hopefully out of interest, not a sense of obligation. I am also grateful to my fantastic LLM students on whom I did impose the obligation to read parts of the book and who engaged with it in a critical way. Finally, I am deeply grateful to the UCL Faculty of Laws and the successive Deans and Vice-Deans who do their best to protect our research time and cultivate a true intellectual community. Research, one must not forget, is not a purely individual endeavour.

This is the first monograph I publish since Ronald Dworkin died in 2013. My first book, on human rights, was based on my doctoral thesis, which was supervised by Stephen Guest and Ronald Dworkin at UCL. My formative years at UCL, first as PhD student then as lecturer, were shaped fundamentally by Ronnie's towering presence, especially the colloquium he ran with Jonathan Wolff. His passing left a profound sense of intellectual loss in me, and I am sure I am not the only one who feels it. Even though I did not set out to defend any of Dworkin's specific claims, this book has his philosophical influence all over it. I dread to think what he would say about the book's argument. He would have drawn a distinction I missed, no doubt. But as his student, I hope he would have been proud of the effort.

I have presented parts of the book on several occasions, though perhaps not enough to save me from all mistakes or inaccuracies. I would like to thank audiences at the Toronto Legal Theory Workshop (2021), the University of Athens Legal Philosophy Workshop (2022), the Oxford Jurisprudence Discussion Group (2023), the UCL Staff Seminar Series (2023), the UCL Ronald Dworkin Colloquium (2024), the UCL workshop on Niko Kolodny's *The Pecking Order* (2024), the King's College London KJuris Seminars (2025), the Queen's Colloquium in Legal and Political Philosophy (2025), and the LSE Private Law Theory Discussion Group (2025). Several colleagues read drafts, made criticisms and suggestions at seminars, or directed me to literature of which I was unaware. I would like to thank in particular Scott Altman, Ruth Chang, Robin Dembroff, David Enoch, Scott Hershovitz, Nicola Lacey, George Pavlakos, Andrea Sangiovanni, Scott Shapiro, Gregg Strauss, Kevin Toh, Andreas Vasileiou, Philippos Vassiloyannis, Emmanuel Voyiakis, Gregoire Webber, Fred Wilmot-Smith, and Lorenzo Zucca. An earlier version of parts of Chapters 4, 5, and 6 appeared in 'Offences Against Status' in the *Oxford Journal of Legal Studies* (2023).

While writing this book, several close friends were subjected to long conversations about status, for which I can only apologise. Nicholas Hatzis was coerced into reading the penultimate version of the introductory chapter and helped me to improve it. Cecile Laborde, whose productivity I cannot ever match, transferred some of her intellectual energy to me, during long discussions about status. Jo Wolff, who once taught me political philosophy, now hears me talk about legal status showing way more interest than he ever did in general jurisprudence (admittedly a low bar among political philosophers). Jo strongly encouraged me to pursue this project and he has been enormously supportive throughout my career (and throughout the Spurs' ups and downs). Kostas Koukouzelis gave me a tutorial (one of many) on Kant, in Mani of all places, and helped me to see better the links with Pufendorf. Nicos Alivizatos, Konstantinos Papageorgiou, and Pavlos Sourlas, my university of Athens mentors, have always been keen to discuss what I am working on, even when I fail to explain it properly. Amalia, David, Dimitris, Douglas, Emmanuel, Ilias, Jackie, Joanna, Katerina, Kostas, Manos, Nafsika, Philip, Panos, Reni, Shelley, and Spyros showed (or feigned) interest in this book, and I hope they will enjoy reading it.

Writing this book was nowhere near as hard as it might otherwise have been, thanks to the support of friends and family. I would like to thank especially Tom Poole and Devika Hovell, whose generosity—especially during the pandemic—was greater than I could ever repay. I am convinced they are time travellers from different eras, having absorbed the best of human culture and virtue. Nicholas Hatzis has always listened patiently to whatever happens to occupy my mind (and soul) and provided wise counselling, free of charge. Dimitris Kyritsis has been a fellow traveller for my whole adult life, and, in both philosophy and life, he always knows just what to say.

Unsurprisingly, the greatest gratitude is to one's nearest and dearest; to my parents, who, tactically, kept asking me 'have you finished your book yet?', succeeding in their intention; to Alexandra, who advised expertly on the cover; and, of course, to Virginia Mantouvalou. Virginia read drafts and explained to me how to improve them. She spotted mistakes, passages of unintended pompousness, and obscure or clumsy formulations. She encouraged me and set me deadlines, knowing my flaws. And she helped me find long stretches of time in summer 2025 to bring this book to completion. Without their love and support, there is nothing that I could ever accomplish. I dedicate this book to Virginia, Ross, and Nina.

Contents

1
WHY STATUS?

1.1 Introduction

In the film *Bicycle Thieves*,[1] we meet Antonio, an unemployed father of two young children in post-War Italy, waiting outside an employment agency. He is badly in need of a job, in conditions of mass unemployment and economic deprivation. Antonio cannot believe his luck when he is offered a job as a poster-hanger. But there is a catch; he must have his own bicycle. After pawning the last remaining items of family silver to get one, he is ready for his first day at work. We find him at home full of excitement, putting on his work uniform and cap. 'Let me see', says his wife. Antonio stands tall in front of her, shoulders back, head held high. 'Wow!', she exclaims. 'Handsome?', Antonio asks her with aplomb and a huge smile on his face. 'You look like a police officer!', his wife replies proudly. Antonio sneaks a quick peak at the mirror, adjusting his cap, before he heads out of the house for his first day at work. This is pretty much the last time we see Antonio happy in the film. After having his bicycle stolen, without which he cannot keep his job, he ends up trying to steal someone else's bicycle in an out-of-character act of utter despair. He gets stopped by an angry crowd of eyewitnesses who abuse and humiliate him. His son is watching in distress, grabbing onto his father's worn-out jacket. 'You should be ashamed', someone scolds Antonio, 'setting such an example for your son'.

The story of Antonio is a story of many statuses: the status of being a parent, responsible for providing for his young children; the status of an employee, whose job description includes the requirement to have a bicycle and without which he faces dismissal by his employer. Like contemporary food-delivery platforms, Antonio's employer externalised the cost of running their business by expecting him to use his own vehicle. But it is also the story of status in a different sense: Antonio's pride and social esteem. The low status, perhaps humiliation, he feels as a working-class menial worker, waiting endlessly outside the unemployment office, while middle-class Italians walk by with their nice suits; and the pride he feels when he gets a job and, as a responsible father, he can finally provide for his family. When all goes terribly wrong for him, Antonio loses not only his job but also his social esteem and good standing in society. He is now a delinquent who committed a crime in front of his own son; he faces the prospect of arrest and imprisonment. In a tragic interplay

[1] Vittorio De Sica, *Ladri Di Biciclette* (1948).

Status in Law and Morality. George Letsas, Oxford University Press. © George Letsas 2026.
DOI: 10.1093/9780198936725.003.0001

of his various statuses, he fails at multiple levels: as an employee, as a citizen, and as a father.

This book seeks to provide a philosophical account of status, as it figures in Antonio's story. In this first chapter, I give an overview of the book and explain the main motivations for writing it. Status is a broad concept, whose boundaries are not clearly defined. If a colleague asks for an update on my status, they want to know something about my situation, relative to some implied context. Am I running late for our meeting? Have I recovered from my illness? Will I be able to mark those essays in time? In a non-technical sense, this Latin word means the condition in which a person, or an object, is. Other synonyms include state, situation, or circumstances. This simple definition would make the concept a rather banal object of philosophical inquiry and certainly not one that I would want to undertake here. Philosophical interest on status has, instead, focused on two narrower senses and it is the interplay between these two concepts that interests me here.

The first is the familiar sense of social status, or what I shall call *rank-status*. This typically refers to the position one holds relative to others within a system of social hierarchy, where persons are ranked comparatively. Such systems were formally embedded in ancient and medieval societies and can still be found in certain parts of the world, such as the caste system in India. Broadly conceived, social status refers to the condition in which people find themselves, relative to others, with respect to important interests such as wealth, occupation, or education. Crucially, the position one occupies with respect to these interests is epistemically accessible to others and one knows, roughly, where everyone stands. This, in turn, affects how one is esteemed by society. High status invites deference and admiration; low status invites indifference, even contempt, as in the tragic end of Antonio's story. This notion of status, in other words, has a social meaning. My red blood cell count is most likely different to yours and we cannot know whose is better unless we volunteer the relevant information. And any comparative ranking here, even if it could be made accessible, would change little in the way others treat us. Obviously, an ideal red blood cell count is not the sort of thing that attracts societal esteem, though of course good health and a healthy appearance might. Contrast this to holding a university degree. Not only is it difficult to hide which university one has graduated from (e.g. in job applications), but also there are formal and informal rankings of universities that make a difference to how one is treated by others. A degree from a prestigious university opens doors that an ideal red blood cell count does not.

In pre-modern times, individuals were born into rigid social statuses, which they often retained for life, unable to escape their confines. How such social hierarchies are produced and maintained has been the subject of philosophical inquiry at least since Karl Marx's[2] class-based analysis and has recently attracted renewed

[2] Karl Marx, *Capital*, Vol. 1 (London: Penguin Classics, 2004).

interest among philosophers.[3] Contemporary egalitarians view social hierarchies with outright scepticism, even when they are less rigid and not imposed institutionally. But the precise conditions under which our circumstances place us in a social hierarchy, and when such a hierarchy is problematic, are not easy to ascertain. Some social hierarchies seem unproblematic, and merit-based ones are a core case. Nobel Prize winners enjoy a higher social status than other academics. They are ranked higher. Thanks to the prize, they will get more publicity, more invitations to speak, more opportunities to access grants and so on. It is less clear to me, however, that other social statuses, such as being awarded a knighthood by the UK government are acceptable (I will argue later that they are not).

This first sense of status, rank-status, is familiar and has a non-technical meaning. We all roughly know what it means, and we have experienced it ourselves. We know what it means to say that one has married above or below their station, or that one has climbed up or down the social ladder. But there is a second sense of status, what I will call *role-status*, which forms the focus of this book. The sense is familiar from law, which uses it extensively to describe the legal position of a person, such as an employee, a refugee, or a minor. It is used to refer to a distinct set of rights, duties, powers, and so on, attached to a class of persons compared to the rest of us. If I possess the legal status of a refugee, it means that I have the right not to be returned to my country of origin and the right to seek asylum in other countries. It also means that others who lack this status, such as economic migrants, do not enjoy this set of rights.

But it is not just law that uses status to refer to a role that comes with rights and responsibilities. We use it more widely. In virtue of his status as a parent, Antonio is responsible for the well-being of his children and has a duty to raise them by instilling the right values and by setting a good example, a status in which he ends up failing badly. Just by using the term 'status' here one understands that we are making a normative point about Antonio's role obligations as a parent. In its most abstract formulation, role-status concerns what philosophers call the normative profile of a person. It is used to convey information about a distinct subset of rights, duties, powers, and the like[4] that a person who holds a certain role possesses. Status is something one holds or possesses, rather than something that one can exercise (as rights are) or fulfil (as duties are). Though such normative positions flow from one's status, status is not the same as those positions. This indicates that role-status performs a special function in our moral practices.

[3] See Niko Kolodny, *The Pecking Order: Social Hierarchy as a Philosophical Problem* (Cambridge: Harvard University Press, 2023).

[4] In philosophical parlance, a normative profile may include several other categories such as immunities, privileges, capacities, and permissions. Though status need not refer to all of them, it is used to denote more than a single token within each category (e.g. a single right). Typically, it cuts across categories, capturing for instance both rights and duties.

These two notions of status, role and rank, are the subject matter of this book. Here is a first approximation:

> **Rank-status**: the position one holds within a ranking scheme of a given society, where a person's esteem is ranked comparatively to that of others.

> **Role-status**: the position one holds within a social interaction between two parties in virtue of which one has a set of rights and duties.

I aim to show that, though they bear many things in common, these two notions should be distinguished. And I shall argue that role-status is the more fundamental idea, one that has been neglected and that should be socially and legally recognised, more than it currently is. But why should anyone care?

Lawyers should, for a start. John Austin, UCL's[5] first professor of jurisprudence, once said that 'to determine precisely what a status is, is in my opinion the most difficult problem in the whole science of jurisprudence'.[6] Law uses status, but not ubiquitously. Pedestrians have legal rights and duties; they have the right not to be run over by motorists and the duty to use designated crossings. But being a pedestrian, unlike being an employee, is not a legal status. Why does law sometimes present rights and duties in terms of status and sometimes it doesn't? Austin, like many other jurists, was genuinely perplexed by this problem, finding no solution. A couple of decades later, in 1861, Sir Henry Maine, Oxford's first professor of Jurisprudence, defined a status as incapacities imposed on people by law without their will, and put forward the thesis that 'the movement of the progressive societies has hitherto been a movement from Status to Contract'.[7] His claim became hugely influential and the subject of some scathing criticism.[8] But his thesis only muddled the jurisprudential waters. In fact, Maine and Austin are largely responsible for the decline of status as a moral idea, which was at the forefront of moral and legal philosophy throughout the seventeenth and eighteenth century.

Though neglected as a jurisprudential problem in the second part of the twentieth century, status has been making a slow comeback recently. Jeremy Waldron remarks that 'the idea of status is an underexplored normative category, both in law and in morality. It used to be spoken of in law much more than it is now . . . more work is evidently needed'.[9] Other scholars complain that a general theory of the continuous salience of status in the Anglo-American legal theory is 'rare' to see.[10]

[5] Then known as the London University.

[6] John Austin, *Lectures in Jurisprudence: Or The Philosophy of Positive Law* (New York: Henry Holt, 1875), p. 355. Status is not even a topic in general jurisprudence these days, let alone its most difficult problem.

[7] Henry Sumner Maine, *Ancient Law* (Oxford: Oxford University Press, 1861), p. 170.

[8] Roscoe Pound, *Interpretations of Legal History* (New York: Macmillan, 1923), p. 62ff.

[9] Jeremy Waldron, *Dignity, Rank and Rights* (Oxford: Oxford University Press, 2012), p. 13.

[10] As remarked by Timothy Lubin, in 'Status in Ancient and Medieval Law: Introduction' 62(2) *American Journal of Legal History* (2023), pp. 61–65.

But moral philosophers too should care about status. They once did very much. Samuel von Pufendorf (1632–1694) called status 'a moral entity' and a 'field for moral persons to exist in'.[11] And he did not just mean our status as humans. He also meant person-specific statuses, such as being a parent, a citizen, or an employee. About a century later, Kant and Bentham, the lead representatives of the two main moral traditions (deontology and consequentialism), both identified status as a distinct category of rights and wrongs. And towards the end of the nineteenth century, a lexical cognate of status, the term *station*, was used by the British idealists to articulate a once influential moral view, namely that one's rights and duties are fully determined by social norms. 'We have found ourselves', F. H. Bradley wrote, 'when we have found our station and its duties'.[12] More recently, Arthur Ripstein[13] included status as the third main category of individual ('acquired') rights, alongside property and contract. These moral philosophers do not agree on what status, as a moral idea, captures, but they all agree that it is an important category of moral rights and wrongs.

Evidently, sociologists too care about status. There is a long tradition in sociology of using the concept of a role to study important social phenomena. Unlike the classical sociologists of the nineteenth century, American sociologists of the twentieth century tended to focus on micro-level inquiries and situational interactions between persons. Erving Goffman made the dramaturgical metaphor of a role central to his analysis.[14] And his work has recently attracted the interest of moral philosophers,[15] deservedly so. But when the anthropologist Ralph Linton first introduced the concept of role to sociology, he noted that 'there are no roles without statuses and no statuses without roles' and that 'role and status are quite inseparable, and the distinction between them is of only academic interest'.[16] Though later sociologists use the term status to refer only to rank-status,[17] the great British sociologist T. H. Marshall was critical of this trend, insisting that status 'has no direct or necessary reference to position on a scale or in a hierarchy. It embraces all relationships, not only those of superiority and inferiority'.[18]

Last, but not least, ordinary people too care about status and not just about rank-status. The rise of large digital platforms, such as Uber and Deliveroo, which mediate between service providers and consumers, has raised concerns about the

[11] Samuel Pufendorf, *Of the Law of Nature and Nations* (Oxford, 1703), Book I, chapter I, § IX. Unless otherwise indicated, references are to the 1703 English translation, published by L. Liechfied in Oxford.

[12] F. H. Bradley, *Ethical Studies* (Oxford: Clarendon Press, 1988).

[13] Arthur Ripstein, *Force and Freedom* (Cambridge: Harvard University Press, 2009).

[14] Erving Goffman, *The Presentation of Self in Everyday Life* (Penguin Books, 1959).

[15] Sam Berstler, *The Philosophy of Erving Goffman* (manuscript on file with author). Thomas Nagel cites Goffman in his influential article: Thomas Nagel, 'Concealment and Exposure', 27(1) *Philosophy & Public Affairs* (1998), pp. 3–30.

[16] Ralph Linton, *The Study of Man: An Introduction* (New York: D. Appleton Century, 1936), p. 114.

[17] See recently, Cecilia Ridgway, *Status: Why Is It Everywhere? Why Does It Matter* (New York: Russell Sage Foundation, 2019).

[18] T. H. Marshall, *Class, Citizenship and Social Development* (New York: Doubleday, 1964), p. 207.

casualisation of work and the lowering of employment standards. Workers who provide services through these platforms have taken legal action against the multinational corporations that own them, demanding the status of an employee. They demand the package of protective rights that law grants employees, such as annual leave and minimum wage. Here, unlike with rank-status, the demand for status is considered a laudable goal from the perspective of social justice. It is not higher societal esteem that Uber drivers demand, but a set of protective rights attached to the legal status of an employee. This demand has a clear moral dimension.

So, lawyers, philosophers, sociologists, and ordinary citizens have turned to status to capture something significant about our social lives. But what exactly? And why has it proved elusive, giving rise to theoretical disagreements and bitter disputes? This book takes up this challenge.

1.2 The Main Argument

The theoretical threads of status are loose, cutting across many disciplines, but they nevertheless make for a rich tapestry that I will seek to weave in this book. My primary aim is to offer a philosophical account of status as a moral idea.

Some elements of the concept of status are abstract and relatively beyond dispute. First, status has a social dimension; it is part of our social lives, of the way we relate and interact with one another. Second, it is *person*-specific: people have different statuses. I am a father, a professor, an employee of UCL, a mortgagee, and a citizen of Greece and the UK—to mention a few. Your list of statuses will be different to mine. Third, status implies some kind of hierarchy or asymmetry. This is obviously the case with social status, or what I call *rank*-status: there is low and high social status and each one of us occupies a point on this spectrum. But asymmetries also exist in *role*-statuses: As an employee, I am obviously less powerful than my employer, but as a father I am more powerful than my children (most of the time). Finally, status has something to do with social esteem, or social recognition. Having a status is not an esoteric attitude, like having remorse or taking pride. One is recognised by others *for* some position or condition one holds. It could be a condition of being worthy of esteem, as in the case of a Nobel Prize. Or it could be a relation one has, such as being a member of a political community, as in the case of citizenship.

As we shall see, different theorists unpack these abstract conceptual points differently. In a nutshell, my own theory—what I call *role*-status—is this: status is an asymmetrical social relation between two parties, one of which (the weaker party) suffers from dependencies or vulnerabilities vis-à-vis the other (the stronger party). This asymmetry triggers distinct moral requirements: first, duties to balance the asymmetry of the social relation through vesting both parties with institutional rights and duties; and second, duties to recognise socially and legally the asymmetrical position of the two parties and to project the value of equality into the relation.

This is a mouthful, I know, and very abstract. More explanation will be given in due course. For now, let me give a brief list of some of the statuses that count as true ones, according to the theory I put forward here: employer/employee, parent/child, citizen/official, doctor/patient, teacher/student, and tenant/landlord. These are social relations that most of us will enter, on either side of them, at some point in our lives, and stay in them for significant periods. They are not episodic interactions. They concern, moreover, certain enduring and non-contingent aspects of our ethical lives: work, family, politics, health, education, and housing. And they are social relations that are asymmetrical: employees, children, citizens, patients, students, tenants are vulnerable or dependent vis-à-vis the other party in the relation: employers, parents, officials, doctors, teachers, and landlords. When one holds one of these statuses, one acquires a set of rights and duties towards the other party, and sometimes towards third parties too. And these are rights and duties we must assign to the parties, through social and legal recognition, *qua* status-holders. A person is entitled to this set of rights and duties *in virtue of* being an employee, citizen, or tenant. Modern law does well to single out employees and citizens as a having a distinct legal status,[19] but less so when it comes to tenants, students, or patients.

But why do these social relations deserve special moral attention? As is common in philosophy, different thinkers get interested in the same idea in roughly the same period and come at it from different angles. In the last couple of decades, the literature on relational egalitarianism, and the revival of the republican tradition have shifted the attention to the question of how we treat each other socially. Philip Pettit has aptly called this the eyeball test:[20] how can we be sure that we look at each other in the eyes in our social interactions? This literature, and the concepts of domination and oppression developed therein, have been very influential, and inspired new ways of doing political philosophy. However, I am not relying on it here to explain why certain social relations are significant from the point of view of social equality. Instead, I draw inspiration from law and the work of Samuel von Pufendorf. The classical approach to status, as found in Roman law and in seventeenth- and eighteenth-century moral philosophy, provides a unique insight into social equality. We might call it 'deontology with a social face'.

The argument I put forward in this book is this: role-statuses pose a distinct social threat to our standing as moral equals. These are interactions in which the weaker party suffers from serious and widely known dependencies or

[19] It is worth noting that before the rise of international human rights, and their effect on domestic law, the older term used for the fundamental individual rights one has against one's government was *civil liberties*.

[20] Philip Pettit, *Just Freedom: A Moral Compass for a Complex World* (New York: W. W. Norton, 2014), p. 16.

vulnerabilities. But they also relate to enduring and significant relations in people's lives, which impact certain objective aspects of our well-being. As a result, two distinct risks emerge: first, that the stronger party will interpret their position as one of superiority and treat the weaker party as inferior, seeking to abuse their position and commit downstream wrongs; second, that the weaker party will internalise the belief that they are inferior and accept unequal terms of social cooperation.

Consider the first risk. We know that the stronger party in these relations is typically inclined to abuse their position and commit several wrongs that may also be committed episodically, outside a relation: they might treat the weaker party unfairly; they might violate their privacy or free speech; they might violate their right to bodily integrity. These wrongs, and the likelihood that they may be committed, differs from one status to another. Employees and tenants face different risks compared to patients and students. This is because each relation exhibits different vulnerabilities and dependencies. Status is not unified by some specific right, such as the right to privacy or bodily integrity, that is found in all relations, nor by the same dependency or vulnerability. It is unified by the fact that the risk of wrongdoing is endemic in these relations because the stronger party tends to exploit the weakness and vulnerability of the weaker party and act as socially superior. The right that unifies status is the more abstract right to equal standing in our social relations.

Within each of these relations a set of prophylactic legal rights and duties is morally required, to reduce the likelihood of wrongdoing and balance the relation. Legal status, understood as a set of protective rights and duties, is a way to prevent wrongdoing that we know is endemic in these relations. For example, employees have a right to form and join trade unions; patients have a right to be informed fully of their medical condition and all available treatments; teachers and doctors have a duty not to engage in romantic relationships with their students and patients accordingly. Status, as a moral idea, justifies a set of legal rights and duties that make it less likely that downstream moral wrongs will occur. Crucially, it is not as if law can ignore status relations: if law says nothing about status, it will simply permit the stronger party to exploit the weaker party, turning a blind eye to its asymmetry. Status therefore is not only an inherently moral idea; because of its relational nature, it is an inherently legal idea too. Law cannot but take sides, either allowing the asymmetry to produce its effects, or balancing it.

To be sure, legal rights and duties could be assigned to weaker parties without recognising any status. This is where the second risk comes in. If the moral concern raised by these asymmetrical relations was simply instrumental, to prevent downstream wrongdoing, we would be unable to explain why law recognises status. Many rights and duties are of this instrumental character without being status-based. For example, contractual parties in certain types of contracts of sale must use specific formalities if the transaction is to be legally valid. The point of such formalities is to prevent fraud. But the parties to such contracts do not hold any status. These formalities are not duties they have in virtue of being buyers and sellers. When someone holds one of these legal statuses, it is seen as normatively grounding the relevant set of rights and duties; hence the familiar locution that one has rights and duties *qua* an employee, or a citizen. We use status when we appeal to it as the ground of a set of rights and duties. But why do we do so?

Status has an expressive, non-instrumental, dimension. The risk that the weaker party faces in these asymmetrical interactions is not just that of being the victim of wrongdoing, in the way one risks being the victim of street crime. We can do all kinds of things to prevent street crime. Recognising the pedestrian as a status, as the holder of rights and obligations is not one of them. The argument I make for the non-instrumental dimension of status is based on people's inherent worth and how it serves as the basis of self-esteem within certain relations. This second risk that asymmetrical relations pose is the risk of being treated by the stronger party—routinely, and not just episodically—as socially inferior and, as a result, of endorsing this inferiority.

Consider some typical attitudes: 'I am your boss, and you work for me, so shut up'; 'I am your landlord, and I can throw you out any time I want, if you carry on being demanding about repairs'; 'I am a police officer, and I can arrest you, if I don't like your tone'. These attitudes are familiar. They need not always result in downstream wrongdoing. The boss might not unfairly dismiss the employee for speaking up. The landlord might not evict the tenant whose lifestyle they disapprove. The police officer might not drag the citizen to the police station just to teach them a lesson. And yet simply by being treated routinely as socially inferior, the weaker party is likely to internalise the belief that they are socially inferior. They will believe that they are below, and the other party is above, and therefore hold fewer moral rights within the relation. They will endorse a social hierarchy.

This might not seem like such a terrible thing, at first. I argue, however, that it is in itself a moral wrong, independently of any downstream injustices. By believing that one is inferior to another, with whom one has social relation, one automatically loses self-respect—that is, the belief in one's inherent worth. For one's inherent worth is not a matter of degree. We all have the same inherent worth and nobody has more than others. By believing that one has less worth than another person, one fails to place value on one's inherent worth. This is a moral mistake, of course, but it has a devastating consequence. By losing one's self-respect within a social relation, one will not insist on equal terms of cooperation with the other party. This is because only people with self-esteem will insist on equal terms of social cooperation. Only people with self-esteem will seek to stand on their rights and demand treatment as an equal. By losing one's self-esteem, one loses this vital moral defence.

Self-esteem (i.e. the belief in one's inherent moral worth) is a vital moral defence against social threats to our equal standing. This is an idea I find in Pufendorf, who—anticipating Kant's argument—stresses that free will is the only thing that is 'truly one's own', and the only basis for self-esteem. Neither intelligence, nor beauty, nor wealth are things for which we have reasons to esteem ourselves. Only our ability to act for reasons, using our free will, is a ground of self-esteem. And free will is something we all have, grounding our natural status as equals. Yet self-esteem is something we can lose, in the sense that we may not actively place worth on ourselves when we enter social relations, even though it is inherent in us. And we might lose it precisely because the other party treats us as inferior in that relation.

So how can status help to protect our self-respect and build this moral defence? I argue that it does so through social and legal recognition of status, as a set of rights and duties attached to a role. There is a strong normative connection between the morality of status and its legal recognition. This recognition serves three important functions. First, it shields the weaker-party's self-respect: it tells them that their vulnerability or weakness is not a ground of inferiority. They possess moral rights, grounded on the value of equality, whose aim is to balance the relation. It tells both parties: 'though one of you is vulnerable or dependent on the other, you are still each other's equals'. Though there is asymmetry in the relation, there is no social hierarchy.

Second, social and legal recognition of status gives moral notice to the parties that their relation is not purely contractual: each status comes with a set of stringent moral rights and duties that cannot be set aside merely because the parties agree to it. This is of crucial significance especially for status relations that parties enter voluntarily, through contract. It helps to prevent the stronger party from seeking to impose and rely on unfair terms and conditions. Even if the weaker party accepts these terms contractually, they are morally invalid, superseded by status. And they should be legally invalid too. Employees cannot contract out of the right to join trade unions. Tenants cannot contract out of the right not to be evicted at a short notice. Patients cannot contract out of the right to be informed about their medical condition.

Finally, the third function relates to the dynamic character of the legal recognition of status. New ways routinely emerge in which the stronger party can abuse their position and commit downstream wrongs against the weaker party. For example, employers can use new technology to monitor employees and violate their privacy. The status of an employee, as a ground of rights, serves as an abstract normative standard which the weaker party can use to identify new threats to their vulnerable position and tackle them. Precisely because status serves to project the value of equality within social relations, it is a dynamic standard, operating as an interpretive concept.[21]

What kind of normative theory am I putting forward? Within a deontological framework, moral rights and duties cannot be grounded on gradual properties that

[21] This is Dworkin's term for concepts that pick out moral values and are subject to substantive disagreement. See Ronald Dworkin, *Law's Empire* (Cambridge: Belknap Press, 1986); Ronald Dworkin, *Justice for Hedgehogs* (Cambridge: Harvard University Press, 2013).

are empirically contingent.[22] I endorse this framework and do not think that my account is in tension with it. According to my account, the ultimate foundation of status, as a moral idea, is our equal worth: our free will is the only thing that is 'truly our own' and makes us all equally valid sources of self-esteem. Neither our free will, nor our self-esteem is a matter of degree; we all have it, and nobody has more than others. Yet the value of moral equality cannot be blind to the social threat that certain stable and enduring asymmetrical relations pose to the weaker party's rights and self-esteem. Pufendorf, who belongs squarely in the deontological tradition,[23] was aware of the need to contextualise the value of equality, taking into account social reality as we typically find it. It is deontology with a social face.

1.3 A Revisionist History: Flipping Status on Its Head

A second aim of this book is to challenge the standard narrative about the history of the relation between status and law. Distinguishing between role-status and rank-status, and defending a moral conception of the former, allows me to tell a different story about the evolution of legal systems. The existing literature on status tells a rather simple story about its place in human history. According to this orthodox story, we used to distribute legal rights and duties according to one's social status: a citizen in ancient Rome would enjoy civil and political rights that other groups, low down in the social hierarchy, such as women, freedmen, and slaves, did not. Ditto for the European nobility during medieval times. These legal systems were said to be based on the belief that one is entitled to a set of rights and duties merely in virtue of one's high social status. Conversely, those low down in the social hierarchy were considered unworthy of certain rights and duties, simply in virtue of the fact that they were held in low esteem. But, this familiar story goes, with the advent of the Enlightenment, and the rise of moral egalitarianism, legal rights and duties were no longer assigned based on social status. In contemporary law, this moral egalitarianism is reflected on the heightened legal significance of human rights law, and the thought that these rights are held by all, simply in virtue of being human. Richard Dagger remarks for instance that 'for the concept of rights to appear and gain purchase, the status concepts had to lose their grip'.[24]

The story is of course part of Henry Maine's well-known thesis that legal systems have historically progressed from a status-based social system to a system based on individual autonomy (contract-based). But similar versions of this story have also

[22] I am grateful to Arthur Ripstein for pressing me on this point.

[23] I here follow Darwall's interpretation. See Stephen Darwall, 'Pufendorf on Morality, Sociability and Moral Powers', 50(2) *Journal of the History of Philosophy* (2012), pp. 213–238.

[24] Richard Dagger, 'Rights', in Terence Ball, James Farr, and Russell L. Hanson (eds), *Political Innovation and Conceptual Change* (Cambridge: Cambridge University Press, 1989), p. 292.

been told by philosophers, such as Jeremy Waldron and Stephen Darwall, among others. Pre-modern legal statuses, Waldron says, were 'sortal'. They 'categorise[d] legal subjects on the *sort of person* they are'.[25] Women, slaves and villeins were deprived of several legal rights and duties that another a group (such as male citizens or nobility) enjoyed thanks to their social status. Similarly, Darwall argues that status-based societies made a fundamental moral mistake: instead of seeing all persons as inherently worthy of respect, they grounded rights on honour, which is not a normative idea. No moral rights and duties can ever be grounded on honour, on his view. In sum, the orthodox story is that legal status used to track rank-status. Whereas in the past, people were given a set or rights and duties merely because of their high rank-status, we now no longer do so. Aristocrats, celebrities, scientific geniuses are not given more legal rights than the rest of us.

Compelling as the above accounts might appear, however, I shall try to show that they are in important respects inaccurate. They portray historic legal statuses as a function of social esteem, an instrument used to embed and reproduce existing social hierarchies based on esteem or honour. They claim that legal status tracked social status. As a historical claim, however, this is misguided. In Roman law, a person did not lose their legal status merely because they lost their social status or honour (what the Romans called *infamia*). We learn very little about social status in Roman society by studying legal status. The three main legal statuses in Roman law (citizenship, freedom and family) were a very poor proxy for social status. Patricians did not enjoy more private law rights than plebeians. Legal status never tracked rank-status directly, as the orthodox story goes. Though there are examples of legal rights that directly privilege groups holding high social status, the typical use of status in law was not premised on societal esteem or honour. Instead, I argue, the central notion of status that law uses is different: it takes a social relation between parties (around labour, politics and family) as triggering a set of moral rights and duties, based on the roles they occupy. The fundamental character of legal status was always role-status, not rank-status.

Drawing inspiration from Roman law, I provide a very different account, one that places role-status at the centre of both pre-modern and modern societies. The transition between the two was not a transition from a society based on rank-status, to a society where everyone has the same status. Rather, the transition that took place was within the confines of role-status. We moved from protecting the *stronger* party in role-status relations concerning labour, politics, and family, to seeking to protect the *weaker* party. Instead of protecting the slave master, we protect the employee; instead of protecting landowners, we protect the tenant; and instead of protecting officials, we protect citizens. This is a more accurate picture, as it allows us to explain why the idea of status has persisted in modern times.

25 Waldron, *Dignity, Rank and Rights*, p. 58

Perhaps the best way to illustrate this claim is the example of labour. In ancient times, labour was mainly done by slaves, who were forced to work and lacked legal rights. They were under the extensive legal control of their masters. In modern times, by contrast, labour is never forced and must always be freely contracted. It is this transition that Henry Maine's motto, 'from status to contract', sought to capture. And undoubtedly the abolition of slavery and forced labour was one of the most progressive legal reforms in human history. What we should notice, however, is that in both ancient and modern times we find at its core the same social relation with two parties: one party provides labour under the direction of another party. This relation is asymmetrical in that one person (the weaker party) is dependent on, or is vulnerable vis-à-vis, the other (the stronger party).

Focusing on the nature of the underlying social relation, rather than the social esteem enjoyed by the parties, allows me to explain why status has persisted through the evolution of legal systems. The difference between ancient law and modern law is not that the former was status-based, whereas the latter is not. This is Maine's thesis, and it is one that has caused great distortion. Being an employee is a legal status in modern legal systems, and a valuable one at that. So is being a citizen, a refugee, a bankrupt, a minor, and a defendant. Contrary to Maine's thesis, the difference lies elsewhere: in ancient times, law sided with the stronger party to the social relation of labour (the slave master), at the expense of the weaker (the slave). In modern times, by contrast, law aims to side with the weaker party to that relation (the employee), at the expense of the stronger party (the employer). Put differently, modern law turned role-status on its head, seeking to protect the weaker, rather than the stronger party. Status has always been with us, so to speak, because the social relations it picks out have always been with us. Law regulates status, but it does not create it. Rather than having abolished it in modern times, we started to turn status upside-down. As we ought to. So here is the main claim this book makes about the historical evolution of status:

> **The Evolution of Status**: Both ancient and modern law regulate status relations. Whereas ancient law sided with the stronger party in these relations, modern law aims to side with the weaker party.

1.4 Why Are There Two Kinds of Status?

This book explores these two senses of status, *rank-status* and *role-status*. The former is based on societal esteem and the latter on the social role one occupies. Of course, for the distinction not to collapse, roles must be understood in a way that makes no reference to societal esteem. In Chapter 7, I provide an account of the ontology of social roles and how certain roles (what I call role-statuses) are inherently moralised. Being a celebrity, for example, is not a role-status as I understand it here. The Kardashians have rank-status and that's what they are known for. They probably also possess various role-statuses (e.g. parents or employers) but that is not why we know them. Occupying a role-status cannot be merely a matter of enjoying high societal esteem, where no moral duties vis-à-vis vulnerable people are attached to one's position. Princess Diana, after her divorce, did not occupy any role, even if she felt compelled to use her fame for good purposes. Her affiliation to the Royal Family gave her rank-status but no role-status.

But are these two senses of status even linked then? And why would it be worth rehabilitating role-status when it can be conflated with rank-status? The two senses of status might appear to some readers as mere homonyms. This raises a threshold objection. Perhaps the issues surrounding the existence of social hierarchies of esteem have little to do with the moral question of what rights are attached to certain roles. After all, numerous employees do not enjoy high rank-status (think of social workers, or street cleaners), whereas several independent contractors, who lack employment status, are high up in the social hierarchy, such as famous painters and musicians. Am I inviting confusion by writing a book on two different concepts which just sound the same?

My answer is that status has an inherent ambivalence, which it shares with the concepts of dignity and respect. The dual meaning of status, rank and role, is part of its nature. It is important to distinguish between them, and not to conflate them, but it is also important to understand why they are connected. This section explains this dual character of status.

One of the things that motivated me to write this book is that the difference between rank-status and role-status has not been made clearly in the literature. The most significant difference is that role-status is the basis of a set of interpersonal moral rights and duties, whereas rank-status has no inherent moral dimension. There are of course moral rights *against* allowing rank-status to impact people's interests in particular ways, which anti-discrimination law protects. But that is not the same as rank-status being the normative *ground* on which a person holds a right. Role-status has a justificatory relation to the relevant rights and duties. One has a right against unfair dismissal *in virtue of* being an employee. Role-status is the more fundamental notion.

And yet role-status and rank-status are unlike 'river banks' and 'money banks'. They are closely connected. The first commonality is to do with the social dimension of status and the asymmetries that it picks out. Both rank-status and role-status are attributes of persons. And they typically overlap. I hold the role-status of a professor, and alongside with it, the rank-status that being an academic attracts (not much in the UK). What we should observe, however, is that both senses of status concern a position of asymmetry between myself and others. In my role-status as a professor, I am in an asymmetrical relation with my students. And in my rank-status as a professor, I am in an asymmetrical relation with other professionals who are esteemed more or less than me. Both statuses are therefore about social asymmetries. These social asymmetries are typically understood as relations in which there are inferiors and superiors,[26] or—as I argue we should better put it—weaker and stronger parties.

Though both these kinds of social asymmetry occupy significant parts of our lives, they do so in different ways. Take rank-status first. Every person has a sense of how their attributes and circumstances are esteemed socially by others. I do not mean that people necessarily obsess over it, or that they think of their rank-status, be it formal or informal, as an important part of their life. Some suggest, plausibly, that it is mainly the middle-class that is perennially afflicted with this obsession.[27] People at the bottom and at the top of social hierarchy might, paradoxically, be very similar in that they are largely oblivious to their rank-status. Those at the bottom may have no aspirations about climbing up the social ladder, or they might feel they are at the top of the ladder that matters for them.[28] And it may never occur to those born with a silver spoon that another life is possible for them. Be that as it may, we are all aware of disparities of esteem and our own position on it. Antonio knows his place in society as an unemployed menial worker. He also knows how his rank-status went up among his family and friends when he got a job; that may matter more to him than what society thinks about menial workers.

Rank-status is both retail and wholesale. It figures not only in how one is esteemed by society in an impersonal sense (e.g. the status of a professor), but also how one is esteemed, as a person, within the smaller social circles in which one moves. I may be indifferent about how British society esteems academics. But I may care deeply about how I am esteemed by my colleagues or by the members of my sports club. People can be indifferent to wholesale rank-status. But it is extremely rare to be indifferent to retail rank-status—that is, to the esteem one enjoys within the small social circles in which we pursue valuable activities. Hierarchies of esteem, formal or informal, inevitably emerge there and they shape one's pursuit of the good.

It is in the nature of societal esteem that it comes in degrees and that people are disposed to rank others based on it.[29] Societies place esteem or disesteem on various other attributes and rank them on a scale. How they do so is a complex matter of social ontology. It includes, at the very least, patterns of social behaviour together with mental states, such as expectations and beliefs, that are widely shared as common knowledge. Profession is perhaps the most common such attribute.

[26] This is Kolodny's position. See Kolodny, *Pecking Order*, p. 87ff.

[27] See Paul Fussell, *Class: A Guide through the American Status System* (New York: Pocket Books, 1992).

[28] On the idea of working-class aristocrats, see E. E. Lemasters, *Blue-Collar Aristocrats: Life Styles at a Working Class Tavern* (Madison: University of Wisconsin Press, 1975).

[29] The property of gradation is not the same as a ranking property. An entity can come in degrees (e.g. blood cells) without being ranked comparatively across persons by someone. Ranking is a deliberate human activity. Rank-status possesses both these properties.

Scientists and doctors are esteemed more than builders and truck drivers.[30] Income or wealth is another common attribute that typically places people on a ranking scale. Both the placing of esteem on individual attributes, and the ranking on a scale, can be formal or informal; it can be top-down, or bottom-up. Government may place more value on science and medicine than on crafts and manual jobs in setting the school curriculum or awarding honours. At their core, however, disparities of societal esteem are bottom-up and relate to most aspects of our social life.[31] Whether within one's one profession, or vis-à-vis all professions, one has a sense of where one stands, whether close to the top, middling, or bottom of the league.

Disparities of esteem based on arbitrary personal characteristics, such as gender or race, are of course inherently objectionable, the root cause of serious forms of discrimination and social injustice. But are merit-based disparities of societal esteem a problem? These appear to be a rigid part of the human condition. I am not an anthropologist, but I would not be surprised if no human society was ever completely devoid of disparities of societal esteem, given human propensity for competition and pursuit of excellence.[32] Perhaps such a society can exist and certainly some people have thought so. But for it to be possible, it would have to suppress our interest in cultivating and expressing admiration for human excellence, since pursuit of excellence is a typical driver for social status. Pecking orders among young children with respect to say, athletic ability, are formed quickly and intuitively, without much mediation by cultural or institutional norms. Sociological research suggests that within controlled social interactions, status hierarchies arise organically, with different character traits being attributed to persons depending on whether they are leaders or followers.[33] I will argue in Chapter 8, that merit-based disparities of esteem are not objectionable when they come about from the bottom-up, through each person's beliefs and preferences, rather than top-down, through government imposition.

Role-statuses, on the other hand, are part of our social lives in a different way. They form part of our *moral* life—that is, of what rights and duties we owe one another. We all occupy roles in our social life within which we face dependencies or vulnerabilities, either ours or of those with whom we, as role-holders, interact. Arguably the most common such role is that of a family member, since we all spend childhood being dependent on parents or other carers. During adulthood,

[30] https://yougov.co.uk/international/articles/33901-scientists-and-doctors-are-most-respected-professi

[31] This is not universally accepted. Variants of the Marxist school of thought hold the view that ideology is a top-down mechanism for reproducing a hierarchy of social esteem and the power that comes with it. I do not accept this view. Within liberal societies that guarantee free speech this view must be rejected, because we must hold people responsible for any hierarchies that they implicitly endorse and reproduce.

[32] For the anthropological claim that humans are naturally disposed to form hierarchies see Christopher Boehm, *Hierarchy in the Forest* (Cambridge: Harvard University Press, 2021).

[33] See Ridgway, *Status*.

this vulnerability flips, as most of us have to care for aging parents or young children. But role-status also consumes our lives outside family bonds. Most of us are employees, earning an income through providing labour to an employer.[34] Most people in the UK aged 16–34 are tenants, relying on either private landlords or the government for housing,[35] and most people in countries such as Switzerland or Germany are tenants.[36] And of course, almost all of us will be patients or students at one point or another in our life.

What is interesting about role-status is that its asymmetry has a *two-way dynamic*. We often move from being the weaker party to a status relation to being the stronger party. A minor might later in life become a parent or a carer. A student might become a teacher. A tenant might become a landlord. An employee might decide to start their own business. And many of us will bounce up and down the same status relation, sometimes concurrently. A doctor might become another doctor's patient. A professor might take up a course in a new discipline. A landlord might decide to move to a new area and rent, becoming some other landlord's tenant. A judge may sue a neighbour in their personal capacity and become a litigant before another judge. This two-way dynamic mitigates the asymmetrical character of status relations. It makes the call for abolishing them altogether weaker. By contrast, hierarchies of social esteem rarely exhibit this two-way dynamic. Though people may skyrocket to fame, or fall from the stars, they don't do so as often and as systematically as we alternate between the weaker and the stronger party in these role-statuses. And of course, moving up and down the ranks of societal esteem does not, other things being equal, change one's moral profile.

In addition to social asymmetry, there is a second conceptual commonality between rank-status and role-status. Rank-status, as a descriptive notion, is constitutively dependent on collective intentionality. Doctors have higher rank-status than builders and they do so *because* most people believe so. By contrast, role-status is not dependent on collective intentionality. As I will seek to show in Chapter 7, one's role or status as a litigant, or a judge does not depend on collective intentionality. And yet, role-status, as a normative notion, requires that we *ought* to recognise socially certain relations. Social recognition is an element in both rank-status and role-status. It is present in rank-status as a descriptive criterion. And it is present in role-status as a normative requirement. Each one of us, through our beliefs and practices, helps to create an unofficial ranking of societal esteem based on perceptions of merit. We are not morally required to do so, but it happens nevertheless, and it can be unproblematic when esteem tracks excellence. Yet it is a matter of moral duty, through our collective institutions, to recognise and place

[34] The average percentage of employed people relative to general population in the OECD countries is 69.4 per cent. See https://www.statista.com/statistics/268127/employment-rate-in-selected-industrialized-countries/

[35] https://www.nimblefins.co.uk/number-homeowners-and-renters-uk

[36] https://uncle.co.uk/renting-around-the-world/

value on role-statuses. One way to put this point is that the social recognition that societies typically place on attributes such as one's achievements or talents (rank-status) should be placed equally, if not more, on statuses such as being an employee or a tenant (role-status).

So, we might say that the deeper connection between role-status and rank-status is this: we recognise social positions and relations, and we place esteem in them. It is sometimes significant that we place esteem on those who merit it—for example, the Nobel Prize winners. But it is not *morally* significant: nobody has a right to have their merit recognised. By contrast, it is morally significant to recognise collectively social threats to one's self-esteem, by recognising socially and legally one's status. Of course, it's not the *rank*-status of employees and tenants that we ought to recognise; it's their *role*-status. We aim to shield the self-esteem of employees and tenants (role-status), rather than boost their societal esteem (rank-status). It is Antonio's self-esteem that is masterfully portrayed in the scene from the *Bicycle Thieves*.

In his major work, *Of the Law of Nature and Nations*, Pufendorf keeps going back and forth between using the Latin word *dignitas*, or what I call rank-status, and the word *dignatio*, or what I call role-status. This is not an accident. Both *dignitas* and *dignatio* involve social recognition of a position. *Dignitas* relates to how we are esteemed by others in our society; *dignatio*, by contrast, is a moral notion, denoting a person's inherent worth and the need to recognise it socially.[37] The failure to appreciate the ambivalence of dignity, which can be used to refer to both *dignitas* and *dignatio*, underpins in my view Waldron's[38] well-known claim that dignity is essentially a matter of rank. Waldron argues that dignity was something that only nobility used to enjoy, and that with the advent of human rights we were all elevated to a high noble rank that we all now enjoy. I think this is a mistake. It is *dignatio* that grounds rights, not *dignitas*. Waldron's account fails to appreciate that *dignatio* was always part of our legal and social practices and that it is a more fundamental notion than *dignitas*.

We should note finally that this inherent ambivalence is not unique to the concepts of status and dignity. The concept of respect is another case, as Stephen Darwall has explained with his very influential distinction between two kinds of respect: recognition-respect and appraisal-respect.[39] All these concepts seek to capture the interplay between the moral and social domain. Just like these are two different types of respect, as opposed to two different concepts, likewise role-status

[37] Niklas Luhmann is probably the first to spot the distinction between *dignatio* and *dignitas* in modern times. See Niklas Luhmann, *Law as a Social System* (Oxford: Oxford University Press, 2004), p. 483.

[38] See Waldron, *Dignity, Rank and Rights*.

[39] See Stephen Darwall, 'Two Kinds of Respect', 88(1) *Ethics* (1977), pp. 36–49. See further the discussion in Section 8.6.

and rank-status are two different types of status. We all have both, and they both relate to social recognition, but they are quite different.

1.5 What This Book Isn't About

There are at least two other senses of legal status that do not concern me here. The first, more narrow one, is that of legal *standing* understood as the right to initiate legal proceedings with respect to a particular set of facts. An informal association, for instance, may lack legal status to initiate proceedings on behalf of its members. This notion relates to the conditions under which one's interests have been sufficiently impacted to justify the judicial resources required to examine whether one's legal rights have been breached.

The second, broader sense, of legal status is that of general legal personhood—that is, the extent to which natural persons, as well as various non-human entities, are generally recognised as capable of bearing legal rights.[40] This second sense overlaps with status but is not the same. I am not interested here in whether, and if so why, entities such as states, international organisations, animals, corporations, or rivers have legal rights and duties. My focus here is narrower, concerned with relations between natural persons[41] whose legal personhood ought to be recognised, and regulated, by law. I am interested in why law picks out certain conditions or relations (e.g. employment) and attaches to them a distinct set of legal rights and duties, different from that of other persons.

In fact, I think that seeing status merely as a way of imposing restrictions on legal personhood, as Henry Maine did, or even of denying legal personhood altogether, is a mistake. It obscures the relational character of status, which law necessarily regulates, either directly or indirectly. By regulating three main statuses (freedom, citizenship, and family), Roman law recognised the personhood of all the parties in the underlying relations (citizens, foreigners, masters, slaves, head of household, women, and dependent relatives) and sided with the stronger party.

Finally, I should be clear that this book is not about all forms of social inequality. Not all violations of equality are status offences. Discrimination based on arbitrary characteristics is another widely known social practice that poses a serious

[40] This second idea has been explored recently in Visa Kurki, *A Theory of Legal Personhood* (Oxford: Oxford University Press, 2019).

[41] I set aside in this book thorny questions regarding the relation between corporations, as legal entities, and the individuals that lie behind them. My main concern is with cases where individuals (e.g. the employee or the tenant) are the weaker party in a social relation, even if the stronger party (e.g. the employer or the landlord) might be a corporation. Obviously, when individual interests are mediated by a corporate structure it might not be easy to identify who the weaker party is in a social relation. A corporation may be too far removed from the individual status-holders whose interests it represents, to count as the weaker party. I am grateful to Seana Shiffrin and Sarah Patterson for discussion on this point.

threat to equality: racism, sexism, homophobia, transphobia, and ablism are all social phenomena that constitute distinct affronts to the value of equality. Their presence is indicated by how law tries to mitigate their pernicious effects. Current anti-discrimination law deems suspect any differentiation based on certain characteristics such as race, sex, religion, transgender status, or sexual orientation.[42] But discrimination cuts across all, or most, aspects of our social lives, applying not only to all relations but also to episodic interactions. A woman may be harassed while crossing the street. A person with disability may be ignored by a shopkeeper. A person belonging to a minority group may be turned down for a loan. This is partly because discrimination operates via *rank*-status (i.e., the societal beliefs held) consciously or unconsciously, regarding who is worthy of esteem. Empirical research shows that if you belong to a class of persons that enjoys low societal esteem, your health is very likely to be much worse than those higher up in the hierarchy. This is so even if you enjoy the same level of healthcare as them. This extraordinary empirical finding means that merely having lower social status *makes* you less healthy. Michael Marmott, whose work on the social determinants of health has been pioneering, has aptly called this social problem the 'status syndrome'.[43]

Role-status, by contrast, requires an ongoing interaction between two parties, one that pertains to certain non-contingent interests of well-being that are stable parameters of our ethical lives: family, work, politics, housing, health, or education. Status offences capture a narrower set of equality-based wrongs, those arising within the context of specific relations that anyone, regardless of their characteristics, can enter (such as employment or tenancy), or that everyone finds themselves (such as citizenship and family). They are to do with the nature of the relation (e.g. labour, family, medicine, teaching, or housing) rather than the personal characteristics of the parties within that relation, such as their gender or race. Status is the ground of *relation*-specific prophylactic rights and duties—that is, rights that concern the specific activity with respect to which the weaker party is vulnerable or dependent. Needless to say, as the literature on intersectionality[44] has shown, the vulnerable position of employees or tenants is exacerbated at a greater scale when one also belongs to historically discriminated or disadvantaged group. But my focus in this book is on seeking to explain why status poses a distinct social threat to equality, different to discrimination. Not all social threats to equality are captured by status.[45]

[42] See, e.g., the UK Equality Act 2010.

[43] See Michael Marmot, *The Status Syndrome* (London: Bloomsbury, 2004).

[44] Kimberlé Williams Crenshaw, 'Demarginalizing the Intersection of Race and Sex: A Black Feminist Critique of Antidiscrimination Doctrine, Feminist Theory and Antiracist Politics', 139(1) *University of Chicago Legal Forum* (1989), pp. 139–167.

[45] This is one point of difference between my account and Kolodny's, who seeks to offer a comprehensive account of moral equality in terms of relations of inferiority. I explore further these differences in Chapter 6.

1.6 A Note on Methodology

It is not clear to me that doing legal philosophy in the analytic Anglo-American tradition involves a choice between different possible methodologies. But I should like to say something about it. People usually have in mind the distinction between normative and descriptive methodologies. And some still defend the possibility of conceptual analysis that is free from any normative theorising. Ronald Dworkin once asked John Gardner at a seminar what the point of conceptual analysis is. Gardner, with his characteristic quick wit, replied that it is like peeling an onion: you expose layers of semantic content of the concept; to which Dworkin said: 'Yes, but at some point, all the layers are peeled, and you realise that there is nothing there.'[46]

I agree with Dworkin that doing legal philosophy without making any normative (by which I mean moral) claims is futile. But I appreciate that other legal philosophers opt for a different approach. My own sense is that conceptual analysis has little currency outside the dispute in general jurisprudence between positivism and non-positivism that we have inherited from the Hart–Dworkin debate.[47] When legal philosophers engage with specific areas of law, they typically seek to understand them—implicitly or explicitly—in the light of the moral values and principles that they instantiate, exercising normative judgment about what is essential or central, and what is ephemeral or peripheral, in those areas.[48] The areas themselves won't make this judgment on behalf of the legal theorist. And any stipulations found within legal practice itself, about what is central and what peripheral, are subject to interpretation since practitioners, just like theorists, can be wrong in exercising that judgment.

So, it is certainly not my aim here to offer a conceptual analysis of status. Nor do I think that there is an identifiable point at which one stops unpacking a concept and starts making normative claims. My approach here is the standard one used in moral and political philosophy, of making first-order normative claims. In that sense, my inquiry is not concept-driven. It is premised on the philosophical claim that the concept of status captures a distinct moral problem: the way in which certain asymmetrical social relations pose a threat to our standing as equals and require a specific form of legal regulation. Ultimately, this book is concerned with the moral problems caused by this type of social relations, rather than a conceptual analysis, a legal history, or a genealogy of status.

[46] This oral exchange took place at a seminar at University College, Oxford circa 2002. It was part of a peripatetic jurisprudence seminar series that Dworkin and Gardner ran jointly, between Oxford and UCL, when I was a doctoral student at UCL. I was in the audience and report here the exchange to the best of my recollection.

[47] For how distorted the reception of that debate has been in general jurisprudence see Nicos Stavropoulos, 'The Debate That Never Was', 130(8) *Harvard Law Review* (2017), pp. 2082–2095.

[48] See, e.g., the approach of Seana Shiffrin in her *Speech Matters: On Lying, Morality and the Law* (Princeton: Princeton University Press, 2014).

Having said that, one needs to start somewhere and to motivate one's inquiry. I begin with the legal use of status, as found in Roman law, and try to see it in its best light, to use Dworkin's familiar metaphor for what he calls an interpretive methodology.[49] This approach involves making choices about what is essential and what is contingent in the relevant practice, as well as what is central and what is peripheral (even if it is essential). Through this interpretive approach, I aim to show that status tracks certain social roles that are morally salient. My argument is not that status is necessarily relational because it was so in Roman law, and modern law is built on Roman law; that would be a daft claim to make. Roman law, just like any historical legal system, had all kinds of morally objectionable contingencies and it could have been wrong about status. Instead, my aim is to use Roman law in order to illustrate a claim whose normative significance is independent of it, namely that certain enduring social relations are asymmetrical, and the law recognises them, inevitably taking sides between the parties. My revisionist account of Roman law is interpretive, not historical. I aim to reconstruct the legal notion of status, with a moral account already in mind, whose merits I will later defend through first-order moral argumentation. But it is nevertheless significant that the best interpretation of legal status also shows it to be relational.

To be sure, the connection between status and a person's moral rights and duties within a relation was not something that the Roman jurists, let alone Roman citizens, strived to understand, or theorise. In fact, as we shall see, they did not even systematically use the word 'status' to describe the legal position of these different classes of persons. They used, instead, the Latin word '*conditio*'. 'Status' began to emerge as a term of art, and to attract intellectual interest much later, in the late Middle Ages. This was when Roman law was rediscovered and drew gradually the attention of the early humanists and natural lawyers, resulting eventually in its reception by European legal systems. In the seventeenth and eighteenth century status solidified as a moral and not just a legal notion.

It is this literature that is my main point of departure. The first rigorous treatment of status in moral philosophy is found in Samuel Pufendorf's *Elements of Universal Jurisprudence* (1660). Pufendorf is now widely seen as a precursor of the Enlightenment movement. Influenced heavily by Thomas Hobbes and Hugo Grotius, he sought to develop a moral science modelled on the juridical concepts of Roman law. 'Status', Pufendorf wrote 'is a suppositive moral entity in which positive moral objects, and, above all, persons, are said to be'.[50] As we shall see in Chapter 3, Pufendorf's philosophical take on status was remarkably original. He

[49] Dworkin, *Law's Empire*.

[50] Samuel Pufendorf, *Two Books of the Elements of Universal Jurisprudence*, translated by William Abbott Oldfather, 1931; revised by Thomas Behme; edited and with an Introduction by Thomas Behme (Liberty Fund: Indianapolis, 2009; hereinafter *Elements of Universal Jurisprudence*), Definition III, p. 26.

got it mostly right too. I will defend his account against Bentham's and Kant's, particularly his claim that citizenship is a status relation.

Philosophy is routinely motivated by puzzles that are not, on their face, about any moral problems. Why does law use status to denote some rights and duties but not others? Why do we use the concepts of status and role to imply that one has a complex package of rights and duties or to make covert moral claims? Why did scholars think that Maine's thesis contributed to legal injustices? One can go some way to addressing these puzzles without endorsing a moral conception of status. My own approach, however, is different: to use these puzzles as indications (rather than proof) that status is a moral idea and, once I have provided a moral account, to use it in order to solve them. Needless to say, those who do not agree with me that status is a moral notion will suggest other ways to solve these puzzles. I wish them well, but I do not think one can go very far without normative theorising. John Austin tried his best to offer a positivistic understanding of status and he concluded that: 'I still find no mark by which a status or condition can be distinguished from any other collection of rights and duties.'[51]

1.7 Chapter Synopsis

Early chapters trace the intellectual origins of status, with a view to highlighting elements that I will later draw on to provide a moral account of status. In Chapter 2, I begin with a reconstruction of the Roman law of status. I mainly focus on the earlier source of Roman law, the *Institutes* of Gaius. My aim is to highlight the fact that the three statuses of Roman law (*libertas*, *civitas*, and *familia*) singled out social relations in the context of labour, politics, and family. These legal statuses far from tracked the social rank or esteem of different classes of persons in Roman society. Status in Roman law was not what Waldron calls 'sortal': it did not predetermine the legal rights and duties of a person at birth, nor did it take a view on the 'sort' of person one is. Instead, it was dynamic and allowed all persons to move up and down, as well as across, statuses. It was surprisingly modern, and this allowed it to be used, centuries later, as the basis of legal systems that recognised the moral value of human equality.

Chapter 3 turns to the work of Samuel Pufendorf, whose work provides the inspiration for the main argument of this book. Pufendorf wrote at a time when Roman law had made a comeback in Europe and was used as a common moral language. I focus on two claims Pufendorf makes. First, that status is a moral entity, grounding rights and duties, and 'a moral field for persons to exist in'. Second, that adventitious statuses, or what I call role-statuses, are unequal or asymmetrical,

[51] John Austin, *Lectures in Jurisprudence: Or The Philosophy of Positive Law* (New York: Henry Colt, 1875), p. 348.

whereas our natural status is one of equality. Building on Pufendorf's work, I argue that role-statuses pose a social threat to our standing as equals. This is so on two grounds: first because the stronger party to these relations is likely to abuse their position and exploit various vulnerabilities of the weaker party; and second, because the weaker party faces the risk of losing their self-esteem. And self-esteem is a vital moral defence. Only persons with self-esteem will insist on equal terms of cooperation. This explains why Pufendorf thought that status is a moral entity, the root of rights and duties: the point of role-status is to protect people against the social threat posed by certain asymmetrical relations. Role-statuses are egalitarian moral fields.

Chapters 4 and 5 flesh out and develop further the moral account of status that I located in Pufendorf's work. After an overview of the distortions caused by Maine's thesis, Chapter 4 leaves the history of status behind. It focuses on contemporary moral complaints, made by ordinary persons, that involve status. This chapter does two things. The first part shows that there are distinct ways in which one can wrong a person by offending their status. More specifically, it identifies three modalities: the failure to recognise one's status, undue interference with the functions of one's status, and status appropriation. The second part of the chapter defends further the distinction between role-status and rank status, the two main concepts with which the book deals, and shows that the three modalities identified involve role-status, not rank-status.

Chapter 5 provides a constitutive account of status relations. It explains the conditions under which a social interaction counts as a status relation and what this entails for the moral profile of the parties. It argues that a relation is a status-based one if and only if it meets the following conditions: first, when it is asymmetrical in that one of the parties suffers from background vulnerabilities or dependencies whose source is pluralistic; second, when it pertains to certain non-contingent and enduring interactions that implicate significant aspects of our well-being, such as work, family, politics, and housing. I then move on to argue that status grounds two sets of requirements: first, the moral duty, legally enforceable, to balance the relation by vesting the parties with prophylactic rights and duties whose aim is to protect the weaker party; second, the moral duty to shield the weaker party's self-esteem and to project the value of equality by recognising socially (and legally) the two parties *qua* status-holders. The most important upshot of status is that parties may not determine freely the terms of their relation. Status supersedes any contractual agreement that is incompatible with the weaker party's rights and their equal standing.

Chapter 6 discusses alternative accounts of status, by way of presenting them as possible objections. The most serious of those is Arthur Ripstein's contemporary restatement of the Kantian approach to status. I seek to distinguish my account from Ripstein's, which I call the fiduciary view. Though I have no quarrel with fiduciary relations, as a distinct category of rights and duties, I think that my account of status is more faithful to the history of status, than the fiduciary view. I then turn to the views of Henry Maine and John Austin, both of whom I hold responsible for the neglect of status as a moral idea. Their positivistic account is superficial, missing the relational account of status and the asymmetry that characterises it. Finally, I discuss the very important recent book by Niko Kolodny, *The Pecking Order*, which seeks to recast the whole value of equality in terms of a claim against social inferiority. Kolodny does not employ the notion of status and the scope of his inquiry is much wider than mine. Though I largely agree with Kolodny's conception of equality, I argue that role-statuses pose a distinct challenge to social equality that his account fails to acknowledge adequately.

Chapter 7 examines the social ontology of roles and seeks to explain why certain roles are role-statuses (i.e. generate a set of moral rights and duties). It argues against the popular view that all roles are created by social or legal norms. To do so, I revisit a neglected idea in moral philosophy, that of role obligations. The idea has somewhat of a bad name in moral philosophy, being associated with Hegel's communitarianism. Against the Hegelian tradition, I argue that role-statuses, as a subset of roles, precede institutional practices and collective intentionality. My account of role-statuses explains the common intuition that certain roles can be used as a justification for one's actions, without any further argument. I argue that these roles, such as being a doctor or a judge, emerged as proto-roles with a view to capturing asymmetrical social interactions. They are inherently moralised in that they function as a shorthand for the rights and duties that are triggered because of the underlying asymmetry. By arguing against social constructionism about roles, I make space for the claim, made by Ronald Dworkin, that legal obligation is moralised, attached to the role of being a citizen. Though we can be social constructionists about many roles (e.g. a Moots Officer or a slave-catcher), we shouldn't be social constructionists about role-statuses. Just like the terms and conditions of the employment relation are not determined entirely through the parties' intentions and beliefs, likewise the terms and conditions of citizenship (i.e. citizens' legal rights and duties) are not determined entirely though the lawmakers' intentions and beliefs. They are both sensitive to the asymmetry of the underlying social relation: employer/employee and citizen/official.

Chapter 8 applies the account of status developed in previous chapters to titles and the social recognition of statuses. It begins by showing that titles are positional social goods whose aim is to distribute societal esteem. It then examines the practice of handing out honorific titles by the government, as is the current practice in the UK, and the justification offered by Montesquieu and John Adams for doing so. The chapter argues that these arguments are instrumental and cannot be based on a putative moral right to be publicly esteemed. In fact, this practice violates the individual moral right to decide for oneself who is worthy of esteem and when and where to express this. The chapter advocates, instead, a public ecology of esteem, where ranking of esteem is informal and diffuse, created from the bottom-up, and independently of government. With respect to other titles however, such as those attached to professionals (medical doctor) and public officials (judge), the chapter argues that they can be justified so long as they are stripped of connotations with nobility and are attached to functions within asymmetrical social relations. The point of social recognition of role-statuses, through titles, is to put the parties under moral notice that the relation is asymmetrical and that the stronger party has the moral responsibility to protect the rights of the weaker party. Role-status titles help to place self-esteem where it belongs, namely with the inherent worth of the weaker party.

By way of an epilogue, Chapter 9 reflects on the politics of status and on why the transition from contract to status remains incomplete. It examines the main obstacles impeding this transition and whether human rights law can fill the gap left by legislative inaction. The book concludes with the hope that a general, role-based, account of status, can be of help to movements for better legal regulation of specific asymmetrical social relations.

2
STATUS IN ROMAN LAW
WHERE IT ALL STARTED

2.1 Some Methodological Preliminaries

Organising law into different categories is a familiar feature of the European legal systems that are based on Roman law and, to a lesser degree, common law. Law presents itself to us as comprising different domains and subdomains. The very term 'legal system' suggests a complex organisational structure composed of various parts that are connected in a rational manner. What purposes are served by law's apparent systematicity is not obvious. There might be plenty. Clearly, it helps to make the transfer of legal knowledge easier by breaking it down into more manageable chunks. Lawyers can become experts in specific areas and ignore others. In that respect, not much is at stake in how we carve up law's categories and different, mutually inclusive, classifications are possible. But another thing might be at play behind law's fondness of systematicity. Some legal classifications may reflect a deeper structure that law has, wherever it exists, even if it is not readily noticeable.[1] Almost all legal systems, for example, have at least a rudimentary distinction between private law and criminal law. Sometimes law makes us compensate others for things we have done to them and sometimes it puts us behind bars. We theorise about the point of the difference between a civil wrong and a criminal wrong, which we take to be fundamental to law.

What does it mean to say that some legal category is part of the deeper structure of law? For one thing, it means that it is not based on contingencies found only in some places or periods, like the legal status of a serf, or internet law, for example. The more abstract the legal category (e.g. 'criminal law'), the more likely it is that it will be ubiquitous in legal practices. But a lot depends on the modality of the necessity claim one is making here. It is one thing to claim that, given the human condition, all legal systems must necessarily contain certain norms (e.g. criminal prohibitions) if they are to be viable.[2] It is a different thing to claim that

[1] Peter Birks once remarked that 'it ought to be possible to take any legal subject and to cut away its detail so as to reveal the skeleton of principle which holds it together', in Peter Birks, *An Introduction to the Law of Restitution* (Oxford: Oxford University Press, 1985), p. 1.

[2] This thesis was defended by H. L. A. Hart, who labelled it the 'minimum content of natural law'. See H. L. A. Hart, *The Concept of Law*, 3rd edn (Oxford: Oxford University Press, 2012), ch. 9. Hart's label was confusing, perhaps deliberately so, given that the sense of necessity involved in his claim is very different to that used by natural lawyers.

Status in Law and Morality. George Letsas, Oxford University Press. © George Letsas 2026.
DOI: 10.1093/9780198936725.003.0002

law necessarily contains certain normative categories, regardless of what any legal authorities have decided.

I am not going to take sides, at least for now, in the familiar debate between legal positivism and its opponents, which has dominated jurisprudence in the last sixty years. Instead, I shall proceed intuitively. Legal systems have used the notion of status since Roman law and continue to do so. Why and how they have done so is my starting point. That's not to say much of course. Some property may be recurrent within a practice but neither central nor essential to it. All promulgated laws are printed on a white piece of paper, but white paper is not part of the deeper structure of legal practice. These are familiar issues. When we seek to make best sense of a practice, we inevitably make choices based on what strikes us as more salient and hence capable of explaining other, more superficial, aspects of the practice. In that sense, my inquiry into the history of status is normatively laden. It is based on the working hypothesis that legal status tracks a distinct moral concern arising in certain enduring relations that have existed in most societies. Think, for instance, of family relations and the status of being a parent, or a guardian. One should expect, as is indeed the case, that almost all legal systems have something to say about what rights and duties arise in family relations. But I should be clear that my aim here is not just to explore whether *this* or *that* status is part of the deeper structure of law; it is mainly to explore whether the law's general use of status, as a way to categorise certain rights and duties, is part of its deeper structure. It is with this purpose in mind that, in this chapter, I trace the intellectual roots of status. What follows is an interpretive reconstruction of the idea of status in Roman law.

2.2 The Two *Institutes*

It is an extraordinary fact about Roman law that it exerted a powerful influence on modern legal systems and modern thinking more broadly, many centuries after it had ceased to be in force. I shall later offer one tentative explanation as to why this happened. But one major part of its influence has been the way in which it classified different areas of law. And interestingly, Roman law largely owes its classifications to the work of individual jurists who sought to systematise law for practical purposes, not least for the needs of a growing Roman Empire. Among them, the *Institutes* of Gaius and Justinian stand out as the most significant. It is also where the legal notion of status originates.

As their name suggests, the two *Institutes* were written with a view to introducing (*instituere*) the basic principles of Roman Law. They were, effectively, law textbooks. Gaius, who wrote the first one,[3] is a mystery figure about whom we know almost

[3] W. M. Gordon and Olivia Robinson (translated and with an introduction by), *The Institutes of Gaius* (London: Duckworth, 1988).

nothing. A talented jurist, he lived in the second century BC. Though his *Institutes* are the oldest substantial source we have of Roman law, they were lost for centuries until they were rediscovered in 1816 in the library of the Verona Cathedral. Unlike Gaius's work, the *Institutes* of Justinian was a group effort. The product of an official law commission established by the Byzantine Emperor Justinian I, it was completed in the early sixth century. The commission was led by Tribonian, a Byzantine jurist, and was tasked with codifying the law. At the time of this major codification, Roman law was about a thousand years old, much older than many contemporary legal systems.[4] It had lived through the transition from the Roman Republic to the Roman Empire. This transition included the rise and spread of Christianity and the move of the imperial seat from Rome to Constantinople.

I mention these changes as an indication of the durability of the main classifications of Roman law. They withstood political, economic, and cultural changes from very early on, even while individual rules within them were modified or repealed. When the palimpsest with Gaius's *Institutes* was discovered in Verona, it was remarkable to see the extent to which the Justinian codification had built on them. For context, there were some 600 years between the two *Institutes*, which included Rome's transition from a Republic to an Empire.

Gaius's influence on the systematisation of Roman law, and its longevity, cannot be overstated. In fact, for all we know, Gaius may well have come up with the main classifications on his own and superimposed them on a disparate set of legal rules and practices.[5] Perhaps the extraordinary chain of events that led to the reception of Roman law by modern legal systems was triggered by a single person's philosophical reflection on the nature of law and its basic categories. Were that to be the case, Gaius can lay claim to being the legal scholar with the most impact ever outside academia. It would be hard to beat his accomplishment. This is a wild and amusing hypothesis, of course. Still, why did his classifications prove so durable? And why did they serve as fertile ground for the reception of Roman law by the modern European legal systems more than a dozen centuries later?

2.3 Status and the Roman Law of Persons

The main classification found in Gaius's *Institutes*, and retained by Justinian, is the tripartite division between the law of persons, the law of things, and the law of actions. 'All the law that we make use of', Gaius says, 'relates either to persons, things, or actions.' The law of persons (*ius personarum*) comes first, and it is where the intellectual history of the concept of status originates. The other two categories comprise what would now be called the law of contract and property (the law of things)

[4] The *Twelve Tables*, which is taken to be the foundation of Roman law, was promulgated in 449 BC.

[5] A point made by W. M. Gordon in his introduction to *The Institutes of Gaius*, p. 8.

and procedural law (the law of actions). By today's standards, the *Institutes* cover the core of private law and civil procedure. They largely leave out matters that fall within criminal and public law.

What is the subject matter of the law of persons? In classical Latin, the word *persōna* means 'mask, character, role'.[6] The etymology of the word is Greek, from the word 'πρόσωπο', which means 'face'.[7] This semantic point is of some significance, since it suggests that the same human being can wear different masks (i.e. occupy different roles) at different times and in different settings. If one's status is a *persōna* then it is not an immutable characteristic. And as we shall see shortly, this is exactly the approach Roman law takes. On the orthodox account of status, by contrast, for which I have taken Waldron as a spokesperson, legal statuses used to be rigid, assigned at birth, and impossible to shake off. As we shall see, this view of status hardly fits Roman law and the choice of the word *persōna* to describe this category of law is not accidental.

In Gaius's *Institutes*, people are classified alongside three axes: freedom (*libertas*), citizenship (*civitas*), and family position (*familia*). With respect to freedom, one was either free (*liberus*) or a slave (*servus*). With respect to citizenship, one was either a Roman citizen (*civus*) or a foreigner (*peregrinus*). And with respect to family, one was either independent (*sui iuris*) or subject to the control of another (*alieni iuris*). These were largely cross-cutting statuses. One could lack Roman citizenship but be free (e.g. the Latins); or one could be a Roman citizen, but under the power of the head of the family (*filiusfamilias*). More importantly, these statuses could change. Slaves could be freed (*manumission*), Latins and foreigners could be awarded citizenship,[8] freemen could lose their freedom (*capitis deminutio*) or be enslaved, and family members could become independent (*mancipation*). These statuses were dynamic and subject to change.

This did not mean, of course, that slaves and women were not systematically dominated and exploited, nor that it was easy for them to change status. It is not as if most people regularly alternated between these statuses. What I want to focus on here is how things look from the point of view of law. Two points are worth highlighting. First, Roman law treated statuses as something that people can change during their lives depending on their circumstances. And second, as far as law was concerned, the same individual could hold more than one legal status at the same time. This means that classical Roman law was a far cry from the notion that Waldron calls 'sortal' status:

> Sortal status represents a person's permanent situation and destiny so far as the law is concerned. It is not acquired or lost depending on actions, growth,

[6] *Oxford English Dictionary*, online edition (www.oed.com).
[7] Literally, the sight we see when we look at someone, from προς (towards) + ωψ (sight).
[8] Caracalla extended citizenship to most foreigners in 212 AD.

> circumstances, or vicissitudes. The idea behind sortal status is that there are different kinds of person.[9]

I am not sure why Waldron says this. The two examples of sortal statuses that he gives come from Apartheid South Africa and nineteenth-century American slavery law. He might be right that these two legal systems, at that particular time, treated status in a sortal way, sorting those who are meant to spend their lives as slaves from those who are meant to be free. But these two legal systems is not where the modern idea of status originates. And Waldron's notion of sortal status finds little ground in Roman law. We might say that Roman law sorted out different kinds of *personas*, not persons. One's legal destiny was not determined permanently, since one could change statuses (personas) during one's lifetime or occupy more than one, depending on one's circumstances.

The dynamic character of status in Roman law also explains a feature that Waldron finds puzzling, namely the absence historically of the idea of 'ordinary' legal status. If status is a role one happens to occupy in some aspect of one's life, a mask one wears, then it does not pertain to all people and at all times. There is no such thing as ordinary or 'general' legal status, simply because there is no single role that every person always occupies in their interaction with others. And hence one should expect to find no discussion of the notion of general legal status or personality, as least not with respect to private law. Even in contemporary private law, one can be a parent and an employer, a permanent resident and a minor, or a citizen and under guardianship. Thus understood, there is no such thing as a 'general' legal status.

Nowadays we do, of course, speak of a 'person' to refer to the condition of being a human. And we also speak of legal personality or legal status in a general sense. We ask, for instance, whether foetuses, animals, or the environment have legal personality. And we know that corporations count as legal persons. But this is because the word 'person' has departed from its original meaning. To see this, consider the connection between respect and personhood. We now say that the law should respect *all* persons, equally. But up until the late nineteenth century, the idea seemed to be the opposite, namely that law should be 'no respecter of persons'. The phrase was not used to condone inhuman treatment in the hands of the law but, instead, to express the normative ideal of equality before the law. This is because in its original meaning, the word 'person' meant 'role' or position in society. And hence the phrase made perfect sense: law should not take notice of people's position in society because doing so amounts to bias or favouritism. The phrase in fact comes from the New Testament, where Paul describes God as a 'no respecter of persons', using the original Greek word

[9] Jeremy Waldron, *Dignity, Rank and Rights* (Oxford: Oxford University Press, 2012), p. 59.

'πρόσωπο'.[10] I shall come back to the relation between status and (legal) personality in the next chapter.

The absence of the idea of ordinary legal status appears morally problematic to Waldron, but it need not be. In the case of Roman law, it was not the product of a belief that some individuals were less human than others or lacked humanity altogether. This false moral belief became, tragically, operative in later parts of human history. The Romans did not deny that slaves were human beings,[11] despite treating them as the object of property rights. They believed that, as Honore puts it, 'we are all free and equal members of a community related by birth'.[12] And when Gaius introduces the legal status of slaves, he makes sure to note that the institution of slavery is contrary to human nature. Roman slavery was no doubt a morally atrocious practice, but it was not perpetrated based on the moral belief that slaves, by nature, were not humans. And it couldn't have been, since any free person could become a slave and any slave could become free.

In modern times, by contrast, when the denial of a group's humanity led to the Holocaust and the other moral atrocities of the twentieth century, it became necessary to appeal to our shared humanity as the basis of moral egalitarianism and of equal legal rights. The connection between humanity and legal equality underpinned the development of human rights law and the progressive legal reforms that it has generated. But historically, it was not the case that denial of equal legal rights was necessarily based on denying a group's humanity. The Roman law of persons was not an attempt to deprive certain groups of legal personhood, and then equate legal persons with human beings. Everyone was taken to be human, and it was considered circumstantial what legal status each individual got to hold.

2.4 The Relational Character of the Law of Persons

One thing that I was struck to discover in researching the history of status was that in the original Latin text, Gaius does not use the word 'status' to describe the law of persons. Instead, he prefers the word 'condicio' throughout, which has the non-technical meaning of 'circumstances'. The word 'status' appears only four times in the original text of his *Institutes*, whereas the word 'condicio' appears over 20 times, all of which are rendered as 'status' in English by modern translators. It is fair to say that status was not a technical term in Gaius, certainly not one which would

[10] Thomas Ethelbert Page (ed.), *The Acts of Apostles* (London: Macmillan, 1886), 10:34, p. 26: 'οὐκ ἔστι προσωπολήπτης ὁ Θεός' (God does not look at people's faces).

[11] See J.-R. Trahan, 'The Distinction Between Persons & Things: An Historical Perspective', 1(1), *Journal of Civil Law* Studies (2008), p. 10; Barry Nicholas, *An Introduction to Roman Law* (Oxford: Oxford University Press, 1975), p. 60.

[12] See Antony Honore, 'The Nature of Slavery', in Jean Allain (ed.), *The Legal Understanding of Slavery* (Oxford: Oxford University Press, 2012), p. 9.

give rise to controversies about its precise meaning and constitute a philosophical problem. It is only in the *Institutes* of Justinian that the word 'status' becomes more common, taking over the word 'condicio'.[13] It is more accurate to say that the law of persons in early Roman law concerned the law of *circumstances*.

What circumstances? Two out of the three axes along which rights and duties were allocated within the law of persons are still used in modern times: citizenship and family. It is circumstantial which country and which family one is born in, and hence which citizenship and family bonds one develops. Moreover, these circumstances change one's normative profile. A citizen enjoys rights (e.g. to vote) and is burdened with duties (e.g. taxation) that non-nationals do not have. Similarly, parents have distinct legal rights and duties with respect to their children, as do spouses with respect to one another. Like contemporary law, Roman law made legally relevant two circumstances that pertain to relations: the political relation between members of a political community and the intimate relations between family members. To be sure, the actual allocation of legal rights and duties within these two relations in Roman law was different compared to nowadays, particularly with respect to the dependence of women and grown children on the head of the household (the *pater familias*). But it is worth noting that two of the three fundamental statuses identified by Roman law—citizenship and family—continue to play a significant role in human societies and are still reflected in modern legal systems. They correspond to nationality law on one hand and family law on the other.

We should therefore qualify the initial observation that two of the three categories in the Roman law of persons referred to circumstances. These are not just any circumstances, like being the victim of an accident or an assault. They are circumstances in which an individual finds themselves in a relation with another, either a political one or a kinship one. These relations are multifaceted. Citizens have a relation with one another in that they are members of the same political community. But this also changes their relation to non-citizens, with whom they interact. The existence of a political community makes certain individuals *fellow citizens* or *compatriots*. And it makes other individuals *foreigners* or *aliens*. These roles are conceptually connected. The fact that A is a foreigner vis-à-vis B means that B is a citizen of a country of which A is not. And the fact that B is a citizen means that there is a determinate group of other individuals (C, D, . . .) who are B's fellow citizens (i.e. citizens of the same country). One cannot be a citizen without fellow citizens, and one cannot be a citizen without there being individuals who count as foreigners. The same applies to family relations. The fact that A is a father or a guardian, means that there is an individual, B, who is A's child or ward. It also means that there is a determinate group of individuals (C, D, . . .) who are strangers (i.e. not in A's family). Conceptually, one cannot hold a family role without being

[13] In the *Institutes* of Justinian, 'condicio' is used almost exclusively to mean a precondition, and 'status' emerges as the main term by which to indicate different legal positions within the law of persons.

related to someone and without there being individuals with whom they bear no family relation.

To be sure, the point just made does not apply when the notions of citizenship and family are used in a metaphorical sense, to refer to the whole of humanity. We can refer to all humans as fellow citizens, as Kantians do, or as family members of the same animal species. This metaphorical use has become more common with the advent of human rights. It is used to place emphasis on moral entitlements that are not grounded on relations, and hence apply universally to all individuals, irrespective of their social relations. But this is not the common use of the word family and citizenship, nor the one that law follows. Crucially, one need not deny the existence of universal moral entitlements by recognising that certain relations, such as citizenship and family, also ground a set of rights and duties.

How about the third classification within the law of persons, that between free persons and slaves? If we examine it closely, we can observe that this classification too is relational. A slave is not simply an unfree person but someone who is in the power (*potestas*) of another, namely the slave master (*dominus*). For an individual A to be a slave, it must be the case that there is another individual (or group of individuals) who is A's master. Here, one might immediately object that the relation between a slave and their owner is very much unlike that between citizens, or between family relatives. This is correct, in that being placed under the arbitrary power of another certainly does not qualify as a relationship, that is, as a valuable bond between two parties; the opposite, it constitutes an appalling injustice and one of the most inhumane forms of exploitation. Nevertheless, there was a standing interaction between slaves and masters, which involved the provision of labour by one party under the direction of another. The slave–master relation was not only legal, a legally protected right to dominate another person with impunity but, in the central case, it also had a socio-economic dimension, namely the direction of the slave's actions with a view to extracting their labour for economic purposes. Despite its involuntary and forced character,[14] this is a feature that it shares with modern forms of employment.

Slaves in ancient Rome were engaged in many economic activities,[15] although the extent to which the entire economy depended on slave labour is a contentious issue in the literature.[16] It seems that a certain amount of work, particularly in agriculture, was also done by Roman citizens who, despite enjoying freedom, were poor. Still, slaves' commercial activity was not negligible, and owners often

[14] Though it should be mentioned that certain instances of slavery in ancient Rome were contractual. See Morris Silver, 'Contractual Slavery in the Roman Economy', 25 *Ancient History Bulletin* (2011), pp. 73–132; Edward E. Cohen, *Roman Inequality, Affluent Slaves, Business Women, Legal Fictions* (New York: Oxford University Press, 2023), ch. 3.

[15] See Richard Gamauf, 'Slaves Doing Business: The Role of Roman Law in the Economy of the Roman Household', 16(3) *European Review of History* (2009), pp. 331–346.

[16] See Chester G. Starr, 'An Overdose of Slavery', 18(1) *The Journal of Economic History* (1958), pp. 17–32.

made available to them a fund, called peculium, allowing them the appearance of an independent businessperson.[17] More importantly, it allowed them, subject to various conditions,[18] to grow this fund and use it to gain freedom (*manumission*) by paying their owner. In general, the practice of freeing slaves is certainly a distinctive characteristic of Roman slavery, compared to later forms of slavery. And it was common enough to make it the subject of legal regulation since early Roman law. Gaius tells us, for instance, that it was not legally permitted to free more than one hundred slaves in one's will.[19] The extent to which manumission took place is, however, disputed in the literature. For some it was 'a far more difficult proposition than the strict letter of the law suggests'.[20] For others, the practice of slaves using their peculium to buy their own freedom was widespread and underpinned by an economic rationale.[21]

My aim here is not to settle empirical controversies regarding the condition of slaves in Ancient Rome. Nor to suggest, as others have, that it was somewhat more humane than later forms of slavery,[22] or than earlier forms of slavery before the rise of Christianity.[23] Roman slavery was no doubt a cruel and brutal institution. Instead, my aim is to cut through the contingencies surrounding the application of the Roman law of persons and reveal the relational character of the categories that it uses. My point is interpretive, not empirical. Seen as relations, the Roman law of persons, including the status of slavery, was not based on the idea that certain people were destined to be owners, citizens, and guardians, while others were destined to be slaves, foreigners, and wards. In this respect, the law of persons was surprisingly modern. There was no fixed view of what a person's place in society should be at birth which informed the allocation of rights and duties. It is noteworthy, moreover, that since the early days of the Roman Republic, citizenship was not understood in ethnic terms, but in terms of residence in Rome. And in the later stages of the Roman Empire, it was granted to people in most imperial provinces. Similarly, slavery was not based on racial characteristics,[24] let alone a claim to racial superiority.

[17] W. W. Buckland, *A Text-book of Roman Law from August to Justinian* (Cambridge: Cambridge University Press, 1963), p. 65.

[18] See Egbert Koops, 'The Practice of Manumission Through Negotiated Conditions in Imperial Rome', in Giuseppe Dari-Mattiacci and Dennis P. Kehoe (eds), *Roman Law and Economics: Volume II: Exchange, Ownership*, and *Disputes* (Oxford: Oxford University Press, 2020).

[19] *The Institutes of Gaius*, paras 42–43.

[20] K. R. Bradley, *Slaves and Masters in the Roman Empire: A Study on Social Control* (New York: Oxford University Press, 1987), p. 111.

[21] K. Hopkins, *Conquerors and Slaves: Sociological Studies in Roman History I* (Cambridge: Cambridge University Press, 1978), pp. 115–132.

[22] Henry Maine makes the assertion that the condition of slaves in the American states influenced by Roman law, such as Louisiana, was less bad than those based on the English common law. See Henry Maine, *Ancient Law* (Oxford: Oxford University Press, 1861), p. 166.

[23] For scepticism about the humanising influence of Christianity on Roman law, see Marcia L. Colish, 'The Roman Law of Persons and Roman History: A Case of an Interdisciplinary Approach', 19 *American Journal of Jurisprudence* (1974), pp. 112–127.

[24] See Hopkins, *Conquerors and Slaves*, p. 127.

I should like to stress that I am not here equating Roman slavery, or forced labour in general, with modern forms of employment. That labour nowadays must always be contracted, never forced, marks an important transition in human history and constitutes major moral progress. But as it is obvious by its very name, forced labour is still labour. And just like modern labour, it involves a relation between two parties: the party producing the labour and the party under whose direction this takes place. Like family and citizenship, labour was seen as an important relation precisely because it generates roles on either side, each of which generates a set of rights and duties. In sum, my reconstruction of the Roman law of persons, as we find in Gaius's *Institutes*, is that it concerned the normative profile of parties involved in three important human relations, revolving around citizenship, family, and labour respectively. In the eyes of Roman law, these relations, and the status to which they give rise, were dynamic rather than static. They were not fixed permanently and they tracked circumstances, rather than rigid individual characteristics.

One might object here that the legal status of women must surely be an exception to the claim I seek to make here, since it was fixed at birth based on gender-based assumptions, and not subject to change. It is no doubt true that women were subject to several permanent incapacities: they were under the legal power of the *pater familias*, they could not hold governmental positions, and had limited rights of inheritance. But here too, we find that Roman law was progressive and nuanced. Many of these legal incapacities applied to all household dependents, both male and female, in virtue of their family role. Moreover, Gaius tells us that adult women who engage in business activities are to handle these commercial affairs for themselves and that the belief that women must necessarily be in guardianship because they are 'light-minded' (*leuitate animi*)[25] is 'specious rather than true'.[26] To modern ears, this is far from a plea for gender equality. Nevertheless, it makes us doubt that, in the eyes of Roman law, women's social role was fixed at birth and was subject to no change. In practice, women played a vital role in the Roman economy. Some commentators go as far as to claim that Roman commercial law purported to be gender-blind.[27] If a woman's circumstances involved engaging in commercial activities then gender, though an impediment, was not insurmountable.

Again, I do not mean to suggest that the treatment of women in Roman times was not appalling, an offence to the values of justice and gender equality. The point I am making is interpretive: the Roman law of persons was primarily concerned with the activities or relations of a person, rather than the kind ('sort' in Waldron's terms) of person one is. One's legal position tracked mainly the nature of the relevant relation, rather than assumptions about some immutable characteristic of individuals. Legally, the fact that a person was engaged in establishing commercial

25 *The Institutes of Gaius*, § 144.
26 *The Institutes of Gaius*, § 190.
27 Cohen, *Roman Inequality*, p. 136.

relations was more important than the fact that the person was a woman or a slave. And although one of the parties to these relations was often legally disempowered and exploited, the relation itself was not constituted by law. My suggestion therefore is that the Roman law of persons got this right: the relations surrounding labour/commerce, citizenship, and family are morally and politically significant and they precede legal regulation. They are not only apt for legal regulation but one of the main areas of social life with which law should rightly be concerned. Roman law innovated by recognising that these three relations are at the core of law.

2.5 Role-Status (*Conditio*) vs Rank-Status (*Dignitas*)

Later, I will argue that the main difference between Roman and modern law concerns *whose* side in these three relations the law takes. Now, I want to turn to another aspect of Roman law that provides support for the relational understanding of status. This is to do with the way in which Roman law treated social status (i.e. hierarchies of societal esteem). Recall that a very popular narrative about premodern societies finds a close co-relation between social status and legal status: the higher one's social status, the greater the legal privileges one enjoyed. And the thing to note about the law of persons in Gaius's *Institutes* is that it seems entirely indifferent to social hierarchies. Legal status far from tracked social status.

Since the first period of Ancient Rome, when it was still a kingdom, Roman society was stratified, marked by the class-based distinction between the patricians and the plebeians. The patricians were said to descend from the founding fathers (*patres*) of Rome. These were the noblepersons that—according to myth—Romulus first appointed to the Senate when he founded Rome. Plebeians, by contrast, who could not claim such noble lineage, were mostly of low socio-economic class. Early on, they lacked political rights and other legal privileges that the patricians enjoyed. For instance, statutes passed by the plebeian assembly were not binding on patricians. Soon after Rome became a republic, however, the plebeians sought political equality, resulting in a long period of conflict between them and the patricians, the so-called Conflict of the Orders (500–286 BC). By the time Gaius wrote his *Institutes*, the plebeians had won the fight for political equality. The only reference in the *Institutes* to the distinction between patrician and plebeians was to remind the reader that the law (the Hortensian Act) had given political equality to plebeians.[28] And other than this, Gaius takes no notice of the differences in societal esteem between patricians and plebeians.

The fact that plebeians achieved political equality did not of course mean that they enjoyed the same social status as patricians. Differences between social esteem

[28] *The Institutes of Gaius*, § 3.

or honour (*dignitas*[29] in Latin) were widespread among Roman citizens. Later on, Roman citizens were roughly divided between those of higher social status (the *honestiores*) and those of humbler status (the *humiliores*). And within each category, there were very many different ranks. Senators and equestrians, for instance, enjoyed the highest social status—constituting what we might nowadays call the elite. Moreover, the rank to which one belonged had legal significance outside the law of persons. In public law, for instance, only certain social ranks were eligible for certain public offices, such as senator. And in criminal law, a 'dual-penalty' system[30] had been developed during the period of the Roman Empire, which provided for much lighter penalties for the *honestiores* than those applied to the *humioliores*. Outside of private law, Roman society was certainly not indifferent to social status.

Still, it is important to emphasise that, as Tristan Taylor rightly observes, 'the legal categories under the Roman law of persons tell us relatively little about social status'.[31] The law of persons, and Roman private law in general, was not based on people's differences with respect to social status, which no doubt existed. We should moreover recall that private law forms the core of Roman law. Property and family law occupy by far the largest part of the canonical sources of Roman law. And herein lies one explanation of the adaptability and endurance of Roman law. Abstracting from hierarchies of social esteem (social status) and focusing instead on social relations (legal status) equipped Roman law with the ability to serve as the basis of modern European legal systems, centuries later. As European societies started to move away from nobility and hereditary privileges and towards moral egalitarianism, the Roman law of persons provided a fitting conceptual apparatus. This is not only because, as I have been arguing, it focused on certain enduring social relations in which people— any people—usually find themselves: citizenship, family, and labour. It was also because its private law was indifferent to the hierarchies of societal esteem.

I have so far been relying on a distinction to contrast the law of persons with the highly stratified character of Roman society. This is the distinction between status understood as social rank or honour (*dignitas* in Latin), and status understood as a role or a position within a social relation (*condicio* in Latin). It is time I reminded the reader of this distinction. For the remainder of this book, I shall call the former *rank-status* and the latter *role-status. Rank-status* is the position an individual occupies within a hierarchy of societal esteem. Other synonyms include esteem, honour, reputation, or simply *social* status. *Role-status*, by contrast, is the position one holds within a relation with another party, in which each party holds

[29] For the view that the Latin word *dignitas* (social esteem or honour) is different from *dignatio* (inherent moral worth), see Chapter 4.

[30] See Peter Garnsey, *Social Status and Legal Privilege in the Roman Empire* (Oxford: Oxford University Press, 1970), chs 4–6.

[31] Tristan S. Taylor, 'Social Status, Legal Status and Legal Privilege', in Paul J. du Plessis et al. (eds), *The Oxford Handbook of Roman Law and Society* (Oxford: Oxford University Press, 2016), p. 349.

a distinct set of rights and duties. Role-status, unlike rank-status, is an inherently normative notion as it bears a close connection to rights and duties. This distinction will inform much of the argument in this book. My argument so far is that the Roman law of persons, where the idea of status originates, was based on the notion of role-status, rather than that of rank-status. I will attend to rank-status in greater detail and offer an account of how the distinction with role-status should be drawn, later in Chapters 4 and 5. For now, there are two more aspects of the law of persons that I should like to mention, as they strengthen further the reading of Roman law put forward here.

2.6 Status-Loss

There is one legal doctrine where it might appear that Roman law does not distinguish between rank-status and role-status. It is known as the doctrine of *capitis diminutio*. 'Caput' in Latin means head and 'diminutio' means reduction or deterioration. Literally translated, the term means that one's head reduces so that one becomes less of a person, or even ceases to be one. Modern translators translate this term as 'status-loss', which seems to suggest that legal statuses were ranked hierarchically tracking some notion of honour or *dignitas*. We shall see, however, that this is misleading.

According to both *Institutes*, there were three degrees of *capitis diminutio*: *maxima*, *media*, and *minima*. The first and most serious one was loss of both citizenship and freedom. This was usually the result of a punishment for a serious wrong committed by a Roman citizen, either free-born or freed. In early Roman law, a person could be punished with enslavement for being caught in the act of stealing or for evading the census.[32] The second, intermediary, degree was also the result of punishment for wrongdoing. It involved the loss of citizenship, but not the loss of freedom. The wrongdoer was stripped of their Roman citizenship, and the rights that go with it, but remained free. For instance, an individual could be banished from their home and effectively turned into a foreigner. Finally, the third degree, which was the most common, involved a change in the position one held within the family. It could come about because of marriage, emancipation, or adoption, among others.

Was *capitis diminutio* an instance of a deterioration or reduction of sorts? Not necessarily. As commentators have pointed out,[33] this hardly applies to the third and most common category. In the *Institutes* of Justinian, we read that *capitis diminutio minima* covers cases not only where an independent person passes into

[32] See Buckland, *A Text-book of Roman Law*, p. 69.
[33] See Henry Goudy, 'Capitis Deminutio in Roman Law', 9(2) *Juridical Review* (1897), pp. 132–142, at 136; Nicholas, *An Introduction to Roman Law*, p. 97.

the authority of another but also, crucially, *vice-versa*.[34] It includes, in other words, the case of an individual who goes from being dependent (*alieni iuris*) on the head of the household to being independent (*sui iuris*). And this change hardly puts one in a worse position than before. The same applies to the manumission of slaves, which Gaius includes as a case of *capitis diminutio minima*, as well as to cases of adoption. Though a status (caput) is there lost, the newly acquired one is no worse, or even better, than the previous one. Gaius observes, aptly, that *capitis diminutio* was 'the exchange of one status for another', a phrase retained by Justinian. In the terms that I have been proposing here, *capitis diminutio* was the exchange of one persona or role for another (i.e. the establishing of a new relation). An individual would lose their 'head' (*caput*), in the sense that they would lose the mask (*persona*) they previously wore and replace it with a new one. This dramaturgical metaphor signified the change in an individual's relations with others. And though the new relation might sometimes be described as worse (for instance when a free citizen became enslaved or banished), what mattered was that this new relation entailed a change in one's rights and duties—a new role.

That *capitis diminutio* was not, in essence, about social rank is also evidenced by a further observation. The mere loss of one's honour (*dignitas*), what I called *rank-status*, did not bring about a change in one's legal position under the law of persons. The *Institutes* of Justinian are clear that *capitis diminutio* does not occur 'where people suffer a setback in honour rather than status'.[35] Losing one's social status did not affect one's legal status in private law. To be sure, loss of honour did have other legal repercussions. Engaging in activities seen by Romans as disgraceful, such as having been convicted of certain crimes or practising certain professions (e.g. gladiator, prostitute, or actor), placed individuals in a disreputable state called *infamia*. This was not a legally defined state but those who were considered as disgraced or disreputable suffered from several legal incapacities to do with public and criminal law. They could not hold public office, bring an accusation in a criminal case, or represent others in court. However, as Robert Knapp notes,[36] these legal incapacities were hardly debilitating for the average citizen. They concerned mainly the elite for whom more was at stake. Individuals of high social status (*honestiores*) who fell into a state of *infamia* were prevented from pursuing activities, such as holding public office, that pertained to their rank and were expected of them. But for the *humiliores*, who were the majority of the population, those activities were in any case beyond their reach and of little interest. With respect to private law, *infamia* was largely irrelevant.

[34] Peter Birks and Grant McLeod (eds), *Justinian Institutes* (London: Duckworth, 1987), § 1.16.5, p. 49.

[35] Birks and McLeod, *Justinian Institutes*, § 1.16.5, p. 49.

[36] See Robert Knapp, 'Legally Marginalised Groups: The Empire', in Paul J. du Plessis et al. (eds), *The Oxford Handbook of Roman Law and Society* (Oxford: Oxford University Press, 2016), p. 362.

2.7 The Explanatory Priority of Status

There is a final aspect of the Roman law of persons that I want to highlight here, because it relates to the way status operates as a conceptual device. As discussed already, status in Roman law was a legally relevant condition or circumstance in which an individual found themselves. On closer examination, this condition involved a relation of that individual with another, each of which occupies a role. These relations generate pairs of roles: citizen/alien, father/child, guardian/ward, master/slave. The law allocates these roles to different individuals, such that the individual is or becomes the role—for example, a citizen, a freed person, or a guardian. Once an individual occupies, in the eyes of the law, that role, then they acquire a set of legal rights, duties, capacities, incapacities, and the like. What we should observe here is that from the point of view of law, the order of explanation is *from* the role-status *to* a set of rights and duties. The role-status is presented as the basis upon which a set of rights and duties is grounded. In the following chapters, I will show how this idea became central in Samuel Pufendorf's work and provide a philosophical defence of it.

Now, the first book of the *Institutes* of Gaius, which is on the law of persons, tells us relatively little about the rights and duties attached to each status. Instead, it concerns mostly the conditions under which one acquires or loses the relevant status. In the case of family relations, for example, a large part is devoted to the conditions under which a newborn child acquires the status of a Roman citizen. This priority of status over rights and duties is a device commonly employed by modern legal systems. Instead of providing a list of rights and duties that an individual has in circumstances X, Y, and Z, the law first describes the circumstances under which a person acquires (or loses) a given status (e.g. an employee). At a second stage, the law proceeds to give an account of rights and duties that pertain to the status. But why is that?

One explanation here, which later appealed to John Austin, is that this is a more convenient way to present the relevant set of rights and duties. Instead of laying out the rights and duties applicable in a set of circumstances, the law creates a shorthand by way of a legal fiction. An employee, for instance, is whoever has been given by law a set of rights and duties in some defined circumstances. On Austin's view, the status of an employee is a legal fiction in that it does not aim to capture some extra-legal entity; it simply denotes the way law allocates certain employment rights. Hence, status has no priority over the related set of legal rights and duties. It *is* that set.

As we shall see later, however, Austin's view cannot fully explain why law places explanatory priority on status. It would make little sense to provide a list of statuses ahead of giving an account of the rights and duties that accompany them if status did not convey some meaningful information about the nature of these rights and duties. A hypothetical might help here. Suppose I tell you that an individual has the status of a Tuesday-born, which is acquired by being born on a Tuesday between 6am and 12pm. You will be at a loss to get a sense of what rights and duties possibly accompany such a status. By contrast, if I were to tell you that an individual has the status of a firstborn child, you will immediately get a sense of what the accompanying set looks like, which concerns the relation between the firstborn child and their family. You will understand that the individual's status is based on a belief that being firstborn should attract certain family privileges (e.g. with respect to inheritance or decision-making) vis-à-vis one's family members. This is because status here operates as the putative *ground* of the related set of rights and duties. The belief, of course, might be false, judged morally. But it is nevertheless a meaningful attempt to ground rights and duties on status.

The relational character of the category of being firstborn not only conveys meaningful information about the accompanying set of rights and duties but also reflects the belief that this relation is normatively significant. To be sure, the actual allocation of rights and duties is morally problematic, as far as privileges go. But it is not mistaken with respect to whether it is morally significant. Being a firstborn may make a moral difference to one's normative profile. In certain cases, it might mean that the firstborn bears duties (rather than privileges) to care for younger siblings or the rest of the family simply because one is older and more capable. Status can have the priority that law gives it, since it points to an underlying relation that serves as a plausible normative basis for allocating rights and duties. To put it differently, not anything can be a legal status. The law of persons in the *Institutes* of Gaius guides us through a complex set of rules about how one acquires or loses different statuses while telling us little about what rights and duties are attached to these statuses. This would not be possible, if we were unable to make sense of the underlying relations that it tracks: citizenship, family, and labour.

2.8 Conclusion

Let me take stock. I suggested that status in Roman law was surprisingly modern and forward-looking. It was not based on notions such as honour, reputation, or rank; instead, it focused on certain enduring relations within individuals' lives. It was relation-based rather than honour-based. I then suggested that this aspect of status explains why it proved appealing to the young European nations emerging out of medieval feudalism and turning against nobility. My account may sound anachronistic to the modern ear, but it is presented here as an interpretive reconstruction of the Roman law of persons. I certainly do not want to place too much emphasis on it. None is needed for the main argument advanced in the book, since that argument is not premised on any historical claims. But it is important to tell a story about why the notion of status was transposed into modern legal systems many centuries later and why it came to be seen as a philosophical problem. Any such explanation must acknowledge that the Roman law of persons, in which the notion of status originates, did not track social hierarchies of esteem, a notion that I have been calling *rank-status*. It focused, instead, on three relations which we still find in most human societies (citizenship, family, and labour) and which generate bilateral roles. This latter notion is what I called *role-status*.

The assumption that legal status was always to do with social hierarchies of esteem, and the way they manifest in law, is not only inaccurate but also a philosophical distraction. It stands in the way of explaining both the continuity and the importance of status in modern legal systems. As we shall see, the relational character of status was neglected by the legal philosophers of the nineteenth century, when status came to be seen as a philosophical problem. And contemporary philosophers typically assume that status is about social hierarchies that should have no place in contemporary legal systems. By showing that status in Roman law was primarily relational, rather than based on honour, I hope to lay the groundwork for a normative argument about the significance of status. The Romans saw that status is a valuable moral notion.

3
STATUS
'A MORAL FIELD FOR PERSONS TO EXIST IN'

3.1 Introduction

There is a notion of status, this book argues, that is fundamentally a moral idea, the basis of a distinct set of rights and duties that people hold within certain relations. In the previous chapter, I traced the intellectual origins of this notion in the Roman law of persons. There, we saw two key ideas emerging, one positive and one negative. The first is that status is *relational*; it concerns certain relations or standing interactions between two parties, each of which occupies a role (*role-status*). For example, one's status as a citizen co-relates with another's status as an alien; one's status as the head of the household co-relates with another's status as family dependent. The second idea is that status, thus understood, does not track hierarchies of societal esteem (*rank-status*). For instance, Roman law considered rank-status to be irrelevant to the allocation of interpersonal rights and duties: losing one's good standing in society (*infamia*) did not entail any loss of private law rights. Role-status tracks, instead, certain enduring interpersonal interactions in which, as we will begin to see in this chapter, certain asymmetries are embedded.

The notion of status that I traced in Roman law did not disappear with the collapse of the Roman Empire. It made a strong comeback when Roman law was rediscovered in Europe in the late Middle Ages. But this time, it had an impact on seventeenth- and eighteenth-century moral and political thought. Philosophers turned to status to identify a distinct moral practice. They did not agree, however, on what that practice is, and modern scholars will struggle to find a fully articulated conception of status within this classic literature. Nevertheless, the prominence that status enjoyed during that period in moral philosophy poses a challenge to Henry Maine's thesis that status was confined to the ancient world. I do not know why Maine neglected this philosophical literature.[1] One possible explanation is that he sought to focus exclusively on legal status. But this

[1] Kant is mentioned only once in Henry Sumner Maine, *Ancient Law* (Oxford: Oxford University Press, 1861) and there is no mention of Samuel Pufendorf. Though Maine discusses Bentham extensively, there is no discussion of Bentham's category of 'Offences against condition' (status).

Status in Law and Morality. George Letsas, Oxford University Press. © George Letsas 2026.
DOI: 10.1093/9780198936725.003.0003

rationale risks resulting in a distorted account of status. Legal status, insofar as it is a distinct idea, cannot be dismissed as a wholly artificial creation of the law. It must pick out a notion that exists independently of the positive law. And if that notion has an inherent moral dimension, as seventeenth- and eighteenth-century philosophers maintained, then it becomes less plausible that it would be confined to ancient law. The simplicity of Maine's thesis no doubt contributed to its popularity, but its lasting influence obscured the true character of status as primarily a moral idea.

3.2 The Comeback of Status

The rediscovery of Roman law was followed by its rapid expansion during the Renaissance, when it became a field of academic study in the newly founded European universities. The Justinian codification grew in significance and came to be known as the *Corpus Iuris Civilis*—the body of civil law. As the primary source for the study of Roman law, it was gradually absorbed by the legal systems of the emerging European states. But it was not just lawyers who turned to Roman law. Philosophers, theologians, historians, politicians, and writers started to grapple with the main categories of Roman law and to interpret them against the background of the gradual secularisation of European politics. Nowadays, law is typically classified under the social sciences but at the time, it was at the centre of all the humanities. Nowadays, legal scholars turn to philosophy to understand, scrutinise, or challenge law, but back then philosophers turned to law to understand, scrutinise, or challenge moral ideas. During that period, and in the run-up to the Enlightenment, Roman law became a common moral grammar, the basis upon which modern moral, legal, and political thought was built.

Why Roman law had this appeal to the humanists and the intellectuals whose work laid the foundation for the Enlightenment is not easy to explain. In the previous chapter, I offered a partial explanation: the progressive character of Roman private law made it fertile ground for the critical moral thinking that followed the Middle Ages and cultivated the movement towards moral egalitarianism. As we saw, the fundamental categories of Roman private law were not tied to hierarchies of societal esteem, what I called *rank-status*. Medieval law, by contrast, was structured around social hierarchy, aiming at protecting the privileges of European nobility. In the telling example given by Jeremy Waldron, medieval English law would allow a nobleperson to sue a commoner for defamation but not the other way around.[2] Unlike Roman law, rank-status was rigidly embedded in medieval private law.

[2] Jeremy Waldron, *Dignity, Rank and Rights* (Oxford: Oxford University Press, 2012), p. 63.

There is another reason, however, behind the appeal of Roman law at the time. Religious matters were largely in its periphery, not only of private law but also of Roman public law.[3] Religious authorities in Gaius's time, and before the split of the Roman Empire, had little political power. By contrast, medieval Europe was founded on Christianity, with the church having extensive legal and political power. Though medieval natural law theories were distinctively theological, the humanist turn to the study of classics during the Renaissance, and the rise of Protestantism, loosened the grip of religion on the humanities. As ideas of moral egalitarianism started to emerge, Roman law served not only as a source of inspiration but also as an antidote to the nobility-based and religion-driven character of medieval Europe.

When scholars began to grapple with the canonical text of the Justinian codification, status emerged as a key notion in both legal and philosophical literature. In law, it figures in the writings of the sixteenth- and seventeenth-century jurists who produced commentaries of Roman law, such as Hugues Doneau (1527–1591) and Jean Domat (1625–1696). It started to intrigue and to puzzle them. In the early part of the nineteenth century, it drew the attention of the great German jurist, Carl Von Savigny (1779–1861) and, in the English-speaking world, Jeremy Bentham. It is no easy task to research the intellectual trajectory of status during that period. As far as I was able to establish, it is Bentham's and Savigny's work that provided the impetus for status to emerge as a philosophical problem in the Anglo-American world. When John Austin popularised status as the 'most difficult problem in the science of jurisprudence' in the late nineteenth century, he was reacting to Bentham's account of status. And he was familiar with Savigny's work, as was Henry Maine and, later, Roscoe Pound.

In philosophical literature, status becomes a powerful moral idea. It figures prominently in the work of the humanist thinker Samuel Pufendorf (1632–1694), whose account will occupy me at some length. Like other modern natural lawyers,[4] most notably Hugo Grotius (1583–1645), Pufendorf drew on the ancient classics to develop a highly systematised account of morality and politics. But the influence of Roman law was also evident later, in Immanuel Kant's philosophy. In the *Metaphysics of Morals*, Kant offered a tripartite classification of rights: rights to persons, rights to things, and rights to person akin to rights to things. As we shall see, tripartite classifications, inspired by the *Institutes*, became a familiar motif in modern political thought. And though Kant did not use the Latin term 'status', his

[3] See Andrew M. Riggsby, *Roman Law and the Legal World of the Romans* (Cambridge: Cambridge University Press, 2012), ch. 20.

[4] On so-called 'modern' natural law theories in general see Richard Tuck, 'The "Modern" Theory of Natural Law', in Anthony Pagden (ed.), *The Languages of Political Theory in Early-Modern Europe* (Cambridge: Cambridge University Press, 2009).

last category (rights to persons akin to rights to things) is nowadays commonly referred to as 'status'.[5]

I have, perhaps, dropped too many names already. My primary aim is not to do history of philosophy but to construct a philosophical theory of status. In the previous chapter, I argued that Roman law identified certain relations as morally significant and as a central domain of human affairs with which law should be concerned. I sought to highlight the relational character of status, as a legal idea. In this chapter, I want to begin to channel seventeenth- and eighteenth-century philosophical theories of status and to identify their strengths and weaknesses. These have been neglected, in large part because of the distorting influence of Henry Maine's theory and his claim that status relations were confined to the ancient world, having been replaced by contractual relations. My focus will be on Samuel Pufendorf, a philosopher whose work is underappreciated in the English-speaking world. There is one normative proposition that I locate in Pufendorf's work, and that I shall aim to unpack in this chapter: status is a fundamental moral entity that serves as the ground of rights and duties. How status serves as the ground of certain rights and duties is not obvious. What does it mean to say that, *qua* an employee, one has the right against unfair dismissal? Is the status of an employee a shorthand for an unstated normative justification? Or could it be self-standing, requiring no further explanation?

The story I will tell in this chapter is this: early modern political thinkers saw status as a significant moral, and not just legal, category. They stressed the significance of the link between the notion of status and a set of moral rights and duties, which precedes law. The three most important thinkers here are Pufendorf, Kant, and Bentham. I will draw on their accounts while building my own theory of status. Despite their differences (and there are many), all three philosophers recognised status as primarily a moral notion, capable of serving as a justification for a subset of moral obligations. All three identified the asymmetrical character of status relations and the challenge it poses to the value of equality. That the moral dimension of status is inextricably linked to the value of equality was obvious to these moral philosophers. But this link was later neglected. With John Austin, and later Henry Maine, there was a substantial shift in the understanding of status and a departure from relational accounts. Both Austin and Maine conceived of status in legalistic terms, as legal notions. They sought to understand it exclusively as a way in which legal institutions allocate rights and duties rather than a subset of genuine moral rights and duties. Once status became detached from its moral roots, its place in

[5] See Arthur Ripstein, *Force and Freedom* (Cambridge: Harvard University Press, 2009). Ripstein takes the term 'status' from Mary Gregor's translation of *The Metaphysics of Morals*. See Immanuel Kant, *The Metaphysics of Morals*, edited by Lara Denis and translated by Mary Gregor (Cambridge: Cambridge University Press, 2017). Thank you to Arthur Ripstein for discussion. Like the first translation of Bentham's early work to French, 'condition' and 'status' were used interchangeably.

the law started to make little sense. It puzzled legal theorists and became a jurisprudential problem. Yet we can only get a clear philosophical sense of status if we return to its original philosophical understanding. The main aim of this chapter is to explain why status is a moral entity and how it is linked to the value of equality. To do so, I will draw heavily on the work of Samuel Pufendorf and his idea that status is a moral field for persons to exist in.

3.3 Status as a Moral Entity

By the middle of the seventeenth century, Roman law was widely taught and studied in Europe. The French jurist Jean Domat (1625–1696) was probably one of the first thinkers to express puzzlement at the notion of status as a legal category, and to identify it as a theoretical problem. In his legal digest,[6] published in 1689, Domat noted that the Roman law of persons concerns the different qualities that individuals have in virtue of which they have different statuses, such as 'a Freeman, a slave, a Father, and a Son'. 'But', he hastened to add, 'we do not there find any thing that points out to us what is common to all these qualities, which might help us to conceive a just and precise idea of what the character necessary to a Quality, so as to be able to say that it concerns, or doth not concern the state of a person'.[7]

Domat was, in one respect, right. If one compares the legal duties involved, statuses are very different from one another. The status of a parent for instance has little in common with the status of a slave. Though parents often complain about the hardship of their predicament, they are not under the legal control of another, as slaves were. Note, however, that in the passage just quoted, Domat introduces a new term, characterising status as a *quality*. But what kind of quality is involved here, such that we can look for commonalities? This question relates to a broader one: what is the ontology of status? How does one acquire it or lose it? Roman law, recall, classified certain legal rights and duties in terms of the persons that hold them. And 'persons' was taken to refer to *personas* (masks) or roles that a given individual holds.

Now, Domat suggests that these roles must refer to some distinguishing quality that the holder has. And this sounds plausible. We say, for instance, that *qua* a father one must look after one's children. The preposition '*qua*' denotes some quality or qualification that an individual possesses. But it is much more than that. It denotes, in these cases, what normative requirements apply to a person in virtue of occupying a role.

Writing in the same period as Domat, the German humanist Samuel von Pufendorf was less interested in an exegesis of Roman law. He refused an

[6] Jean Domat, *Lois Civils dans leur Ordre Naturel* (1689). References are to the English edition, *Civil Law in Its Natural Order*, translated by William Strahan (London, 1722).
[7] Ibid., p. 17.

appointment in Roman law at the University of Heidelberg, citing his disagreement with the various ways in which Roman law diverged from natural law.[8] Instead, Pufendorf sought to develop a natural law theory of ethics and politics. His work, neglected for a long time, has attracted much philosophical attention recently.[9] And he has a lot to say about status too. He is, in fact, the first philosopher to develop a systematic account of status as a moral idea. With Pufendorf, a new idea emerges: status is not the mere creation of the law but a moral entity. And it is not just any ordinary moral entity; it is fundamental, the basis of moral persons and moral actions. Pufendorf's thoughts on status are dense, yet fascinating. They form a constant theme in his moral and political writings, from his early treatise, *Elements of Universal Jurisprudence*, to his final essay on the topic, *On the Natural State of Men*.[10]

Status, Pufendorf tells us in his early work, is 'a suppositive entity because it is made the basis of positive moral affairs, so that on it they rest such moral existence as they have, and erect their actions and their effects'.[11] I came across Pufendorf's definition at a late stage of writing this book and after I had published an article defending a moral account of status.[12] Pufendorf's formulation excited and fascinated me. It departs from the legal origins of status and treats it as a fundamentally moral construct. There is a lot to unpack here, and it requires a closer look at Pufendorf's philosophy. Like with all great thinkers, the line between exegesis and reconstruction is thin and competing interpretations are to be expected.

Pufendorf treats status as a fundamental moral idea from the start, without a discernible rationale. He does not motivate his account with examples of different statuses and how they ground rights and duties. Instead, he begins with an abstract characterisation of status, and proceeds to specific statuses only after he has developed a general model. His starting point is that status is a moral entity in contradistinction to a physical or a natural entity (I shall use these adjectives interchangeably)—say a rock or a human body. Moral entities, of which status is a central case, are 'modes superadded to natural things and motions, by understanding beings, chiefly for the guiding and tempering the freedom of voluntary actions'.[13] Pufendorf insists on a strict separation between natural and moral entities. Unlike

[8] See Leonard Krieger, 'History and Law in the Seventeenth Century: Pufendorf', 21(2) *Journal of the History of Ideas*, pp. 198–216, at 205, fn. 22, citing: Pufendorf to Thomasius, 16 Oct. 1688, in Varentrapp, ed., 'Briefe', Historische Zeitschrift, LXX, 36–37; 1 Dec. 1688 and 9 Apr. 1692, in Gigas (ed.), Briefe Pufendorfs, 32, 67; Pufendorf, *Eris Scandica*, 125.

[9] See, among others, Stephen Darwall, 'Pufendorf on Morality, Sociability and Moral Powers', 50(2) *Journal of the History of Philosophy* (2012), pp. 213–238; Knud Haahonssen and Ian Hunter (eds), *The Cambridge Companion to Pufendorf* (Cambridge: Cambridge University Press, 2023).

[10] *Samuel Pufendorf's Of The Natural State of Men, the 1678 Latin Edition and English Translation Translated, Annotated, and Introduced by Michael Seidler*, Studies in the History of Philosophy, Vol. 13 (Lewiston: Edwin Mellen Press, 1990).

[11] Pufendorf, *Elements of Universal Jurisprudence*, p. 26.

[12] George Letsas, 'Offences Against Status', 43(2) *Oxford Journal of Legal Studies* (2023), pp. 322–349.

[13] Samuel Pufendorf, *Of the Law of Nature and Nations* (Oxford, 1703), p. 2.

natural entities, moral entities are imposed ('superadded') onto the natural world through the decision of reasonable agents, out of 'their own free will'. Though the role of moral entities is to guide human action, they do not inhere in anything physical.

Talk of humans imposing moral properties on natural properties might suggest that Pufendorf took moral judgments to be mere expressions of human emotions or desires. But Pufendorf was a firm believer in moral objectivity. Though not physical, he took moral entities to be no less real. He rejected the common conviction that in morality 'there is no firm and infallible certainty, and that all knowledge of such matters rests upon probable opinion only',[14] which he thought was based on a misunderstanding of Aristotelian ethics. And he held that, just like with the natural sciences, it is possible to do moral science by demonstrating the necessity of certain relations between moral propositions. One could demonstrate, for example, that theft and robbery are 'against the Law of Nature'.

Just like Hobbes before him, Pufendorf sought to develop a moral science by analogy to the natural sciences. In his early work, he employed a mathematical method, whereby necessary connections can be established ('demonstrated') by a set of axioms.[15] His book, *Elements of Universal Jurisprudence* (note the ambition of the title) is arranged as a series of definitions and axioms, from which concrete moral propositions are said to flow, through syllogism. Quite astonishingly, Pufendorf wrote this book within eight months while imprisoned in the Copenhagen town hall during the first Nordic war between Sweden and Denmark.[16] In the *Elements*, Pufendorf argues that human action is something more than bare physical movement, since it involves the exercise of the will, as well as the reason 'by which the action as decided by the will is conceived'. Being reason-based, human action has a non-physical dimension; it is something humans impose on the physical world, rather than contained in it. It is, moreover, 'imputative', in that we must impute a reason, 'an inclination of the mind', to bodily movement if we are to attribute actions to individuals at all. And since morality concerns the 'inclinations of the mind' and 'the habits of life', Pufendorf concludes that human action is moral, by which he means that it has necessarily a moral dimension. Put differently, no human action is a purely physical event, a material motion ('locomotive' as Pufendorf puts it) occurring in the natural world; rather, it contains already the properties which lead us to characterise it in moral terms.

We can place Pufendor's view within contemporary meta-ethics, allowing a more precise analysis of its philosophical implications. He is a non-naturalist in

[14] Ibid., p. 7.

[15] Pufendorf was heavily influenced by his friend, Erhard Weigel, a professor of Mathematics at the University of Jena. Weigel had sought to marry the Euclidean method of doing mathematics with Aristotle's analysis. See Erhard Weigel, *Analysis Aristotelica ex Euclide Restituta* (Jena: Grosium, 1658).

[16] See Ian Hunter, 'Introduction', in Knud Haahonssen and Ian Hunter (eds), *The Cambridge Companion to Pufendorf* (2023), p. 12.

that he takes moral properties to be discontinuous with natural properties.[17] Unlike naturalists, non-naturalists believe that moral properties, such as wrongness, are not reducible to, or identical with, natural properties. Roughly understood, natural properties are those that are studied by the natural sciences (e.g. physics) and whose existence can be established using empirical methods. Moreover, Pufendorf is a moral objectivist since he takes moral properties to be real and no less objective than natural properties.

It is less clear, however, what relation Pufendorf sees between the moral and the non-moral properties of action. He thinks that we impute to action various moral *qualities*, such as 'modes', 'affections', and 'effects', including rights and obligations flowing from it. For example, we impute to an act of robbery that it is unjust, a breach of someone's right. And he believes that this imputation would be impossible if there was no moral entity inherent in the act and upon which imputations about rights and duties are based. The imputation must have a basis, a ground on which these moral qualities stand. And that basis cannot be the physical aspects of the act, because—being physical—they cannot provide moral support. Pufendorf concludes that human action must have a formal element, a 'positive form, from which, as from a root, spring those affections, properties, and consequences of which we must treat here'.[18]

Pufendorf's account postulates a complex relation between action, its moral qualities, and their grounding. Precisely because human actions are the product of the will, they have a non-physical dimension which is imposed on the physical. Actions are imputed to agents and this imputation is a mark of their moral, non-material dimension. Moreover, acts have moral qualities and effects. But for these qualities and effects to obtain there must be some base-level entity which serves as the object of qualification, and which produces the relevant effects. If there are moral qualifiers, there must be something that they qualify. Pufendorf thinks that they do not qualify the physical dimension of the act, but he does not explain why. Instead, he thinks that they qualify some underlying moral entity, a 'substance', which serves as the root of moral qualities. Though this substance inheres in the action, it is imposed by us (superadded), rather than being part of the physical world.

Human action, then, has three layers for Pufendorf: first, a material element which extends in the natural world; second, a moral substance ('a root') that is embedded in the physical action and upon which various qualities and effects of the action are grounded; and third, the actual moral qualities and effects that the action produces. It is the second and third layers that are most significant for Pufendorf: insofar as human action produces moral effects, it is a 'positive moral

[17] I take this formulation from Victor Moberger, 'The MacKiean Supervenience Challenge', 22 *Ethical Theory and Moral Practice* (2019), pp. 219–236.

[18] *Elements of Universal Jurisprudence*, p. 22.

entity' that belongs in 'the class of things moral, not of things in nature'. Any human action for Pufendorf contains this two-tier moral structure.

The argument Pufendorf gives for why moral qualities need a basis, or ground, proceeds by analogy to physics. Just like quality and quantity don't exist independently but are properties of physical substances, likewise, moral qualities and 'affections' (such as rights and duties) do not exist independently but are properties of moral substances.[19] Hence, moral entities can be of two kinds for Pufendorf: either the 'root' or 'substance' of an action, or the various 'modes' (qualities, affections, and effects) that 'spring' from the root or qualify the substance. In *Of the Laws of Nature and Nations*, he writes:

> Now though moral entities do not subsist of themselves, and for that reason ought not in general, to be ranked under the class of substances but of modes; yet we find many of them to be conceived in the manner of substances, because other moral things seem to be immediately founded in them, just as quantities and qualities inhere in the real substance of bodies.[20]

Pufendorf thinks that qualities of moral actions, including the rights and duties they generate, must be properly grounded on some underlying moral substance, if they are to be non-arbitrary. Moral qualities and effects are not base-level moral entities; they require another entity, a fundamental substance, on which to be grounded. Pufendorf denied, in other words, that moral rights and duties are fundamental moral categories. They are grounded on something else altogether.

Pufendorf moves on to introduce the notion of status, which he takes to be a base-level entity, upon which various moral qualities, including moral persons, are founded. Status he tells us, is a 'suppositive' moral entity (i.e. it sits below ('sub') other posited qualities). It is the basis of moral affairs—that is, of claims we impute regarding the person who takes a given action using their will. Just as space 'sits below' natural objects and substances, likewise status 'sits below' two moral entities: persons and actions. Whereas persons and actions are positive entities, status is a 'suppositive' entity; it is more fundamental, being the root of moral claims about persons and actions.

The analogy between status and space receives a longer treatment in *Of the Law of Nature and Nations*. There, Pufendorf argues that moral entities are similar to natural substances in one respect, namely that they have properties, such as qualities and quantities. And just as natural substances are contained in space, likewise moral entities are contained in statuses. Status, Pufendorf claims, may be defined by analogy to space:

[19] According to Thomas Behme, Pufendorf took this analogy from the work of his friend, Erhard Weigel.

[20] Pufendorf, *Of the Law of Nature and Nations* (1703), Book I, chapter I, § VI, p. 3.

> As space seems no principal and original being, but is devised to be as it were, spread under other things, to hold and sustain them in some particular manner; so the several statuses were not introduced for their own sakes, but to make a field for moral persons to exist in.[21]

Pufendorf adds, crucially, that 'peculiar rights and obligations accompany each status.'[22] The moral space of status not only encompasses moral persons, but also grounds a distinct set of rights and duties.

I consider Pufendorf's analogy with space to be the most significant insight in the history of the concept of status. It captures, in a single phrase, the core thesis of this book: status is the field for moral persons to exist in. What this means, I shall argue, is that status marks out distinct roles or domains ('fields') of personal interactions in our lives, where a unique set of rights and duties applies, in the same way in which space marks out a unique field on which an object sits. Status 'holds and sustains' moral persons holding roles with a distinct set of rights and duties. Put differently, statuses mark out discrete moral fields, within which specific role obligations are held. Morality is not an unvaried, homogenous domain; it is demarcated by statuses, fields where persons interact holding specific roles. As we shall see, the moral reason why these fields are discrete is that they pose a distinct threat to the value of equality.

Pufendorf's account stands in stark contrast to attempts to unpack status as a quality attached to natural persons. He considers status, not as a moral quality, but as the moral space on which moral persons, and their qualities, are founded. The difference is subtle but significant. On one view, which we found in Domat, status is a quality attached to a person, understood in naturalistic terms. Like a mask one puts on, this view understands status in descriptive terms as a material property attached to physical beings. This is a familiar account that, as we shall see, was defended by John Austin. On the alternative view, which Pufendorf puts forward, status is the moral basis (the root) of a person. But the person here is understood in moral terms, as the holder of a set of rights and duties, rather than in physical terms. On Pufendorf's view, status is part of the moral explanation of the rights and duties that a person enjoys when holding a role. Indeed, Pufendorf is keen to stress that statuses do not have a physical existence. When he says that statuses are a 'field' or 'space' in which moral persons exist, he does not mean to refer to the physical space they occupy or the material interactions in which they engage. To illustrate this point, he stresses a disanalogy between status and physical space: if one removes the object that occupies a given space, Pufendorf says, the space itself will persist being 'a kind of immoveable substance extended primarily and of it itself',

[21] Ibid.

[22] *Of the Law of Nature and Nations*, Book I, chapter I, § IX, p. 4.

but if one removes a person that occupies a status then 'the status itself is in manifest danger of losing its own existence'.

Pufendorf's claim that status serves as a type of moral foundation ('a root') introduces a number of concepts (moral space, moral persons, moral actions) and a whole new set of questions. What is a moral person, if not a natural being? In what way are moral properties, such as rights and duties, *grounded* on status? How many statuses are there and is there a finite number? Are there rights and duties *not* grounded on status? Pufendorf's account is scant on detail but there is one distinction he draws that is of great significance and to which we need to turn.

3.4 Natural and Adventitious Statuses

Status is a moral entity, a moral field that 'holds and sustains' persons. It is the root from which other moral entities, including rights and duties, stem. That is still quite abstract. It is still not obvious how status serves as a moral field in which persons exist. To be sure, when a person occupies a status, there is an obvious sense in which they 'exist' in that space. When a person has children, for example, parenthood is the moral field in which they exist. This, however, comes close to a tautology. But status according to Pufendorf is also meant to 'hold and sustain' those who occupy it, and to justify the rights and duties that they come under.

As we shall see in more detail in Chapter 7, status—much like the idea of a role—often appears to have an intrinsic justificatory power. We appeal to it *simpliciter* to justify our conduct. If Antonio in *The Bicycle Thieves* were to be asked why he was so desperate to keep his job and provide for his family, he might simply reply, 'because I am a father'. He need say nothing more. Common sense morality treats roles as foundational justificatory elements in justifying the duties that pertain to them. Yet as philosophers, we should be able to say more than that. What is it about parenthood that grounds these duties? What motivates people to take action *qua* parents, often as extreme as a decent man like Antonio committing theft? It is true, of course, that the need for normative justification cannot go on indefinitely. Some normative explanations, like the moral value of equality, must be close to axiomatic, in that they are not derived from further premises. But is status the sort of normative explanation that tells us everything we would want to hear to assess the moral quality of an act? This is unlikely. Perhaps this is the case with parenthood,[23] but it is hard to see how it applies to other statuses, like employment status. It is not obvious what Antonio's employer should, *qua* employer, do when Antonio has his bicycle stolen. Does Antonio have a right not to be dismissed? Or does his employer have a duty to provide him with a bicycle? Unless we know why

[23] For an argument that parental obligation forms a basic, non-consensual type, on which other obligations can be modelled see Nancy Hirschmann, *Rethinking Obligation: A Feminist Method for Political Theory* (Ithaca: Cornell University Press, 1992).

employment status grounds a set of bilateral rights and duties, we cannot just invoke it one way or another.

Pufendorf does not directly explain how status justifies rights and duties. But the answer lies in his discussion of humans' natural equality and in a crucial distinction he draws between *natural* and *adventitious* statuses. This distinction has since become a recurrent theme in philosophical thinking. In his 1955 article 'Are There Any Natural Rights?',[24] H. L. A. Hart distinguished between general rights and special rights. The former are defensive rights against interference that everyone holds equally and are addressed against everyone else. Broadly conceived, they are the rights we have 'simply in virtue of being human'. This is now the familiar idea of human rights, the thought that there is a fundamental set of rights grounded on our status as humans.[25] It has become the focus of much philosophical attention in the last few decades, after the development—and unquestionable success—of the human rights movement.[26] Special rights, by contrast, arise out of either promissory agreements or as Hart puts it, of 'some special relationship in which they stand to each other'. The idea of a special relationship seeks to capture *role*-specific rights that not everyone has. It is the idea that forms the subject matter of this book. Pufendorf's term ('adventitious') for this category of rights and obligations, is inspired. It captures the fact that we stumble into these role-statuses and not all of us occupy them. Here is how Pufendorf seeks to draw the distinction:

> **Natural status**: the universal condition of humanity in which every person exists and upon which the obligation to observe the laws of nature is founded.[27]
>
> **Adventitious statuses**: the condition in which a particular person finds themselves because of either (i) a voluntary act (such as promise or agreement)[28] (ii) a particular condition or state[29] or (ii) a command of a superior or law,[30] and upon which non-universal rights and obligations are founded.

[24] H. L. A. Hart, 'Are There Any Natural Rights?', 64(2) *The Philosophical Review* (1955), pp. 175–191.

[25] Allan Gewirth, *Human Rights: Essays on Justification and Applications* (Chicago: University of Chicago Press, 1982).

[26] See James Nickel, *Making Sense of Human Rights* (Oxford: Blackwell, 2007; James Griffin, *On Human Rights* (Oxford: Oxford University Press, 2008); Charles Beitz, *The Idea of Human Rights* (New York: Oxford University Press, 2009).

[27] Pufendorf, *Elements of Universal Jurisprudence*, p. 27 ('it involves the obligation of observing the law of nature both towards himself and towards other men'); Pufendorf, *Of The Law of Nature and of Persons*, Book I, chapter I, § VII, p. 3 ('the very being of man is a status, obliging to certain duties, and giving a Title to certain rights').

[28] Pufendorf, *Of The Law of Nature and of Persons*, Book III, chapter VI, § III, p. 3 ('Adventitious Obligations, are such as fall upon Men, by the Intervention of some Human Deed; not without the Consent of the Parties, either Express, or at least Presumptive'); Book III, chapter V, § I, p. 205 ('All adventitious obligations proceed, either from a simple, or from a mutual act; of which the former is properly call'd a free Grant or Promise, the latter a Pact or Covenant').

[29] Pufendorf, *On the Duty of Man and Citizen According to Natural Law* (Cambridge: Cambridge University Press, 1991), p. 56.

[30] Pufendorf, *Elements of Universal Jurisprudence*, p. 109 ('Adventitious obligations are those which are voluntarily assumed by men after birth, or else are enjoined by the command [imperio] of a superior, or by law').

Examples of obligations founded on one's natural status, according to Pufendorf, are the obligation to treat others as one's equal,[31] to cultivate and preserve sociality,[32] to cultivate peace, and not to injure others unjustly.[33] Unlike Hobbes, Pufendorf believed that these obligations exist in the state of nature before the creation of any political authority. Examples he gives of adventitious statuses, on the other hand, are one's political status (citizen), one's economic status (master or servant), one's family status (husband, parent, child) and one's religious or governmental office. The parallels with the three main categories of status in Roman law (*civitas*, *libertas*, and *familia*) are striking.

Adventitious statuses, or as I call them here *role*-statuses, are not held simply in virtue of being human. Nor are they purely contractual. Pufendorf, does not count promissory obligations as grounding an adventitious status. Being a promisor or a promisee is not a status; nor is being a tortfeasor.

Still, the contrast between the two kinds of status, natural and adventitious, is not clear. Pufendorf tries to draw the contrast between them in several ways. Whereas natural status is 'congenital' or 'connate', adventitious statuses— he claims—are voluntarily assumed 'after birth'.[34] Rights and obligations grounded on natural status are owed by 'every man to every man', but those grounded on adventitious status obtain only 'towards certain men on the basis of a particular condition or state'. And whereas the former are 'absolute', the latter are 'hypothetical'.[35] Commentators interpret Pufendorf's notion of adventitious statuses as artificial, created by humans through institutions or conventions.[36] I do not think this is an accurate characterisation, but the distinction is far from clear and none of Pufendorf's attempts to draw it succeeds. Here is why.

First, not all adventitious statuses are voluntarily assumed. The obligations of slaves who are captured in warfare towards masters are not, as Pufendorf himself points out.[37] Second, some adventitious statuses ground 'congenital' or 'connate' obligations, such as the obligations of children towards their parents. Pufendorf believes, for instance, that family obligations are 'perpetual', holding for the duration of one's life and not merely until the child reaches adulthood.[38] Finally, adventitious statuses do not necessarily presuppose the agreement ('deed') to form political authority and state institutions. Pufendorf takes issue with an historical account of how humans left the state of nature. He thinks that the idea that rational and self-sufficient individuals, with no bonds with one another, came to agree on

[31] Pufendorf, *On the Duty of Man and Citizen According to Natural Law*, p. 61.
[32] Ibid., p. 35.
[33] *Elements of Universal Jurisprudence*, p. 31.
[34] *Elements of Universal Jurisprudence*, p. 109.
[35] *On the Duty of Man and Citizen According to Natural Law* (1991), p. 56.
[36] Ian Hunter, 'Human Nature, the State of Nature and Natural Law', in *The Cambridge Companion to Pufendorf*, p. 119.
[37] Ibid., p. 130.
[38] *Of The Law of Nature and of Persons*, Book III, chapter IV, § VII, p. 204 ('Among adventitious obligations, we commonly reckon perpetual, the obligation of children towards their parents).

forming a state is a fiction. It never actually happened. On his view, the state of nature, as a historical stage, consisted in a gradual evolution from a small family unit to multiple different families separated from each other.[39] These family members were tied by 'special paternal, marital or master/slave bonds' and these bonds 'can never be removed from the human race as a whole'. For Pufendorf, family bonds and labour relations are not the product of organised societies with institutional structures. He views these adventitious statuses as *pre*-political and hence no more artificial than humans' natural status.

To gain a better understanding of the distinction between natural and adventitious statuses, and of how they generate rights and duties, we need to take a closer look at Pufendorf's discussion of natural status and the equality that pertains to it. The key idea is that adventitious statuses pose a challenge to our natural equality. Pufendorf was one of the first philosophers to identify clearly, and seek to reconcile, two enduring aspects of the human condition: moral equality and hierarchical social relations. Whereas natural status is inherently *equal*, Pufendorf holds that adventitious statuses are inherently *unequal*. Though empirical differences (e.g. in strength or intelligence) between humans do not affect our natural status as equals, certain encounters (advents) create asymmetrical social relations. But to see why these relations pose a threat to equality, we need first to understand Pufendorf's argument for why our natural status is one of equality.

3.5 Equality and the Moral Defence of Self-Respect

Pufendorf's argument for moral egalitarianism begins with the claim that the distribution of physical and intellectual abilities among humans is unequal. He makes this claim in criticism of Hobbes, who argues that natural equality consists in the fact that humans are roughly equal in strength and prudence and hence pose an equal threat of killing each other. Pufendorf objects, however, that humans are equal in a *normative* sense, despite being unequal in a *descriptive* sense. 'A more prudent person,' he writes, 'cannot claim for himself a right to rule a more imprudent one without the latter's consent.' Even if one agrees with Hobbes that rough equality of natural abilities can deter assaulting one another, Pufendorf argues, 'the equality we are dealing with here, and which is of the highest importance for humankind to keep intact, is nevertheless of a different kind'.[40] 'Different' kind here means normative, as opposed to empirical.

[39] *Samuel Pufendorf's On the Natural State of Men, the 1678 Latin Edition and English Translation Translated, Annotated, and Introduced by Michael Seidler*, Studies in the History of Philosophy, Vol. 13 (Lewiston: Edwin Mellen Press, 1990), § 7, pp. 117–118.

[40] *The Political Writings of Samuel Pufendorf*, edited by Craig L. Carr and translated by Michael J. Seidler (Oxford: Oxford University Press, 1994), p. 160. (Hereinafter *The Political Writings of Samuel Pufendorf*.)

Pufendorf makes several points to support the view that humans are equal in a normative sense. Just because some people may excel in honour or wealth, he argues, does not mean that they do not have the same duties as everyone else. They do not, for instance, have a licence to injure others. It is absurd, Pufendorf says, to believe that nature has given the more intelligent sovereignty over the more 'dull'. Humans enjoy equal natural freedom, which cannot be diminished without their consent. And hence forced slavery (i.e. slavery imposed against a person without their consent) is a violation of natural equality.

But why does Pufendorf think that we are all equal despite disparities of physical and intellectual abilities? Stephen Darwall[41] has argued that the answer lies in his idea of *sociability*, which Pufendorf defines as follows: 'a kind of disposition whereby a man is understood to be joined to every other man by ties of benevolence, peace and charity, and therefore by mutual obligation'.[42] Darwall attributes to Pufendorf the view that the natural state of human beings is sociable in the sense that it involves the recognition of mutual rights and obligations. On this interpretation, it is not that humans are naturally inclined to socialise with others and build social bonds; rather, it is that it is inherent in our social relations that we recognise each other as holders of rights and obligations. For Darwall, Pufendorf's sociability is a moralised term: it means that we relate to others in a way that recognises that they are morally entitled to a certain treatment (e.g. not to injure them) and to respect them as persons, while expecting that they ought to do the same to us. We are sociable in the sense that we recognise each other as a valid source of moral obligation, and we hold each other accountable for meeting these demands.

While I agree with Darwall's conclusion, I find the above argument incomplete. It is not clear why sociability involves the duty to recognise others as equally entitled to respect. And if it does so involve, why *must* we take a sociable attitude? Why must we recognise each other as valid sources of moral demands, and do so equally?[43] We need to explain, in non-theological terms, why we ought to relate to others in ways that recognise them as equally worthy of respect. And I believe that we can find in Pufendorf an argument for why humans ought to respect each other as equals. The argument I will reconstruct, and will attribute to Pufendorf, puts a gloss on Darwall's argument from sociability. It is based partly on what Pufendorf says about self-esteem and partly on his discussion of Descartes' idea of generosity.

[41] Darwall, 'Pufendorf on Morality, Sociability and Moral Powers'.

[42] *Of The Law of Nature and of Persons*, Book II, chapter 3, § 15, p. 108.

[43] Darwall is right that the answer cannot be found in Pufendorf's theological voluntarism. It cannot just be the case that we ought to be sociable because God commanded us. For where does the duty to obey God's commands come from? If God is to have this authority over us, it must be the case that humans already have an obligation to abide by whatever God commands. It must be the case, in other words, that there is already a sociable moral relation with God, out of which reciprocal rights and obligations flow. Sociability, in other words, precedes God's will and hence the latter cannot justify the former. That is Darwall's argument.

Pufendorf begins the section on natural equality with a discussion of self-esteem, and how sensitive people are about it.[44] And later in the same chapter, he draws on Descartes to argue that natural equality is violated when people, through arrogance (*superbia*),[45] think that they are better than others. The argument is proto-Kantian[46] and it runs as follows:

Premise 1. Having the faculty of free will is a reason to esteem oneself.[47]
Premise 2. No other attribute (e.g. wealth, honour, beauty, wit) is truly one's own except the faculty of free will.[48]
Premise 3. One ought to esteem oneself only for what is truly one's own.
Premise 4. One ought to recognise that just like there is reason to esteem oneself, others too have the same reason to esteem themselves.[49]
Premise 5. All humans possess the faculty of free will.
Conclusion: We are equal in that we are all valid sources of self-esteem.

As Darwall observes, Pufendorf anticipates Kant's distinction between price and value. Wealth, honour, beauty, and wit are things that can be measured and priced. Each one of us have these attributes in varying degrees. But they are not valid sources of self-respect because they are not 'truly one's own'. Being rich or intelligent are not reasons to esteem oneself. Only the faculty of free will (i.e. our autonomy) is a valid source of self-esteem, or as we should better put it, self-*respect*. Free will is a faculty that we all have, and it does not come in degrees. Recall that for Pufendorf, the exercise of our will is what makes our action moral: we use our will to act for reasons and we can only understand human action by imputing reasons to it. And since our free will is the only thing that is 'truly our own', its value is unconditional: it is not commensurate with external human qualities (i.e. qualities that are not truly our own) and does not compete with them. Though we can be better than others *descriptively*, in all kinds of respects, we are not better than

[44] *Of The Law of Nature and of Persons*, Book III, chapter 2, § I, p. 174.

[45] *Of The Law of Nature and of Persons*, Book III, chapter 2, § VI, p. 178: 'This rule of equality is likewise transgressed by pride, when a man for no reason, or without sufficient reason, prefers himself to others, bearing a lofty carriage towards them, as base underlings, unworthy of his consideration or regard.'

[46] Not all commentators agree that Pufendorf endorses the Kantian view that human beings possess intrinsic value. For the contrary view see Heiki Haara and Kari Saastamoinen, 'Esteem and Sociality in Pufendorf's Natural Law Theory', 32 *British Journal for the History of Philosophy* (2024), pp. 265–283.

[47] *Of The Law of Nature and of Persons*, Book III, chapter 2, § VI, p. 179: 'The only just cause of esteeming ourselves arises from the lawful use of our power of free choice, and from the command and authority we exercise over our will.'

[48] Ibid: 'the true notion of generosity which prompts a man to value himself as highly as in reason he ought, to consist in this, that he acknowledge nothing to be truly his own but this free disposition of his will'; 'besides the actions which depend on that faculty there is nothing in us that can properly merit praise or dispraise'.

[49] Ibid: 'those who have a true sense of themselves are easily inclined to think that every man judges of his own worth in the same manner since there is nothing in this notion that has any dependence on external things or persons'.

others in the sense that matters—that is, *normatively*. This normative equality is 'of a different kind', and 'of the highest importance for humankind to keep intact'.

Pufendorf moves on to connect the idea of natural equality with the value of dignity. 'The very word man' (*hominis*), Pufendorf observes, 'is thought to contain a certain dignity'. It is a dignity that we all have and have equally ('I am as much of a man as you'). Pufendorf here uses the Latin word *dignatio* as opposed to the word *dignitas*. And some commentators argue that *dignatio* denotes the intrinsic value of human beings whereas *dignitas* denotes the societal esteem, or as I call it *rank*-status, that is contingently placed on people.[50]

The argument from self-esteem is incomplete, however, since it says nothing about how we ought to treat one another. And Pufendorf falls short of inferring directly that we ought to respect others equally because we ought to respect ourselves. This would seem like an obvious move, deriving duties to respect others from duties to oneself, given that we are all valid sources of self-esteem. Instead, Pufendorf makes a point about the link between self-esteem, esteem, and social cooperation:

> Now since human nature belongs equally to all men, and since one cannot lead a social life with someone by whom one is not esteemed at least as a man, it follows as a precept of the natural law that 'Everyone must esteem and treat other men as his natural equals, or as men in the same sense as he.'[51]

Pufendorf argues not only that we are valid sources of self-esteem but also that we expect others to esteem us accordingly (i.e. *qua* human beings). When others do not recognise the respect that we take ourselves to have *qua* humans, we refuse to socialise with them. This is not only a normative point, but also a point about human motivation. A person who esteems oneself will not tolerate being treated by others as lacking the dignity inherent in all humans. Self-respect provides us with a vital moral defence in our social interactions with others. By contrast, a person who does not value themselves as having free will, might well accept to socialise with people who treat them as inferior. Self-esteem is therefore not only normatively important, but practically important too. Social cooperation on equal terms is only possible between persons who have self-esteem. But at the same time, Pufendorf observes that our sense of self-esteem is fragile. He calls it 'delicate' and points out that we are often more outraged when others do not respect us as humans than

[50] Niklas Luhmann, *Law as a Social System* (Oxford: Oxford University Press, 2004), p. 483. See more recently, Jonathan Barrett, '*Dignatio* and the Human Body', 21(4) *South African Journal on Human Rights* (2005), pp. 525–546; Evadne Grant, 'Dignity and Equality', 7(2) *Human Rights Law Review* (2007), pp. 299–329. Haara and Saastamoinen dispute that there is sufficient textual evidence in Pufendorf for drawing the conceptual distinction between *dignitas* and *dignatio*. They are right that Pufendorf is not consistent, often using the two terms interchangeably.

[51] Book III, chapter 2, §1 (translation is from *The Political Writings of Samuel Pufendorf*, p. 159).

when they harm our body or property. We dread being treated by others as if we are not valid sources of self-esteem, as lacking the dignity inherent in human beings. And we care about this more than we care about injury to our bodies or damage to our property.

Pufendorf does not explain why we care so much that others recognise us as valid sources of self-esteem. But the link he draws between self-esteem and social cooperation is crucial. Self-esteem is a condition, both normatively and practically, of social cooperation on equal terms. A person who lacks self-esteem will not necessarily insist on equal terms of cooperation. Denial of our self-esteem by others threatens it, making it fragile. What kind of threat is this, though? Normatively speaking, one can never cease to be a valid source of self-respect because free will is inalienable, the only thing 'truly one's own'. Yet one can stop *believing* that one is a valid source of self-respect. One may, mistakenly, treat oneself *as if* one's free will is not as valuable as that of others; even worse, one might treat oneself as if one does not have free will *at all*. Though this is a morally mistaken belief, it is a mistake that one may end up making under unfavourable social conditions. And in this sense, it is possible to lose one's self-respect and lose it *because* others deny it. The threat is social, posed by how others treat us in our social relations with them.

The fact that self-respect is something inherent in human beings and yet something one may lose is a fundamental antinomy[52] of the moral condition. It reveals the important interplay between self-respect and being recognised as worthy of respect by others. If others deny or fail to recognise one's self-respect, then one is likely to lose it. Apart from the dramatic impact this has on a person's moral psychology, it affects the way that person socialises with others. Without self-respect, one will not necessarily insist on equal terms of social cooperation. Instead, one might accept hierarchical social relations that make one inferior to others. This is why being treated with disrespect outrages[53] us over and above the violation of our rights to bodily integrity and property. To be the victim of a rights violation is bad enough; but to lose the belief that one is a valid source of esteem is much worse. It is one of the worst forms of dehumanisation.

The upshot of Pufendorf's argument, as I interpret it, is that an egalitarian society must ensure that people's fragile self-esteem is properly cultivated and protected against social threats. A society of equals is only possible if people have self-esteem—that is, if they actively assign value on themselves. And since how others treat us affects our self-esteem, we must ensure that there is proper social recognition of everyone's dignity, including within asymmetrical relations. *Dignatio*

[52] I am very grateful to Kostas Koukouzelis for suggesting this apt term (antinomy) to express the point. The paragraph draws heavily on extensive discussions we had about the nature of respect in the Kantian tradition, from which I benefited enormously.

[53] It is interesting to observe here the common roots between *dignatio* (which Pufendorf prefers to use here over the word *dignitas*) and *indignation*, the reactive attitude that follows the violation of one's moral rights.

is not only the quality of being worthy of respect but also the fact, or process, of actively placing respect.[54] Without actively placing respect (on oneself and others), there is great danger that hierarchical social relations will emerge, since people will not insist on equal terms of cooperation. Sociability demands not only mutual respect of rights and duties but also ensuring that people actively treat themselves as a valid source of self-esteem. To ensure that this is the case, social recognition of the value of equal dignity is essential.

The upshot of the argument I find in Pufendorf is that *dignatio* is not only a moral value but also it must, at all times, be a social value. It must be projected collectively, through our representative institutions, so as to ensure that people will always insist on equal terms of cooperation. This dual character of *dignatio*, moral and social, explains why the early modern thinkers oscillated between dignity as social esteem or honour (*dignitas*) and dignity as the inherent worth of persons (*dignatio*). Though each one of us has inherent value, we collectively must also *place* value, actively recognising each role-holder as a valid source of self-esteem. Inherent dignity without social recognition is insufficient to ensure equal terms of social cooperation. Though it is a mistake to think, as Waldron does,[55] that dignity just means social rank or honour, it is nevertheless true that dignity must have a social, or collective, dimension if it is to protect our self-respect and our equal status.

3.6 Adventitious Statuses as Social Threats to Equality

Pufendorf's normative argument for moral egalitarianism, as I have reconstructed it, is premised on free will, as the only inherently human attribute, coupled with the claim that it forms the basis of one's self-esteem, and through it, the mutual recognition of respect that should govern social relations with others (sociability). Building on Darwall's argument, I highlighted the importance that self-esteem plays in Pufendorf, as a precondition—both normative and practical—of social cooperation on equal terms. It is interesting, however, that Pufendorf does not merely describe the natural state of equality positively as the moral relation between persons who are equally valid sources of self-esteem. He also defines it negatively as the state of not being subject to anyone's authority:

> A second way of considering man's natural state is to contrast it to the civil state, and to think of everyone being his own master and subject to no human authority.[56]

[54] *Oxford Latin Dictionary* (Oxford: Clarendon Press, 1968), p. 542.

[55] Waldron's treatment of dignity in *Dignity, Rank and Rights* is remarkably narrow, focusing on *dignitas*, or what I call here rank-status. He does not discuss Pufendorf, whose concept of 'dignitas' is one of inherent worth.

[56] *Samuel Pufendorf's On the Natural State of Men* (1990), § 7, p. 117.

Pufendorf thinks that we are each other's equals when we are 'our own masters', capable of exercising our own free will and natural liberties. But he also thinks that adventitious statuses are inherently unequal because one subjects oneself to the will of another and, in that sense, is *not* one's own master. Adventitious statuses are unequal for Pufendorf in that they have superiors and inferiors. Within a state, officials command others through law and having a law for Pufendorf necessarily entails having superiors and inferiors.[57] Moreover, the head of the household is superior to every other family member,[58] and the master is superior to the servant.[59] Considered in our natural status, we are all equal in our self-worth and 'our own masters'. But once we start interacting with others socially, various social relations of inferiority/superiority emerge, the most significant ones having to do with citizenship, labour, and family.

This contrast between natural equality and unequal social relations should appear puzzling at first. Humans do not lose their equal dignity when they enter adventitious statuses, since free will is inalienable, the only thing 'truly one's own'. To be sure, there is a sense in which adventitious statuses are unequal: some people (officials, parents, masters/employers) are in the practice of telling others what to do. But this is a descriptive statement, identifying an asymmetry in certain social practices. Pufendorf's argument for natural equality, by contrast, is normative: we *ought* to respect each other as equals because we all have free will and should respect ourselves. It is only if we assume that adventitious statuses necessarily violate our normative status as equals, that there is a contrast here. But do they?

In the field of political philosophy, this question has been posed in terms of the legitimacy of political authority. Traditionally, the question conceives of politics as based on a fundamental tension: how can free and equal citizens subject their will to that of a ruler, becoming their inferior? The traditional approach conceives of the relation between government and citizens in hierarchical terms, as a vertical, top-down, forcible imposition of the will of superiors over that of inferiors. The command theory of law, which we have inherited from Hobbes, is a corollary of this traditional approach, treating law as orders made by a sovereign and backed by threats of using force. It is therefore no accident that some philosophers have argued that individual autonomy is incompatible with political authority, endorsing anarchism.[60] But the problem, if there is one, is much wider. As Pufendorf points out, authority relations precede the state, and they are found in numerous interpersonal interactions, some of which are contractual (employer/employee) and some of which are not (parent/child). If we should be anarchists about the state,

[57] *Elements of Universal Jurisprudence*, p. 202.

[58] Ibid., p. 88.

[59] Samuel Pufendorf, *On the Duty of Man and Citizen*, edited by James Tully (Cambridge: Cambridge University Press, 1991), p. 129 ('in this contract the master has the superior standing').

[60] See Robert Paul Wolff, *In Defense of Anarchism* (Berkeley: University of California Press, 1998).

we should be *global* anarchists—that is, oppose all adventitious statuses, some of which are central to human life.

The question of global anarchism is a genuine one, which I will pick up in later chapters. Pufendorf says very little about why we should tolerate adventitious statuses, given that he thinks they are inherently unequal. I will argue later that adventitious statuses are roles that all of us will occupy at some point in our lives, sometimes as the weaker party and sometimes as the stronger party—a fact that mitigates their asymmetrical character. But for now, let us assume, as Pufendorf does, that global anarchism is false and that adventitious statuses can in principle be morally justified. Pufendorf insists that natural law governs adventitious statuses and places limits to how parties may treat one another.

Here, there is a range of philosophical approaches that those who reject anarchism might take to reconcile natural equality with adventitious statuses. At one end of the spectrum is the view that these relations are *pro tanto* unequal but can nevertheless be justified *all things considered*. Though one's self-respect is necessarily compromised when one subjects one's will to that of another, especially when one has no choice, this view holds that there are benefits to be gained by doing so. For instance, in the case of the forced relation between citizen and government, there are benefits with respect to producing vital social goods that humans need. Ditto for the parent/child relation. Still, the forced imposition is something to regret; in a morally perfectly world, we wouldn't have superiors, such as rulers, parents, or employers. But in our non-ideal world inferiors benefit from having their equal status compromised. This, more traditional, view deems asymmetrical social relations as a necessary evil at best, something to be tolerated because it produces morally beneficial effects. Call this the *vertical approach* to status.

At the opposite end of the spectrum is the debunking view that these relations are hierarchical only presumptively, or prima facie. If the right conditions are met then these relations are not objectionable, *even though* they are asymmetrical. This second view does not assume that a person's equal standing is necessarily compromised just because one is weaker, or more vulnerable, and has reason to pay attention to another person's instructions. Nor does it assume that in an ideal world, there would be no political authority, parenthood, or employment. The mere fact that citizens, children, and employees have reasons to pay attention to what someone tells them to do, does not make them *inferior*. They can still relate to the stronger party as equals. It is only when the stronger party abuses their position and violates the weaker party's self-respect that these relations degenerate into relations of hierarchy or subordination. From a normative perspective, these relations are asymmetrical but need not be hierarchical, having superiors and inferiors. The proper way to view them, on this second approach, is as relations of equal standing, where—because of some asymmetry—one of the parties is vulnerable to being *treated* as less than an equal by the other (even though one is not). But when parties treat each other as they ought to, then these relations are properly egalitarian. Citizens, children, and employees do not *obey* anyone. When government, parents, and employers behave as they ought to, they are each other's equals. In the case of law, for instance, this second approach treats it horizontally, as principles governing an association between equal citizens, as opposed to commands issued by rulers.[61] Call this the *horizontal approach* to status.

Pufendorf takes the vertical approach. He thinks that obligations owed to someone who has authority over us are obligations of inequality, making the person in authority our 'superior':

> We call the obligation of inequality that which makes him to whom something is owed by us in virtue of it our superior, and brings some authority or sovereignty upon us. Such is subjection, or that obligation by which a man is bound to furnish what has been enjoined upon him by another in virtue of his sovereignty.[62]

I am not quite sure why Pufendorf endorses the vertical approach since it is in tension with his argument for moral egalitarianism. Unlike Hobbes, Pufendorf insists that our equal status is normative, grounded on our free will and self-esteem. It is the inalienable dignity that inheres in human nature. But if adventitious statuses violate our equal status, morally speaking, then why are they to be tolerated? The thought that adventitious statuses—though inegalitarian—may benefit us, all things considered, seems implausible. Our status as an equal is not the kind of moral norm that can be easily overridden by other considerations. It is true, of course, that adventitious statuses are characterised by empirical asymmetries. But why do these asymmetries pose a normative threat to people's equal standing? Pufendorf tells us that other empirical inequalities, such as being less intelligent, wealthy, or strong than others, do not violate our equal standing. But then why should one's diminished physical liberty as an employee or a citizen do so? The question is even more pressing in cases where one uses their free will to agree, contractually, to assume an adventitious status.

Pufendorf is of course aware of the distinction between normative and descriptive notions of equality. He uses it to criticise Hobbes for committing a category mistake. Hobbes had argued that the equality humans enjoy in virtue of their roughly similar physical strength in the state of nature, disappears in the civil condition, replaced by institutional inequalities. But Pufendorf objects that this comparison is inapt because the inequality that emerges within political communities

[61] The horizontal approach is found in Ronald Dworkin's theory of law as integrity and Arthur Ripstein's Kantian theory of law. See Ronald Dworkin, *Law's Empire* (Cambridge: Belknap Press, 1986); Arthur Ripstein, 'Authority and Coercion', 32(1) *Philosophy and Public Affairs* (2004), pp. 2–35. For discussion of the role that coercion plays in these conceptions of law, see George Letsas, 'Force, Coercion and the Law: A Philosophical Framework', in Nicoletta Bersier, Christoph Bezemek, and Frederick Schauer (eds), *Sanctions: An Essential Element of Law?* (Geneva: Springer, 2025).

[62] *Elements of Universal Jurisprudence*, p. 109.

is not one of physical strength. He thinks, contra Hobbes, that inequalities within a political community arise because some are esteemed, or 'dignified', more than others.[63] But one would have expected Pufendorf to say the exact opposite, namely that dignity is a normative state that humans retain, whatever external asymmetries (e.g. in esteem or power) political communities might introduce as an empirical matter. And Pufendorf has already told us that inequalities to do with strength, beauty, or prudence are external and not 'truly one's own' and that the equality that inheres in human nature is 'of a different kind'. At least Hobbes is consistent in comparing external aspects of the human condition: physical strength in the state of nature and political power in the civil state. By contrast, Pufendorf seems to compare the equal dignity in the state of nature with disparities of esteem or power (*rank*-status) within a political community. And he has already told us that asymmetries with respect to external human qualities, of which rank-status is one, do not compromise one's status as an equal. If Hobbes's comparison is inapt, then so is Pufendorf's: the dignity we have in virtue of being human cannot be compared with the social esteem in which some are held by others within a political community.

Though Pufendorf's position appears inconsistent, there is a genuine philosophical problem with which he is grappling: our normative status as equals is inalienable and does not change based on empirical contingencies, including of course societal esteem (rank-status). And yet empirical asymmetries with respect to certain human attributes do seem to be normatively relevant from the point of view of equality. We do not think that disparities of physical strength, intelligence, or beauty is the sort of thing that should make us worry. But we do think that having the status of an employee, a family member, or a citizen poses a threat to our equal status. The reason cannot be that employers, parents, and rulers are deemed by society to be more admirable than others. For the same applies to those who are more intelligent or beautiful. Besides, family and employment relations for Pufendorf arise before the establishment of political authority and before the development of societal norms around what's admirable. And Pufendorf claims that statuses are *moral* entities, the ground for rights and duties.

There is another reason why the claim that authority relations are inherently unequal is too quick. One may exploit *any* empirical asymmetry to violate another person's rights. I may exploit my physical strength to assault and injure you, or I may exploit my intelligence to defraud you. Pufendorf does not regard these asymmetries as sufficient to establish unequal social relations of superiority and inferiority. I am not inferior to you if, being weaker, you injure me in a fist fight.

[63] *Of the Law of Nature and Nations*, Book III, chapter 2, § 2: 'Civil law does not make one man stronger than another, but more dignified.' (Translation from *The Political Writings of Samuel Pufendorf* (1990), p. 160.)

So, what is it about adventitious statuses that raise concerns about our standing as equals and ground, as Pufendorf insists, relation-specific rights and duties?

3.7 Why Adventitious Statuses Pose a Threat to Equality: Two Grounds

Unlike Pufendorf, I do not think that the asymmetry in those relations concerns the phenomenon of authority and consists in the fact that one subjects their will to the will of another.[64] Instead, I think that adventitious statuses pick out certain enduring and non-contingent social relations in which one of the parties is weaker than the other, suffering from dependencies or vulnerabilities. Children depend on their parents, or carers, for food and shelter. Citizens are vulnerable to being coerced by their government into taking some action. Employees depend on their employer for income and other social goods, while having less bargaining power in typical market conditions. Like Roman law, Pufendorf singles out these three relations as central cases of status: government/citizen, master/servant (or, in modern times, employer/employee) and parent/child. Unlike episodic interactions (e.g. buying something from a seller, or injuring someone negligently) these relations are expansive, both in terms of time and in terms of ethical significance. Citizenship, family, and employment are typically an important parameter for people's pursuit of the good, throughout their lives. My view is that these expansive social relations pose a threat to equality for two reasons.

The first reason, which I will develop in more detail in the next chapter, is that the stronger party will become aware of, and be inclined to exploit, the vulnerability of the weaker party. Exploitation, domination, oppression, and tyranny are familiar terms that we use to describe serious wrongs that are typical within enduring social relations. These terms seek to capture the fact that the wrongdoer is not simply evil, or opportunistically selfish, but deliberately *abuses* their position within a relation, exploiting the vulnerability of the other party. We do not say that a fraudster abuses their position or acts against their role. But we do say that a doctor in the public sector abuses their position when asking a patient for a bribe to expedite their operation. 'What kind of a doctor are you?', we might say. Both the doctor and the fraudster make themselves impermissibly rich at the expense of another, but only the doctor abuses their position. Adventitious statuses are not therefore unequal by nature. They become unequal when the stronger party abuses their position and commits a downstream wrong. I shall call relations where parties hold these roles *asymmetrical*, as opposed to unequal. They are asymmetrical

[64] The idea that authority relations are defined in terms of subjecting one's will to the will of another has now become commonplace in moral and political philosophy, in large part thanks to Joseph Raz's influential treatment in Joseph Raz, *The Morality of Freedom* (Oxford: Clarendon Press, 1986).

in that one party suffers from dependencies or vulnerabilities vis-à-vis the other. And yet, it is nevertheless possible for the two parties to relate as equals subject to certain conditions. One such condition is that we collectively ensure that the relation is properly regulated so that the stronger party does not abuse their position. This is the core idea behind the horizontal approach to status relations.

This first reason why adventitious statuses pose a threat to equality is not Pufendorf's. He follows the vertical, authority-based account of adventitious statuses, and holds that adventitious statuses are inherently unequal, simply because they involve telling others what to do. But the second reason why adventitious statuses pose a threat to equality follows from the argument of self-esteem that I attributed to Pufendorf. Given how enduring adventitious statuses are, the stronger party is likely to treat their power as a reason to deny the weaker party's self-esteem and to exploit their vulnerability. Correspondingly, the weaker party runs the risk of treating their vulnerability as a reason to lose their self-esteem. This, no doubt, is a moral mistake. Vulnerability and dependence do not entail inferiority and power does not entail superiority. But it is a moral mistake which is nevertheless common within these asymmetrical social relations.[65] And when it occurs, the weaker party no longer has the motivation to insist on equal terms of cooperation. They lose a vital moral defence. They might then accept as legitimate rules and practices that are incompatible with one's dignity. Children might accept corporal punishment or abuse. Citizens might accept censorship or police brutality. Workers might accept servitude or inhuman working conditions. Adventitious statuses pose a threat to equality for the additional reason that they pose a standing threat to one's self-esteem. By contrast, a breach of contract between commercial parties, or a negligent act between strangers, do not pose that threat.

Of course, the stronger party may not actually abuse their position. They might be benevolent. Employment need not degenerate into servitude. Government need not degenerate into tyranny. The argument I am putting forward is not instrumental, namely that loss of self-esteem within adventitious statuses is more likely to result in downstream wrongdoing against the weaker party. I want to make the stronger claim that, other things being equal, the very loss of self-esteem within an asymmetrical social relation makes that relation unequal.[66] To internalise the belief that one is not a valid source of self-esteem within an asymmetrical relation *is* to be inferior to the other party, even if no downstream wrongs are committed by the stronger party. This is because the weaker party loses a vital moral defence: the motivation to insist on equal terms of cooperation. The value of equality requires

[65] This is an empirical claim for which I need not say much here. Slavery, tyranny, and domestic violence—just to mention a few grave status wrongs—have existed throughout human history and continue to exist in the modern world.

[66] Kolodny is right to argue that not all objections against inferiority can be analysed in terms of rights violations, at least not when we understand rights in a narrow sense, to encompass rights of private and criminal law. See Kolodny, *Pecking Order*, part I.

not only that the stronger party within an adventitious status respects the weaker party's rights, but also that the weaker party enjoys active self-respect. Precisely because one may lose one's self-respect because others deny it, it is morally imperative that the value of equality is adequately projected within these asymmetrical social relations. What is needed is proper social recognition of the vulnerability of the weaker party, which should include, at the very least, legal regulation of the bilateral roles in the relation. Apart from diminishing the likelihood of downstream wrongs (such as exploitation), and protecting the rights of the weaker party, legal regulation also projects the value of equality within adventitious statuses. By doing so, it ensures the active strengthening of the weaker party's self-respect. That is my argument, details of which will be further developed in Chapter 4.

Pufendorf is therefore wrong to say that adventitious statuses necessarily have inferiors and superiors. Physical attributes are asymmetrically distributed, and this fact does not, other things being equal, make some persons superior to others. The savvy fraudster or the muscular assailant are not superior to their victims. Likewise, the employer is not superior to the employee, merely because the employer possesses a material resource on which the employee depends. But the employer will become the employee's superior if the employee were to lose their self-esteem within the relation, that is if they were to internalise the belief that their dependence *makes* them inferior. When this happens, the employee loses a vital moral defence against the employer.

What we should say, therefore, is that adventitious statuses are only unequal, having superiors and inferiors, when they are left unregulated by our collective institutions,[67] or worse, when the regulation favours the stronger party. When the law favoured the stronger party, we had masters and servants. When the law favoured the rulers, we had monarchs and subjects. But since employment status became properly regulated by law, we have employers and employees, not masters and servants. And since citizenship status became properly regulated by law, we have citizens and representatives, not monarchs and subjects. When role-statuses are as they ought to be, employees and citizens remain their own masters, even though they hold adventitious statuses; they relate to each other as equals.

3.8 Conclusion: Role-Statuses as Egalitarian Moral Fields

So why is status a moral entity, a field for moral persons to exist in, as Pufendorf claims? The simple answer is that status is a shorthand for the moral value of

[67] Perhaps that is what Pufendorf should be interpreted as saying. At the time he was writing, neither employment nor citizenship was properly regulated by law. This charitable interpretation is more consistent with his claim that natural law governs adventitious statuses and places normative limits on them.

equality. It underpins our natural status of humanity, in that we are all valid sources of self-esteem. And it underpins the various adventitious statuses that we may enter, in that they pose a social threat to our natural status as equals. The stronger party is likely to treat the weaker party *as if* they have no self-esteem. Correspondingly, the weaker party may internalise the false moral belief that they are inferior to the stronger party. They might *lose* their self-esteem and by doing so, lose a vital moral defence they have in their social interactions with others. When this happens, the weaker party will not necessarily insist on equal terms of social cooperation. As a result, the stronger party is likely to commit downstream wrongs, such as abuse or exploitation. The relation degenerates into an unequal one, described by familiar terms such as domination or subjection.

So Pufendorf is right to claim that adventitious statuses are roots, or grounds, of a set of moral rights and duties. The aim of these rights and duties is to protect the weaker party and project the value of equality within the relevant relation. Key among those is the duty to protect and promote the weaker party's self-esteem through social recognition and legal regulation. Status 'holds and sustains' the weaker party by sending them the following message: 'you may be the weaker party in this relation but that does not make you inferior, lacking rights against the stronger party; you are still each other's equals'. And it 'holds and sustains' the stronger party by sending them the following message: 'you may be the stronger party in this relation but you have no right to exploit the weaker party; you are still each other's equals'.

4
THE MODALITIES OF OFFENCES AGAINST STATUS

4.1 Introduction

If status is the root of a set of rights and duties, grounded in the value of equality, then it follows that one can wrong a person by offending[1] their status. In this chapter I analyse further this claim. First, I explore the modalities of status offences, using examples from current affairs. I identify three: (a) failure to recognise a status (b) undue interference with the functions of one's status and (c) status appropriation. The way in which status operates, as a moral idea, employs distinct modalities compared to the familiar notions of rights and duties. Second, I draw with more precision, and defend, the distinction between role-status and rank-status. In the first two chapters, I traced the intellectual origins of role-status in Roman law and the work of Samuel Pufendorf (1632–1694). But Roman law is far from everyone's favourite subject. And Pufendorf's aphorism that status is a moral field may sound too obscure to modern ears. I want to take a step back and begin to motivate the claim that the idea of status still has moral and political currency. My focus will be on what I call role-statuses, and what Pufendorf calls adventitious statuses, rather than our natural status.[2]

Nowadays, the claim that status is the ground for rights and duties will appear either trivial or objectionable at first. It is trivial if we interpret status to mean the dignity and inviolability inherent in all human beings.[3] On this interpretation, largely familiar from deontological ethics, *all* moral wrongs constitute an offence against status. The claim will sound objectionable, however, if status refers to one's high ranking within an arbitrary scheme of social ordering, what I have been calling rank-status. The value of human equality is nowadays taken, rightly, to condemn preferential treatment of a group (e.g. the gentry or the aristocracy) simply in virtue of its perceived social superiority. By promoting the idea of offences

[1] I use the term 'offence' in the sense familiar from legal doctrine, to refer to a family of deontic wrongs (as in 'offences against the person').

[2] As I will explain in Section 5.9, the philosophical emphasis on our natural status, as the exclusive ground of the extensive rights one finds in human rights treaties, is a mistake.

[3] On the status-based theory of rights, see Thomas Nagel, 'Personal Rights and Public Space' 24(2) *Philosophy and Public Affairs* (1995), pp. 83–107; Frances Kamm, *Intricate Ethics* (Oxford: Oxford University Press, 2007).

Status in Law and Morality. George Letsas, Oxford University Press. © George Letsas 2026.
DOI: 10.1093/9780198936725.003.0004

against status, one risks being perceived as an apologist for unjust orders of social ranking. Status, it seems to many nowadays, is something either we all have or no one should have.

This approach to status dominates contemporary philosophical thinking. It underpins the development of human rights law and adds to its legal and political currency. We are nowadays suspicious of person-specific entitlements, and rightly so. But this dominance comes at a cost; it eclipses the older notion of status that is person-specific, or as we should better put it, *relation*-specific, but nevertheless has genuine moral appeal. By status, we can refer to the set of moral rights and obligations a person holds in virtue of the social position or role that they occupy. This notion is unlike the dignitarian concept in that not everyone has it. But it is also unlike the ranking concept in that it is not morally objectionable. Doctors, teachers, officials, and parents hold social roles in virtue of which they have distinctive obligations, rights, privileges, powers, and the like. *Qua* doctor, one has the obligation to respect patient autonomy, the privilege not to testify in court about a patient's communications, and the power to prescribe medication. What I have in mind here is not the descriptive fact that doctors are treated as having these rights and duties, but a *normative* fact that—morally speaking—this is as it ought to be. This role-based notion of status has been neglected and my aim is to rehabilitate it. The neglect has been unfortunate and has led to theoretical distortions and moral mistakes. If I were to blame someone for this neglect, it would be the person whose name has been associated the most with the idea of status in modern times.

4.2 Henry Maine's Wrong Turn

Before I look at the modalities of offences against status, using contemporary examples, it is worth looking briefly at what happened to the idea of status after Pufendorf's seminal treatment. The idea of status as a set of rights and duties attached to one's social role remained a philosophical concern in the eighteenth century, during the Enlightenment. Status figures in both Immanuel Kant's and Jeremy Bentham's work, published roughly the same period, even though they are the lead exponents of the two main rival moral theories, deontology and consequentialism. In the *Doctrine of Right* (1797), Kant identified a new category of private law rights, separate from contract and property, which he labelled 'rights to persons akin to rights to things'.[4] This Kantian category comprises three domestic relations: master/servant, spouses, and parent/child. Similarly, Bentham, in his *Introduction to the Principles of Morals and Legislation* (1789) singled out offences

[4] 'Von dem dinliche Art persönlichen Rect', see Immanuel Kant, 'The Metaphysics of Morals', § 22, in Mary J. Gregor (ed.), *Immanuel Kant: Practical Philosophy* (Cambridge: Cambridge University Press, 1996), p. 426.

against 'condition', as a category of private (civil) wrongs, separate from offences against the person, property, and reputation. Though much more expansive than Kant's category, Bentham's primary examples of status-based relations were the same as Kant's, namely family relations (children/parents and spouses) and the relation between the head of the household and domestic workers. However, both Kant and Bentham narrowed Pufendorf's list of statuses and excluded from it the status of a citizen. I will defend Pufendorf's wider approach, adding to his list several other relations such as doctor/patient, teacher/student, and landlord/tenant. A general theory of status should include the status of citizenship (official/citizen), which Pufendorf included as a core case. As I will later explain, we gain much by treating political obligation as an instance of status.

Kant and Bentham were, however, the last philosophers to treat status as a moral category until Arthur Ripstein's contemporary restatement of Kantian philosophy.[5] After Kant and Bentham, status as a moral idea got distorted and then neglected. What exactly happened in the intervening two centuries is not easy to explain but Henry Maine has a lot to do with it. In 1861, Maine put forward a historical claim: he argued that status was a device used by ancient law to impose on people rights and duties based on their social status, and that this device was later replaced by contractual rights available to all, irrespective of their social status. In legal terms, Maine treated status as speaking to contractual *incapacities* imposed coercively by law upon a subgroup (e.g. slaves or women) regardless of their volition. These incapacities were seen as the negation of contractual freedom, the capacity to shape one's legal rights and obligations through the exercise of one's will.

Though Maine was careful to point out that Roman private law was already moving in the direction of modern law, he failed to appreciate the inherent moral dimension of status, as capturing asymmetrical social relations. As I argued in Chapter 2, this moral dimension of status was already present in classical Roman law. Instead, Maine treated status as a historically bounded legal device. His focus on contractual incapacities imposed regardless of one's will (e.g. on slaves or women) eclipsed the relational character of status and, in turn, the asymmetrical character of status relations. Meanwhile, historicism started to gain prominence in legal theory, which gradually became detached from moral and political philosophy, particularly in continental Europe. The German school of historical jurisprudence turned to Roman law to defend the descriptive claim that legal systems are a living instrument that reflects the prevailing social, cultural, and other norms of a community. By the start of the nineteenth century, long before Henry Maine's thesis, the German jurists of the historical school, such as Gustav Hugo,[6] were already treating status as synonymous with legal capacity.

[5] Arthur Ripstein, *Force and Freedom* (Cambridge: Harvard University Press, 2009). I discuss Ripstein's very important restatement of status in more detail in Chapter 6.

[6] See Gustav Hugo, *Civilistisches Magazin*, Vol. 4 (1815), as cited by Friedrich Carl Von Savigny in *A System of Modern Roman Law* (Connecticut: Hyperion Press, 1867), p. 324.

The turn to legal historicism and formalism had a very unfortunate impact on both the legal theory of status and legal practice. Consider theory first. Scholars who tried to find a unified account of status in the idea of legal incapacity, or similar concepts, struggled. Some examples help to illustrate this point. The status of citizenship, for example, comprises a set of rights and duties. But it has nothing to do with any incapacities imposed on citizens.[7] This gradually encouraged the view that status simply means legal personhood or legal standing. But this meant that slaves in the ancient world lacked legal status, which made little sense. As explained in Chapter 2, Roman law recognised and regulated the relation between slaves and masters; it did not pretend that no such relation existed. Moreover, many of the statuses that the law recognises are taken up voluntarily, defying Maine's definition. Coverture, the legal position of a married woman, was a widely recognised legal status. Ditto for the status of a public official or a criminal.[8] One enters these statuses through a voluntary act. This, in turn, encouraged another view—entertained by John Austin—that status just is a set of rights and duties attached by law to a group of persons. But then it was a mystery why law made being a citizen, an official, or a married woman a status but not being a mortgagor, a landowner, or a motorist. These struggles prompted Austin's aphorism that 'to determine precisely what a status is, is in my opinion the most difficult problem in the whole science of jurisprudence'.[9] Without piercing the doctrinal veil, to expose the moral character of the underlying social relation, the concept of status gradually appeared criterionless.

Maine's narrow-minded historicism also affected legal practice, and not in a good way. In one of the most deplorable judgments in the history of American law, *Lochner v New York*[10] (1905), the US Supreme Court struck down as unconstitutional restrictions imposed by the state of New York on the number of hours employees at bakeries may work (no more than 60 hours a week). The Supreme Court held that the restrictions violated freedom of contract as protected by the due process clause of the 14th Amendment to the US Constitution. In 1911, the New York Court of Appeals[11] also relied on the due process clause to strike down as unconstitutional a statute imposing liability without fault on employers for workplace injuries suffered by employees. During this *Lochner* era, American courts blocked socially progressive legislation that aimed at protecting workers by imposing limits on freedom of contract. One might think that this was to do with the

[7] See the critique of Savigny against Hugo, in Savigny, *A System of Modern Roman Law*, p. 325.

[8] As pointed out by Allen in C. K. Allen, *Legal Duties and Other Essays in Jurisprudence* (Oxford: Clarendon Press, 1931), p. 37.

[9] John Austin, *Lectures in Jurisprudence: Or The Philosophy of Positive Law* (New York: Henry Colt, 1875), p. 355. Status is not even a topic in general jurisprudence these days, let alone its most difficult problem.

[10] *Lochner v New York*, 198 US 45 (1905).

[11] *Ives v South Buffalo Railway Co.*, 94 NE 431 (NY 1911).

liberal ideology prevalent at the time. But as the great American scholar Roscoe Pound pointed out, the opposition to this progressive legislation '[w]as not due to class bias, or economic associations or social relations of the judges, nor to sinister influences brought to bear upon them'.[12]

Instead, Pound argued—in a scathing critique of Maine's thesis—that the courts' opposition 'grew out of their acceptance of the doctrine that the evolution of law was a progress from status to contract'. According to Pound, American courts interpreted restrictions on contractual freedom as an attempt to restore status, and hence to return to the unjust legal systems of the pre-modern world. The judges were 'imbued with genuine faith' in Maine's doctrine of progress from status to contract. Maine had managed to convince legal scholars that restrictions on contractual freedom are regressive, a return to the injustices of ancient law.

In sum, historicism obscured the relational character of status and the fact that it tracks asymmetries with certain social relations. Coupled with a positivistic understanding of status, as a content-independent shorthand for referring to any given set of posited legal rights, status disappeared from legal and political theory. More importantly, it contributed to judicial trends that caused injustices to status holders: employees were deprived of rights that, as we shall see, are essential to their status. Rehabilitating status as a moral idea is not only a theoretical task but also it has practical significance.

4.3 The Modalities of Status Offences

Let us make a fresh start. Status is not a legal device developed by some legal systems to deal with contingent social hierarchies of esteem. It is a moral entity. To understand why, we need to look afresh at status-based moral claims made today and their various modalities. Consider the following three cases from current affairs, which I will treat as paradigmatic:

1. A multinational ride-hailing company refuses to accord its drivers employment status and treats them as self-employed contractors. Drivers complain that this is unjust.
2. The government imposes tasks of immigration enforcement on academics, requiring them to monitor attendance of overseas students. Academics complain that this is incompatible with their status as lecturers.
3. Healthcare practitioners lobby successfully to be able to use the title 'doctor'. Medical doctors complain that this offends their status.

[12] Roscoe Pound, *Interpretations of Legal History* (New York: Macmillan, 1923), p. 62ff.

What, if anything, can justify these complaints? Why should institutions recognise statuses in the first place? Contemporary political philosophy studies extensively the ethical issues surrounding specific statuses (e.g. that of a refugee or an employee), but it is much less common to reflect on status as a general moral category. I begin by presenting three different ways in which status can give rise to a moral offence, drawing on the cases above.

4.3.1 Failure to Recognise One's Status

Take the first claim of wrongdoing, the failure to recognise one's status. Uber, a multinational corporation, argues that its drivers are self-employed contractors rather than employees, and deprives them of employment protection. Being an employee is a recognised legal status that vests workers with several rights, such as sick leave, paid holidays, and protection against unfair dismissal. Uber bases its argument on the claim that it merely mediates between drivers and passengers. The drivers have challenged this claim in court, on the ground that Uber's role is much more dominant than a mediating one.[13] They argue that they ought to have the same package of workplace rights as other workers, and demand that the government (i.e. the legislature and the courts) recognise their status as employees.[14] Much like Antonio's employer in the *Bicycle Thief*, Uber and other online platforms seek to externalise costs with a view to increasing profits.

The Uber drivers' complaint is not based on some legalistic technicality. It is not the case that Uber is disregarding some statutory provision which clearly stipulates that ride-hailing companies count as employers. Nor is their complaint merely one of equal treatment under law. If the law did away with the status of an employee altogether, then others too—and not just Uber drivers—would complain that law fails to accord them the protection to which they are morally entitled. The core of the Uber drivers' grievance is that they ought to be recognised as employees because they already possess the attributes that normatively justify having this status in law. They are alleging not only a legal wrong, but also a moral wrong. We may, tentatively, put this point as follows: Uber drivers claim that they are entitled to the legal status of an employee because they already possess the underlying *moral* status.

[13] See *Uber BV v Aslem* [2021] UKSC 5. The claim in English law was made under the status of 'workers' rather than employees, a separate statutory category which, however, is still afforded employment protection.

[14] This complaint is common in the so-called gig economy. In various forms of what is called precarious work (e.g. fixed-term contracts, agency workers, zero-hours contracts), workers complain that they offer employers (usually major companies) essential services on a par with those of permanent employees, but without the protection that those employees enjoy. See Valerio De Stefano, 'The Rise of the Just-In-Time Workforce: On-Demand Work, Crowdwork, and Labor Protection in the Gig-Economy', 37 *Comparative Labor Law & Policy Journal* (2016), pp. 461–471.

What is important to note here is that the idea of a moral entitlement to a status underlies many other historic grievances against government. It was once the norm in Western legal systems to refuse to recognise children born out of marriage as legitimate. As a result, these children were deprived of several rights that pertain to the legal status of a legitimate child, such as rights to inheritance or child maintenance. As modern attitudes towards the institution of marriage started to shift, the failure to accord legal status to children born out of marriage was seen as an injustice and a human rights violation. In 1979, Alexandra Marckx took her nation state, Belgium, to the European Court of Human Rights for failing to recognise, upon birth, a legal bond between her and her mother. In a landmark judgment, the Court found a violation of the right to family life and paved the way for the recognition of legal status to all children born out of marriage in Europe.[15]

As the failure to recognise one's status as a child is primarily a moral complaint, it need not involve any legal institutions. In the early years of granting legal recognition to children born out of marriage, many moral conservatives would have continued to treat these children as illegitimate family members. They would have excluded them from family gatherings and conversations, and expressed moral disapproval towards their biological parents. Such behaviour was wrongful, even though the law fully recognised the legitimate status of children born out of marriage. We find, in this case, a clear instantiation of the idea of moral status and the wrong in failing to recognise it.

The wrong of failing to recognise one's status, be it personal or institutional, need not involve a material setback to the victim's interests. It can be expressive. Suppose that grandparents include a child born out of marriage in all material family benefits. But they refuse to address the child as 'grandchild' and the child's parents as 'mother' and 'father'. They pointedly use their first names instead. They treat the child as the passive recipient of benefits, rather than the holder of rights grounded on the child's position. The child would rightly complain that the grandparents fail to show respect for their status as a family member. Their status entitles them not just to material benefits, but also to the recognition of the relation they have to other family members.

We should add to this first category of offences against status cases of withdrawing, rather than withholding, the recognition of status. An example is the practice of banishment. Since ancient times, political communities would expel individual members deemed unwanted or dangerous, and withdraw their status as citizens. The practice continued for centuries until the late nineteenth century and the emergence of nation states. It is nowadays generally accepted that citizenship ought to be a secure status, at least for native-born citizens.[16] Arbitrary

[15] See *Marckx v Belgium* (1979) Series A no. 31; *Keegan v Ireland* Appl. No. 16969/20 (ECtHR, 26 May 1994); *Odievre v France* Appl. No. 42326/98 (ECtHR, 13 February 2003).

[16] See Matthew J. Gibney, 'Should Citizenship Be Conditional? The Ethics of Denationalization', 75(3) *Journal of Politics* (2013), pp. 646–658.

revocation of one's status as a citizen is considered unjust and not just in breach of international law standards. As with previous examples, citizenship is not just seen as a mere creation of the law, but primarily as a moral status held by members of a political community.

4.3.2 Undue Interference with the Functions of One's Status

The second category of offences against status covers cases where one is put by others in circumstances that prevent, or unduly burden, the exercise of the functions of one's status.

In 2014, government in the UK started to introduce measures that require employers, landlords, and universities to check the immigration status of employees, tenants, and students respectively.[17] The official rationale was that sectors which benefit from immigration must share the burden of immigration enforcement. Many complain, however, that the real point of such measures is to create a hostile environment towards immigrants.[18] Universities are required to monitor attendance of overseas students and report absences to the government that are in breach of visa regulations. In practice, the burden falls on lecturers to monitor class attendance, through taking a register. Some universities have asked lecturers to take drastic measures of enforcement to counter the possibility of fraudulent absences, such as checking the photo ID of overseas students in class. Many academics complain that such measures are incompatible with their status as teachers and educators.

The academics' complaint is an implicit appeal to the set of normative functions that are attached to their role. The relation between teachers and students is typically unequal. Students value the judgment of their teachers for several intrinsic and instrumental reasons. Not only does their academic progress depend on it, but so do first-personal attitudes like self-esteem. Teachers, on the other hand, have responsibilities towards their students (such as to facilitate their pursuit of knowledge), powers (such as to set assignments), permissions (such as to request an explanation for an absence), and the like. Part of these normative functions includes the duty not to exploit students and to establish trust in the relationship with them. The exercise of this duty is inhibited when universities require academics to check the photo ID of students on a visa during class, as part of immigration control. When UK-based academics complain that it is not their job to be immigration officers, they do not mean that it is beneath them to carry out mundane administrative tasks. Their complaint is that asking students to prove that they are who they claim

[17] See Immigration Act 2014; Immigration Act 2016.
[18] See Melanie Griffiths and Colin Yeo, 'The UK's Hostile Environment: Deputising Immigration Control', 41(4) *Critical Social Policy* (2021), pp. 521–544.

to be amounts to a form of mistrust, which is incompatible with the role of an academic teacher. The same cannot be said of border guards, whose power to check people's passports raises no eyebrows.

4.3.3 Status Appropriation

The third category of status offences comprises cases that I will call *status appropriation*. It is the wrong of seeking and/or achieving social recognition of a status to which one is *not* entitled.

Various experts complain that complementary and alternative medicine therapies—such as homeopathy, nutritional therapies, acupuncture, and chiropractic treatment—are often placebos, not based on medical evidence.[19] But they are also concerned about the use of the title 'doctor' by healthcare practitioners who are not medical doctors.[20] The concern is partly motivated by the fact that the use of the title is often illicit, made by unscrupulous practitioners who aim to deceive the public about their medical qualifications and who pose a threat to patients' health.[21] But sometimes the concern is wider. In the United States, nursing schools nowadays offer a professional doctorate in nursing practice (a DNP). This is not equivalent to a PhD, but it nevertheless confers on graduates the title 'doctor'. Nursing practitioners think it is important that holders of a DNP are able to use the title 'doctor' in their nursing practice.[22] But medical doctors are worried that losing the exclusive use of the title 'doctor' within the healthcare sector will result in losing control over the profession, with nurses gaining powers to treat patients directly, without a referral by a medical doctor.[23] They believe that, because of their extensive training, they should be the sole gatekeepers of patients' entry into medical care.

The doctors' claim, just like the previous ones, may or may not be justified. What interests me here is its character. It is true that, due to their extensive medical training, there is a set of medical functions that are unique to the status of medical doctors. They clearly have standing to complain if patients are harmed or receive inadequate care by practitioners who have lower qualifications. But they also have standing to complain if other healthcare practitioners appropriate their title. The

[19] See R. B. Bausell, *Snake Oil Science: The Truth about Complementary and Alternative Medicine* (Oxford: Oxford University Press, 2007).

[20] See David Colquhoun, 'Doctor Who? Inappropriate Use of Titles by Some Alternative "Medicine" Practitioners', 121 *New Zealand Medical Journal* (2008), pp. 6–10.

[21] See A. Gilbey, 'Use of Inappropriate Titles by New Zealand Practitioners of Acupuncture, Chiropractic, and Osteopathy', 121 *New Zealand Medical Journal* (2008), p. 15.

[22] See Nancy Dirubbo, 'Words Matter', 31 *Journal of the American Association of Nurse Practitioners* (2019), p. 280.

[23] Gardiner Harris, 'When the Nurse Wants to Be Called Doctor', *New York Times*, 1 October 2011, www.nytimes.com/2011/10/02/health/policy/02docs.html (last accessed 14 December 2022).

use of the honorific title 'doctor' in the healthcare sector is regarded as a recognition of their role and the special responsibilities that they have towards patients. When other professionals appropriate that title without having the respective responsibilities, doctors feel that the importance of their role is diminished.

The logic of the doctors' complaint is similar to arguments made in the context of merit-based competitive practices, such as sports and exams. It is often argued that it offends the status of a winner of a competition if everybody is called a 'winner' or gets a trophy.[24] Insofar as the winner of a competition has the right to the recognition of their achievement (say, because it was the implied agreement between contestants and the judges of the competition), giving everyone a prize amounts to an injustice towards those who excelled. Likewise, insofar as we owe collectively a duty to recognise the importance of doctors' role, then allowing others to appropriate their title could amount to an injustice against them. Finally, the wrong of status appropriation can be personal, rather than institutional. It would arguably offend one's family if a third party fraudulently appropriated the title of one of its members, even if the appropriation caused no risks of harm, reputational or otherwise.

4.4 The Distinction between Rank-Status and Role-Status

The plausibility of the idea of offences against status as a category of moral wrongs depends on whether status can be understood as an attractive moral idea. The preceding section explored cases of people expressing moral-reactive attitudes of indignation and anger with respect to their status. Underlying these cases is the *role-based* account of status. Employees, teachers, doctors, and parents hold social positions which shape the way they are required to behave. 'Role' was once seen as synonymous with status[25] and while there is a rich tradition in moral philosophy around the idea of role obligations,[26] it has not been tied to the notion of status. I am here hoping to connect the two strands, particularly because the idea of role obligations does not immediately imply hierarchy or ranking.[27] By contrast, a large part of contemporary discourse about status regards it in ranking terms. We hear that private jets and yachts are status symbols, that people in capitalist societies

[24] Betty Berdan, 'Participation Trophies Send a Dangerous Message', *New York Times*, 6 October 2016, www.nytimes.com/roomfordebate/2016/10/06/should-every-young-athlete-get-a-trophy/participation-trophies-send-a-dangerous-message (last accessed 14 December 2022).

[25] Linton, who introduced the concept of role in sociology, wrote that 'Role and status are quite inseparable, and the distinction between them is of only academic interest', see Ralph Linton, *The Study of Man: An Introduction* ((New York: D. Appleton Century, 1936), p. 114.

[26] See Chapter 6.

[27] Michael Hardimon discusses both concepts but distinguishes them on the basis that not all statuses are roles. See Michael Hardimon, 'Role Obligations', 91 *Journal of Philosophy* (1994), pp. 333–363. He has in mind, however, the natural status of human beings and notes, rightly, that being human is not a role.

suffer from anxiety about their social status,[28] and that one's social status determines the level of health one enjoys.[29] Many people see status as a problematic idea, in tension with the aspirations of an egalitarian society.

The examples discussed in the preceding section are so far insufficient to distinguish role-status from rank-status. Uber drivers demand the recognition of a set of rights but, at the same time, are in a lower socio-economic position than, say, doctors or lawyers. The demand for the status of employee might be seen as an aspiration for a higher social ranking. Likewise, doctors have a high socio-economic ranking and their complaint about status appropriation might be seen as an attempt to maintain it, by putting other healthcare professionals down. To sharpen the moral dimension of status, we need first to distinguish it from the problematic notion of ranking people.

The distinction between role-status and rank-status is not easy to draw. Both notions track social positions, and both can be attached to the same person. Moreover, both involve social recognition. But they are quite different. *Role-status* refers to the position one occupies within a pattern of social interaction. *Rank-status*, by contrast, refers to the position one occupies within a social ordering of esteem or prestige. The former notion seeks to capture standing interactions with certain morally salient characteristics, most notably the presence of a package of rights and duties.[30] The latter notion, by contrast, seeks to capture society's beliefs about someone's prestige or esteem. Consider Jeff Bezos. He has rank-status in that he is a celebrity that enjoys wide societal recognition that most people do not. But he also has role-status in that he is the CEO of one of the largest corporations in the world, employing 1.6 million workers.

4.4.1 Rank-Status

The contemporary meaning of rank-status is perhaps best exemplified in Michael Marmot's empirical thesis that one's social status determines the level of health one enjoys. Marmot's research has shown that the determinants of health are primarily social, rather than medical. The level of health one enjoys across their lifetime does not depend on some absolute level of material resources or healthcare, but on the relative position one occupies along a social gradient. Things like education, occupation, or class background serve as grounds of societal esteem which sort people out on a gradient. For each of these grounds, the higher one's position on the gradient, the better their health. This empirical co-relation is universal, found even in

[28] See Alain de Botton, *Status Anxiety* (London: Penguin Books, 2005).

[29] See Michael Marmot, *The Status Syndrome* (London: Bloomsbury, 2004).

[30] Not all roles are statuses. Some roles involve very little interactions with others (e.g. a gardener or a commuter) and some do not capture patterns of social interaction that trigger reciprocal rights and duties over and above what was agreed (e.g. a musician).

countries with a strong welfare state and egalitarian ethos, like Sweden. Marmot calls this empirical finding the *status syndrome*.[31]

Rank-status, thus understood, has several characteristics. It is primarily a descriptive notion in that it purports to report a social fact about the attitudes of a given society towards different groups of people, based on attributes such as one's education, occupation, or class. We collectively can be wrong about who should have high social status, but not about who currently has it.

Furthermore, rank-status tracks an attitude shared by most people at a given place and time, which I will call societal esteem. The attitude possesses positive valence at one end (admiration) and negative valence at the other (contempt). It is both emotive and propositional in content. On the emotive side, it is characterised by the desire—or, if not feasible, the counterfactual wish—to possess certain attributes that a group in their society possesses (or, at the low end of the scale,[32] the desire to avoid them). People might desire to be admitted to a top university or wish they had been born into an upper-class family. The desire or wish may, but need not, be malicious, harbouring hostile feelings towards those who possess the attributes. It need not be a form of invidious envy.[33] Its main object is not the holder of the attribute, but the attribute itself. Nor is it necessarily a moralised attitude, like resentment. It might coincide with the desire to emulate, if possible, those who possess the attribute. Most often, it consists in pleasant feelings, particularly a sense of superiority, at the thought of imagining oneself possessing it.

On the propositional side, the attitude contains two main elements. First, an element of common knowledge. One knows that most people in one's society also desire or wish they possessed the attribute. This comes about mainly through the public manifestation of how desirable the attribute is. Typically, societal esteem is not a privately held attitude. For someone to enjoy rank-status, it is not enough that most people have entertained the thought that they are more, or less, esteemed than others. The thought must drive some external behaviour which is publicly recognised as expression of the relevant attitude. This usually takes the form of a disposition to communicate, through conventions or norms of etiquette, that one is aware of another's position in the social hierarchy.[34] When the attributes are not immediately visible, rank-status holders typically make sure to exhibit them

[31] Marmot, *The Status Syndrome*, p. 8.

[32] For ease of exposition, I will focus on the positive valence of the attitude. The emotive and cognitive side of disesteem can be adapted accordingly.

[33] For the distinction between benign and invidious envy, see D. M. Farrell, 'Of Jealousy and Envy', in G. Graham and H. LaFollette (eds), *Person to Person* (Philadelphia: Temple University Press, 1989). I follow here the view that benign envy is not envy at all. See J. Darms and A. Kerr, 'Envy in the Philosophical Tradition', in R. Smith (ed.), *Envy: Theory and Research* (Oxford: Oxford University Press, 2008).

[34] I draw here on Erving Goffman's deeply perceptive analysis of role behaviour, in Erving Goffman, *The Presentation of Self in Everyday Life* (London: Penguin Books, 1959). Goffman's analysis, however, contains elements of both rank-status and role-status.

through signs, implicature or—in the case of material possessions—conspicuous consumption. It is the element of common knowledge that the familiar practice of constantly relabelling certain jobs (e.g. relabelling 'secretary' to 'personal assistant') seeks to escape, so as to shield workers from the low social esteem that their job (wrongly) attracts.

Second, the cognitive aspect of societal esteem contains an element of positionality.[35] One finds the attribute desirable mainly because not all those who desire it can have it. The desire is motivated by the thought that, by having what others want but cannot have due to scarcity, one is superior to them. Rank-status has a 'rub-it-in-their face' dimension. Most people value becoming a parent and owning a Picasso, but only the latter carries high social status because, unlike parenthood, very few of those who desire it can have it. Scarcity can be institutional (e.g. degrees or prizes), material (e.g. diamonds or land in prime location), or biological (e.g. ancestry or good looks). It would be a mistake to think that societal esteem tracks only desert-based attributes. Good looks or inherited wealth often attract societal esteem even though there is nothing one has done to deserve them. Nor is it necessarily the case that the attributes which attract social esteem correspond to objectively valuable qualities. A society may esteem media celebrities who, as the popular saying goes, are famous for being famous.

Here are then the main characteristics of rank-status:

> **Rank-Status**: descriptive (social fact); emotive (admiration/contempt); collective intentionality (widely held beliefs); epistemic (common knowledge); positional (not everyone who desires it can have it).

Related notions to rank-status include honour, prestige, or cachet. When philosophers tackle the notion of status, they usually have this notion in mind. And they tell a familiar story about how status figures in human history. The idea that we transitioned from a ranking morality to an egalitarian morality is a familiar motif in political theory. It employs the contemporary notion of rank-status and projects it backwards as an account of the unjust pre-modern societies against which egalitarianism emerged. There have been two different ways to describe this transition. The first is as an extension in the scope of a legitimate moral outlook. Jeremy Waldron has argued that dignity used to be tied to the rank of nobility (e.g. dukes, earls, and prelates), but with the advent of human rights the idea of dignity as rank

[35] Economists use the term 'positional good', but there is no agreement on its precise definition, particularly about whether the good must be desired *mainly* or *solely* because of its positionality, or whether it is enough that it has some positional aspects. See Michael Schneider, 'The Nature, History and Significance of the Concept of Positional Goods', 45(1) *History of Economics Review* (2007), pp. 60–81. I follow here the narrower definition that the good must be desired mainly because of its positionality. For the use of the wider definition, see Harry Brighouse and Adam Swift, 'Equality, Priority and Positional Goods' 116(3) *Ethics* (2006), pp. 471–497.

has now been extended to everyone. 'We look *up* on each other,' Waldron says, 'as if we are all earls, rather than peasants.'[36]

The second, more robust, way has been to regard the modern outlook as a full-blown rejection of rank as a moral idea. In Richard Dagger's words, 'for the concept of rights to appear and gain purchase, the status concepts had to lose their grip.'[37] On this second view, the problem with rank-status was not that few people got to be earls and dukes and most people were peasants; rather, the problem was the very thought that being an earl or a peasant has anything to do with one's moral entitlements. Stephen Darwall's well-known account of morality as a second-personal standpoint is an example of this more robust view.[38]

These two approaches seek either to purify or to condemn the inegalitarianism of rank-status. I want to suggest, instead, that rank-status, as we understand it now, never had the historical significance that political philosophers nowadays attribute to it. What was central in pre-modern times was not rank-status but role-status, and it is no less central today. What happened is not that we gradually moved away from status, as Maine claimed. Rather, we flipped status on its head: societies used to side with the stronger party to status-relations; now we side with the weaker party. Role-status is the basic concept.

4.4.2 Role-Status

It is true, of course, that dukes, earls, and prelates enjoyed high societal esteem in pre-modern times. But crucially, they also occupied a social position as owners of large estates that controlled production. That social position placed noblepersons at a standing interaction with the people who worked in those estates and whose livelihood depended on it; they were key players in a pattern of social interaction. They had role-status and not just rank-status. And the former, being more fundamental, was the basis of the latter. This is manifested in the concept of *noblesse oblige*. Nobility had the capacity, due to their socio-economic power, to affect the well-being of dependent parties, and in virtue of that capacity, they acquired a set of moral responsibilities.[39] The societal esteem they enjoyed supervened on this role.

36 Jeremy Waldron, *Dignity, Rank and Rights* (Oxford: Oxford University Press, 2012), p. 59.

37 Richard Dagger, 'Rights', in Terence Ball, James Farr, and Russell L. Hanson (eds), *Political Innovation and Conceptual Change* (Cambridge: Cambridge University Press, 1989), p. 292.

38 See Stephen Darwall, *The Second Person Standpoint: Morality, Respect and Accountability* (Cambridge: Harvard University Press, 2009). Darwall has sought to contrast morality with rank-determining attitudes like esteem, annoyance, or contempt. He calls such attitudes *third-personal* because they are not used as the basis for making demands on people; rather, they merely report the perception of merit or demerit one has towards third parties. Morality, by contrast, involves what Darwall calls a *second-personal* perspective, a practice of placing demands on one another. Darwall reaches the conclusion that societies organised around the idea of rank-status are orders of 'honor respect', which—he claims—is not an inherently normative idea.

39 I am grateful to Chris Essert for discussion on this point.

Role-status picks out very different social facts to rank-status, as early sociologists pointed out. T. H. Marshall, writing in the middle of the twentieth century, complained about using status to denote 'a position in the hierarchy of social esteem'. He expressed his preference for the traditional use of the term, as used by lawyers and earlier sociologists, which has 'no direct or necessary reference to position on a scale or in a hierarchy'.[40] Marshall sought to defend the older use of status by sociologists, who were interested in standing social interactions one has with others, in virtue of their role. Role, in this sense, is a set of normative requirements about how a person should treat others, in virtue of some enduring aspect of the role-holder's circumstances, such as one's profession, vocation, circumstances, capacities or age. Though societal esteem is inevitably attached to roles (no less than to everything else we do), it is not a constitutive part of them.

For example, there is a whole range of obligations that one owes students, *qua* teacher, which have nothing to do with the societal esteem attached to the role. Teachers' esteem might go up or down, as it has done historically, without affecting the core of the teacher's role obligations. Contrariwise, a person may enjoy high societal esteem without having any standing social interaction with anyone. A modern-day aristocrat who leads a solitary life off the proceeds of the family wealth may enjoy high social esteem without having a social relation with anyone outside close family and friends. There is no one to whom that person owes a set of obligations *qua* aristocrat; no set of role obligations attached to their rank. By contrast, it is constitutive of being an employee, a doctor, or a teacher that one has a standing social interaction with employers, patients, and students respectively.[41] The concept of role-status has a constitutive dependence on stable and widely known social facts about the background circumstances of the role-holder.

I should emphasise here that I use the term 'role' in a thin sense, to mean simply a distinct pattern of social interaction, rather that the collective beliefs, expectations, norms, etc., with respect to how parties within that pattern ought to behave.[42] I explore the social ontology of role-status in more detail in Chapter 7. Suffices to say

[40] Marshall wrote: '"Status", as used by Linton, Parsons and others, has no direct or necessary reference to position on a scale or in a hierarchy. It embraces all relationships, not only those of superiority and inferiority. But "social status" is now in general use to denote position in the hierarchy of social prestige . . . My own preference is for the retention of the term "status" as used by Linton and Parsons, that is without any necessary reference to hierarchical position.' See T. H. Marshall, *Class, Citizenship and Social Development* (New York: Doubleday, 1964), p. 207.

[41] That such roles track existing social relations can be further evidenced by the fact that people who achieve an institutional qualification (e.g. doctors or lawyers) yet never practice are reluctant to self-identify socially as role-holders. They typically use locutions such as 'I qualified as a lawyer, but do not practice'.

[42] I depart here from the widely held view that roles are necessarily social kinds, identical with a set of descriptively identified mental states of collective intentionality. People may be in massive error about what a particular role-holder is required to do. For an account of roles as social kinds, see John Searle, *The Construction of Social Reality* (New York: Free Press, 1995). For a discussion of Austin's equivalent thesis about legal status, see C. K. Allen, *Legal Duties and Other Essays in Jurisprudence* (Clarendon Press, 1931), ch. 2.

here that I am interested in a subset of roles, those that are bilateral and inherently asymmetrical, such as the roles of employer and employee. This conception allows us to compare the role of nobility who owned large estates with that of multinational corporations, even though background cultural norms surrounding the role-holder are, of course, very different between, say, the Duke of Westminster and Jeff Bezos.

4.5 Differences between Role-Status and Rank-Status

The precise connection between role-status and rank-status is much more complex than the preceding remarks suggest. But the two notions are sufficiently distinct to allow us to draw several significant contrasts. First, role-status cuts across social ranking. The status of an employee is possessed by esteemed professions such as doctors, lawyers, and judges. But it is equally possessed by cleaners, waiters, and rubbish collectors. Likewise, the status of a self-employed contractor is currently assigned to certain low-income jobs, such as Uber and Deliveroo drivers. But it is also possessed by famous painters and musicians.

Second, role-status is relational rather than holistic. The Uber drivers' claim for employment status concerns the bilateral relation they have with Uber, and the way it is regulated by law. By contrast, the social prestige attached to, say, the CEO of a multinational corporation is a function of the relative societal esteem CEOs enjoy vis-à-vis all other professions in society.

Third, role-status is not commensurable. It is not possible to compare role-statuses, understood as a package of rights and duties attached to different social roles, in the way it is for rank-statuses. It makes little sense to say that the status of an employee is better or worse than, say, the status of a citizen or a parent. Each status contains a package of rights and obligations that is unique to the role and incommensurable with the set attached to other roles.[43] By contrast, status as a ranking notion is directly commensurate to the degree of societal esteem one enjoys relative to everybody else.

But the most important difference lies in the way the two notions relate to the value of equality. Rank-status, as explicated here, is clearly not a morally acceptable basis for recognising moral rights. If it is used in this way, it can only offend the value of equality. Nobel-Prize winners, let alone rich CEOs, do not possess additional moral rights compared with you and me. Things are even worse when

[43] It is possible, however, to compare the ethical significance of the interests underlying different statuses. We might say that the interest in being a family member is greater than the interest in being employed. But that is different from saying that we can compare and rank the packages of rights and duties attached to the status of a parent and an employee. For example, it is not possible to compare employees' right not to be unfairly dismissed with children's right to be educated. I am grateful to Massimo Renzo for discussion on this point.

rank-status does not even track merit but is used instead as a way to discriminate against whole categories of persons: women, minorities, immigrants, people with disabilities, people with a given sexual orientation, or those who defy traditional gender norms. Role-status, by contrast, inherently raises the important moral concern of whether the two role-holders in an asymmetrical social relation treat each other as equals. The value of equality is only pertinent to rank-status as a result of a moral mistake. But it is fundamentally pertinent to role-status. It would be a moral mistake to ignore it.

Are there any commonalities between rank-status and role-status? Or are they mere homonyms? The very fact that one might conflate them suggests that they are not. We don't conflate riverbanks with financial banks. I already mentioned that both notions relate to social positions one occupies: within a ranking of societal esteem in one case and within a standing social interaction in the other. Both positions contain asymmetries, but of a quite different sort. Yet there is one more commonality that I want to highlight here and return to it later: how we should distribute societal esteem collectively is itself a normative question. People have their own individual beliefs about who is estimable and who is not. Taken together, they generate rankings and social statuses. But should the government interfere with this process? Should it try to *place* esteem on certain social positions? I will argue that government must not in general interfere with the bottom-up distribution of merit-based esteem; but it ought nevertheless to recognise role-statuses. That recognition, which should mainly take the form of legal regulation, is a requirement imposed by the morality of status. Though not quite a form of rank-status, the duty to recognise role-statuses brings the two concepts closer together and explains why people might conflate them. They both relate to how we collectively—through government—recognise the significance of certain social positions. Government ought to say silent on whether being a doctor is more estimable than being a builder. But it ought to take a stance on the relation between employers and employees: it ought to recognise the vulnerable position of the latter and protect the status of being an employee.

5
THE NATURE OF STATUS RELATIONS

5.1 Introduction

Employees, teachers, and doctors have statuses, sets of rights and duties attached to their position. These statuses are not a reference to a background ranking of societal esteem. They are not morally objectionable. In fact, they can be offended and give rise to a legitimate moral grievance. But when does one acquire a status? Who has it and why? And how many statuses are there? This chapter explores the conditions under which certain social relations become status-based. The thesis I attributed to Pufendorf, that role-statuses pose a social threat to equality, is a key part of my argument.

Pre-modern law protected and solidified the prevailing socio-economic power of nobility over whole classes of persons, such as slaves, servants, or peasants. But it did so with a view to regulating a pattern of social interaction with certain morally salient characteristics, most notably the dependency of these classes on landowners.[1] Modern law does the same when it seeks to regulate the power of large multinational corporations, such as Uber and Amazon, over precarious workers. The difference between ancient law and modern law is that the latter, unlike the former, seeks to balance this unequal relation and protect the weaker party. The transition at issue here relates to role-status, not rank-status. And it is far more complex than philosophical preoccupation with rank-status suggests. Law can, as it did in ancient times, intervene and protect the position of owners of large economic resources against vulnerable workers. It can also, as it did in the early period of liberalisation, stay out of the employment relation and treat it as purely contractual, turning a blind eye to its underlying asymmetry. Or it can, as it does in late modernity, intervene with a view to protecting the weaker party through the creation of employment status. The historical progression has been to turn the role-status relation on its head, by seeking to help the weaker, rather than the stronger, party.

[1] This explains why ancient legal statuses were a poor proxy for societal esteem. According to Tristan S. Taylor, 'Social Status, Legal Status and Legal Privilege', in Paul J. du Plessis et al. (eds), *The Oxford Handbook of Roman Law and Society* (Oxford: Oxford University Press, 2016), 'the legal categories under the Roman law of persons tell us relatively little about social status'.

Status in Law and Morality. George Letsas, Oxford University Press. © George Letsas 2026.
DOI: 10.1093/9780198936725.003.0005

Jeremy Bentham was the first philosopher to use the phrase 'offences against status' to describe a separate category of legal wrongs.[2] Bentham captured very well the idea that status picks out unequal social interactions which precede the law. Unlike Austin, he did not believe that status is simply a taxonomical concept which law uses to group together rights and duties for the sake of convenience. He observed in this respect that when a power is vested in a superior for their own benefit, the superior is called a *master* and the inferior is called a *servant*. But when the power is vested in a superior for the benefit of the inferior, then the former is called a *guardian* and the latter is called a *ward*.[3] We might say, using Bentham's distinction, that the transition that took place historically is that masters became guardians and servants became wards. The distinction suggests that status relations display a stable social asymmetry across time, having stronger and weaker parties, and that the law can either protect this asymmetry or seek to mitigate its effects.[4] It is this asymmetry that I take to be the core of the moral dimension of status, and that has been overshadowed by the emphasis on rank-status.

5.2 The Pluralistic Basis of Status Asymmetries

What is asymmetrical about role-status relations? The main idea is that one party suffers from vulnerabilities or dependencies vis-à-vis the other.[5] These two terms are not synonymous, but nevertheless capture a unified source of moral concern. Dependency, as I understand it here, refers to objective needs that everyone has (e.g. for food and shelter) but which some classes of persons (such as children) cannot satisfy on their own, having instead to rely on others. Vulnerability refers to weaknesses of one group relative to another, with respect to the aim of a particular social interaction (such as employees vis-à-vis employers).

[2] This was originally published in French as 'Vue générale d'un corps complet de législation' and appeared in Jeremy Bentham, *Traités de legislation civile et pénale*, edited by Étienne Dumont (Bossange, Masson et Besson, 1802). The French word Bentham used for status was *condition* ('contre la condition'). In the English edition by John Bowring, this was translated as 'offences against condition'. It was clear, however, that the two were treated as synonymous at the time as in discussing the French edition, Austin uses the term 'status', rather than condition. 'Offences Against Condition' receives a longer treatment by Bentham in *The Collected Works of Jeremy Bentham: An Introduction to the Principles of Morals and Legislation* (Oxford: Clarendon Press, 1996), ch. XVI (hereinafter *IPML*). Some passages from the French edition, however, do not appear in *IPML*. I am grateful to Philip Schofield for very helpful discussion and guidance on Bentham's writings.

[3] See Bentham, *IPML*, 238.

[4] This explains why the use of status to pick out morally evil legal statuses of the past (such as villeinage or tutelage) is not conceptually a mistake. The ancients correctly identified an asymmetrical relation, but made a moral mistake about how to regulate it.

[5] I shall set aside here the rare cases of standing interactions where both parties suffer from vulnerabilities and dependencies, as is the case, for instance, with friendship and spousal relations. These cases also fall within the category of status because there is reciprocal asymmetry that triggers egalitarian requirements.

Consider again the case of employees. It is well known that lack of bargaining power within a market economy makes them vulnerable to accepting unfair or unjust terms of employment. But it is also the case that people depend on employment to promote several instrumental and intrinsic interests. Employment is a social relation that forms a significant part of the employee's well-being. Most people socialise through their work, and one's performance at work is a significant source of self-esteem. Unemployment typically carries a social stigma. These background economic and social factors, creating vulnerabilities and dependencies on the part of employees, are constitutive of the employment status. They are encapsulated in the powerful motto of the International Labour Organization that 'labour is not a commodity'.

The central cases of status relations display similar characteristics. To be a teacher is to engage in a pattern of social interaction that is shaped by the economic and social significance of education. Students' sense of self-esteem, as well as their future success in life, depends on the judgment of their teachers, who are typically more mature. Based on their knowledge and expertise, teachers are in a position of power whose limits they might be disposed to exceed for personal gain.

Looking at most of the statuses that the law recognises, one observes that they too involve social relations that are marked by background dependencies and vulnerabilities. Infancy, insanity, refugee, and bankruptcy would be the obvious ones. But the same holds for the statuses of being a citizen and being an alien. Being a citizen or an alien is not only a legal relation. As a matter of social fact, both are subject to the coercive power of a state and, in the case of aliens, they do not even have the capacity to affect how that power is exercised, say, through voting or other political action.

It would be a mistake to restrict the relevant dependencies and vulnerabilities solely to economic and political factors. Clearly, the cases of employees and refugees fall into this category. But some factors are cultural, to do with the social importance attached to the relevant social interaction. For instance, nowadays there is significant social importance attached to education and employment and conversely, social stigma attached to illiteracy and unemployment. Other factors relate to psychological dispositions that are common to most societies throughout history. There is a natural disposition, for instance, to feel embarrassed and ashamed when exposing one's ill-body to others. This disposition makes patients vulnerable vis-à-vis doctors, regardless of the background social conditions surrounding the practice of medicine. It is important to stress that the vulnerability of patients is not only to do with the lack of expertise. Even expert doctors cannot operate on themselves. They too must consult a doctor and face the vulnerability of having to expose their ill-body.

The relation between family members, particularly that between parents and children,[6] is perhaps the clearest case of status. It features in Pufendorf's,

[6] On the duties of parenthood see Gregg Strauss, *Reconstructing Parentage* (Cambridge: Cambridge University Press, 2025); Scott Altman, 'Parental Control Rights', in Lucinda Ferguson and Elizabeth

Bentham's, and Kant's lists. It is not contractual, insofar as one is born into an existing family—biological or adoptive—which one has not chosen. Young children depend on their parents for food and shelter. This vulnerability flips, as parents age and rely on their children for care. But family vulnerabilities are not only biological. The need for human intimacy generates emotional dependency on one's nearest and dearest.[7] This vulnerability can be abused and exploited and, sadly, often is. Property and financial considerations also come into the relation, reaffirming the point that vulnerabilities and dependencies in such relations are of a pluralistic character.

Like parent/child, the relation between officials and citizens is not contractual either. One is born into a state and, few exceptions aside, one cannot leave by freely choosing to take up citizenship at another state. Citizens' main vulnerability relates to the use of collective force by officials, often at the request of another citizen. The police can come into my house and arrest me in the middle of the night; they can detain and imprison me. Bailiffs can seize my possessions to satisfy my creditors at their request. The stronger party in this social relation is not only the officials who can direct the use of collective force, but also the citizen who can initiate this at their request. If I can get officials to detain you, simply because I do not agree with your political beliefs, then I am the powerful party in an asymmetrical relation. But there are dependencies too. Citizens depend on collective institutions for the provision of public goods, such as health, education, and public order.

Pufendorf thinks that the asymmetry between rulers and citizens is 'the greatest inequality' that is introduced by the civil state, compared to the state of nature.[8] Tyranny, authoritarianism, police brutality, and corruption are evils that come about because rulers exploit the vulnerabilities and dependencies of citizens. Citizenship, as a status, is fundamentally a way to register the asymmetrical position of persons subject to the collective force of state institutions. It is a progressive notion whose point is to protect citizens against tyranny and to project the value of equality in the relation between citizens. It tells officials: 'you may be stronger than me, but you are not superior to me. Your role is to treat me as an equal'.

Finally, some vulnerabilities are not relative to specific background conditions or social meanings, but have mainly a biological basis, such as infancy or lack of mental capacity. I want to advocate here a type of pluralism about the empirical sources of vulnerability and dependency, departing from a monistic account that

Brake (eds), *Philosophical Foundations of Children's and Family Law* (Oxford: Oxford University Press, 2018).

[7] For the connection between intimacy and parental rights see Scott Altman, 'The Pursuit of Intimacy and Parental Rights', in Andrei Marmor (ed.), *The Routledge Companion to Philosophy of Law* (London: Routledge, 2012).

[8] Samuel Pufendorf, *Of the Law of Nature and Nations* (Oxford, 1703), Book III, chapter II, § 9, p. 182.

focuses solely on economic and political factors.[9] What is essential to status is that the relevant relations with vulnerabilities and dependencies are both enduring and widely known. As Niko Kolodny rightly emphasises, relations of inferiority, or as I prefer to call them of asymmetry, must be genuine interactions or relations.[10] They must display a degree of regularity, rather than being episodic. The reason for this requirement is the one offered in the previous chapter: enduring relations pose a serious risk to the weaker party's self-esteem: the weaker party is likely to be treated as inferior by the stronger party, and to internalise this mistaken moral belief. By doing so the weaker party loses a vital moral defence: to insist on equal terms of social cooperation within that relation.

5.3 The Non-contingent Character of Status Relations

Consider the universality and timelessness of the three main categories of status that we found in Roman law and in Pufendorf's work: citizenship, family, and labour. Most human societies that have existed had these three types of bilateral relations. You are someone's daughter or son, you are some country's national, and you are someone's employee or provider of services. The near ubiquitous character of these relations concerns significant aspects of the human condition. Some are to do with basic needs: without care by others, infants and children will not survive; without social cooperation, the mass production of certain basic goods, such as food, is not possible. Others are to do with objective interests of well-being, such as health, education, housing, and sociability or intimacy. In modern-day conditions, for instance, it is impossible to pursue meaningfully one's interests in privacy and intimacy without secured housing.

Role-statuses concern relations that engage central components of our ethical lives. The statuses of doctor/patient implicate one's interest in health and bodily integrity. The statuses of teacher/student implicate one's interest in education and knowledge. The statuses of parent/child implicate one's interest in forging relations of love and intimacy. The statuses of employer/employee implicate one's interests in self-realisation and sociability. I do not mean to suggest that these interests directly generate moral requirements. Indeed, I think it is a mistake to think that the point of status-based moral rights and duties is to make sure that these interests are adequately promoted. This teleological view cannot explain why, in principle, an employer may dismiss an employee, or a landlord may evict a tenant, since these

[9] The Marxist tradition offers such a monistic account, focusing on how the economic structure creates vulnerabilities which are further reinforced and solidified by prevailing legal and political norms. But see Chapter 6 for why certain juridical relations, such as being a trustee or a bailee, are excluded from my account.

[10] Niko Kolodny, *The Pecking Order: Social Hierarchy as a Philosophical Problem* (Cambridge: Harvard University Press, 2023), p. 89.

can have detrimental effects on people's interests. Nor do I want to suggest that one cannot lead an ethically fulfilling life if one is unemployed or homeless. It is possible to make alternative choices, such as leading a nomadic life or living in a nature commune, that are ethically equally enriching. The moral basis of status is not the fact that these relations are essential to a flourishing life.

My view is different: for the vast majority of people in modern-day conditions, the pursuit of certain fundamental interests is necessarily mediated by certain relations. We set out to choose and pursue a conception of the good life through the relations we have with our family, our teachers, our doctors, our employers, and our government. And we enter this process on an unequal footing, as weak parties to the relation: as children, students, patients, employees, and citizens. The pursuit of the relevant interest (e.g. in intimacy, knowledge, health, sociability) makes us vulnerable or dependent on others, who are likely to exploit it. An employer who is not allowed to dismiss freely an employee, might incur a financial cost but they will not suffer in their pursuit of sociability or self-realisation. By contrast, the employee who loses their job will suffer a substantial setback to these interests. The stronger party to status relations either does not pursue the same fundamental interest as the weaker party, or they do not rely on the relation to the same degree as the weaker party for pursuing that interest. This asymmetry, which is constant in modern times and widely known, creates social conditions that—if left unregulated—will inevitably result in exploitation. When entry to the relation is voluntary, as in employment or tenancy, the weaker party is likely to accept voluntarily unfair or unjust terms, having no meaningful alternative. When the relation is non-voluntary, as in family or citizenship, the weaker party is likely to endure abuse without fighting for their rights. Ultimately, status-based rights are based on the value of equality and more specifically, the duty not to exploit another person's vulnerability, taking oneself to be superior to them.

We can imagine, of course, abolishing these relations and some philosophers have made arguments to this effect. Empirically, this might be feasible, though perhaps not for all three relations at the same time. State institutions could be abolished, replaced by informal small-knit communities. Artificial Intelligence (AI) robots could do all the labour needed to produce goods and services for humans. Family could be abolished, with children raised by the state or a collective. It is possible to imagine different ways in which basic needs and fundamental interests of well-being can be served. But any alternative relations we can imagine, or create, will either reproduce existing vulnerabilities (e.g. of infancy) or create new ones (e.g. dependence on AI bots and their manufacturers). I therefore find the argument for abolition naïve at best, assuming that the baseline is a world in which social relations that implicate fundamental interests of well-being can be purely symmetrical. There is no symmetrical baseline.

Moreover, there is another reason against abolition, what I called in Chapter 1 the *two-way dynamic* of status relations. Many of us will move from being the weaker party in a status relation to being the stronger party. A minor might later in life become a parent or a carer. A student might become a teacher. A tenant might become a landlord. An employee might decide to start their own business. And some of us will bounce up and down the same status relation, sometimes concurrently. A doctor might become another doctor's patient. A professor might take up a course in a new discipline. A landlord might decide to move to a new area and rent, becoming some other landlord's tenant. A judge may sue a neighbour in their personal capacity and become a litigant before another judge. In other words, nobody is immune from the risk of occupying the weaker side of these relations at some point in their life.

The better approach is to treat status relations as a central parameter of our ethical lives that raises moral concerns and needs to be kept in check collectively. The fact that there is no symmetrical baseline, combined with the two-way dynamic of status relations, makes status an enduring aspect of our moral practices.

5.4 Non-instrumental Wrongs, Prophylactic Duties and Duty of Social Recognition

The presence of vulnerabilities and dependencies increases systematically the likelihood of moral wrongdoing within the relevant pattern of social interaction. Wrongs such as exploitation or abuse can occur episodically, outside standing social interactions. A savvy scammer may exploit my momentary lapse of judgment and get me to give my bank details. An aggressive stranger on the train may abuse me and get me to vacate my seat. But in the context of role-status, these wrongs become substantially more common because the relevant social interaction is enduring and inherently asymmetrical. Teachers are prone to exploiting students. Employers are prone to treating employees unfairly. Doctors are prone to abusing patients. Though these wrongs are not unique to the underlying social interaction, they are nevertheless central to it. The endemic risk posed to the weaker party is constitutive of the relevant role. It is part of what makes the social roles of, say, patients or students distinct.

Why is there an endemic risk? As mentioned several times already, asymmetrical social relations pose a social threat to a person's self-esteem. The stronger party is likely to interpret their position as one of superiority and treat the weaker party accordingly. In turn, the weaker party is likely to internalise the mistaken moral belief that they are inferior. The loss of self-esteem that accompanies this internalisation deprives the weaker party of a vital moral defence: to insist on equal terms of cooperation. As a result, the stronger party is more likely to abuse their position and exploit the weaker party.

The endemic risk of exploitation and other wrongs has important implications for the moral profile of both parties. It triggers a set of additional rights and duties on both sides. Within role-status, this package of rights and duties, a core feature of role obligations, is grounded on the idea of equality: its point is to balance the relation at the moral level. Contemporary philosophers rightly emphasise the relational character of equality.[11] We should here be careful, however. As Pufendorf points out, our natural status as equals is not dependent on any relation. We are all equal in that we are valid sources of self-esteem, possessing free will. The relational character of equality is manifested in how various social relations *threaten* our natural equality, creating conditions under which people will be treated by others as, and consider themselves to be, inferior. It is not that we cannot understand our equal status except in relational terms; rather, it is that certain relations pose known and enduring social threats to our equal status, by threatening our self-esteem.

Some of the status-based rights and duties are mainly instrumental, a prophylactic measure to reduce the likelihood of wrongful harm. The right of employees to form and join trade unions, for example, is of this instrumental character. It strengthens the bargaining power of employees and therefore reduces the risk of downstream wrongs such as unfair dismissal or exploitative wages. These rights differ from one role-status to another. Tenants have the right to assert their right to possession and block the landlord from entering the premises. Citizens have the right not to have their premises searched without a judicial warrant and the right to be taken to a judge promptly following arrest. But other status-based rights and duties are of a non-instrumental nature.

Consider the duty of doctors not to engage in an intimate relation with their patients. This is not merely a means to prevent or minimise exploitation, for instance imposing treatments to which the patient has not consented, or extracting monetary gain or other favours. The mixing of different roles creates a heavy moral burden of having to integrate competing moral demands within one's life. But within status relations, this burden falls unevenly on the weaker party. The patient would have to assess how *their* illness affects the intimate relation they have started with their doctor. That is much harder than the balancing the doctor has to do. Even when the patient can successfully navigate through the demands of the two roles without suffering any wrongful harm, they have nevertheless been placed under an additional moral burden. Doctors have a duty not to compound the already asymmetrical position of patients by inflicting this extra burden.[12]

[11] See Samuel Scheffler, *Equality and Tradition: Questions of Value in Moral and Political Theory* (Oxford: Oxford University Press, 2010); Elizabeth Anderson, 'What Is the Point of Equality?', 109 *Ethics* (1999), pp. 287–337.

[12] I offer this equality-based account as an explanation of the common intuition that certain interactions, such as starting a romantic relation with one's student, are incompatible with the nature of one's role. For a similar claim about the role of teachers, see Amia Srinivasan, *The Right to Sex* (New York: Farrar, Straus and Giroux, 2021), ch. 5.

As this duty applies even in the absence of any risk of wrongful harm, it cannot by explained by the moral principles underlying the downstream wrongs.

But the most significant non-instrumental requirement is the duty to project the value of equality within the relation. Recognising publicly the statuses of the two parties is inherently significant. It registers publicly that certain interpersonal interactions are asymmetrical and that there is moral imperative to balance them, not only on the part of the stronger party, but also collectively, through political action. This public recognition performs an expressive function. It is itself a form of balancing the unequal relation, quite apart from any beneficial effects. As argued in the previous chapter, it provides the weaker party with a moral defence: it protects their self-esteem and thereby makes it possible that they can insist on equal terms of cooperation. It tells the weaker party: 'you may be vulnerable to the stronger party, but you are their equal'. Without social recognition of their vulnerability, the weaker party is likely to interpret their position as one of inferiority, losing their self-esteem. By doing so, they will be deprived of a vital moral defence: to insist on equal terms of social cooperation. Only persons with self-esteem will insist on equal terms of cooperation.

The duty of social recognition explains why titles are so important to status. Suppose we had no separate titles for the parties to an employment contract. But they nevertheless agree on fair terms, including all the employment rights that contemporary law imposes. Despite this, the relation remains asymmetrical. The worker's inequality of bargaining power and dependence on employment will persist and be known to the parties. The worker will interpret the terms of their contract as either benevolence on the part of the employer or sheer luck. By contrast, by being recognised publicly as employees, they become aware that they are entitled to these terms because of their vulnerable position. As weaker parties typically suffer from multiple vulnerabilities, the normative principles underlying the threatened downstream wrongs (such as fairness or autonomy) are too diffuse to serve this expressive function. Presenting the set of rights and duties that status relations trigger under a single heading (e.g. employee, refugee, patient, or student), as the law does, serves this important normative function. It calls our moral attention to an asymmetrical relation while leaving open what specific rights and duties are triggered within it. This is particularly important in light of the fact that the background social factors which create vulnerabilities are dynamic and their effects on the asymmetry of the relation require constant moral attention.

Consider again the Uber case. Drivers are not merely campaigning for a beneficial legal regulation, in the way a particular sector might campaign for a state subsidy. Their vulnerability within the gig economy is well established and systematic. The claim that they already possess the status of an employee is also an appeal to the moral responsibility on the part of others (Uber and the courts) to recognise their vulnerability and act as the guardian of their interests. A benevolent owner of a business may grant precarious workers a number of benefits (such as periodic holidays with pay) out of charity, not duty; a government may abolish employment protection, but strike a deal with the business sector to provide tax reliefs when they treat contractors *as if* they had employment status. In both these cases, the employment relation would suffer from the point of view of the value of equality, even if the position of contractors was materially no worse than that of (protected) employees. The public recognition of the role of the employer projects the following message to the employee: 'You may work for someone, but you are still their moral equal.'[13]

When Antonio, in *Bicycle Thieves*, admires himself in the mirror sporting a uniform, the income that he will secure is not the first thing on his mind. His pride is that he is an *employee*: a person with self-esteem, holding a role that society and the law recognise as distinct, bearing a set of rights and obligations. Legal recognition of role-status is therefore more than an instrument to prevent downstream wrongs. The value of equality triggers a number of non-instrumental requirements, the most important of which is the duty to recognise one's role—that is, to register publicly the asymmetry of enduring social relations and to project the equal dignity of the parties, shielding the weaker party's self-esteem.

This duty of social recognition is manifested in the way in which status is invoked as a normative justification. We could, in principle, say that people who provide labour have several rights grounded in a plurality of values, such as fairness or privacy. But this does not capture the fact that employees' rights aim at balancing an asymmetrical relation with employers. By saying that *qua* an employee, a person has a right not to be unfairly dismissed by the employer, we acknowledge this asymmetrical relation and we project the value of equality within it. We use status as an abstract normative basis for whatever rights are practically needed to balance this asymmetrical relation, from the point of view of social equality.

5.5 Rights for Stronger Party?

As role-status is grounded on the value of equality, it might appear paradoxical that it should generate rights on the stronger party. But the rationale is still to balance the relation at the moral level. By interfering with the moral responsibilities of the stronger party towards the weaker party, one wrongs both. The distinction between instrumental and non-instrumental rights applies here as well. Some duties of non-interference minimise the risk of wrongful harm inflicted by the stronger party against the weaker party. Universities, for instance, undermine the responsibility lecturers have towards students by imposing on them tasks of immigration enforcement. They exacerbate the risk that overseas students will be excluded or

[13] For an egalitarian account of the employment relation along similar lines, see Sabine Tsuruda, 'Working as Equal Moral Agents', 26(4) *Legal Theory* (2020), pp. 305–337.

discriminated. The stronger party to a status relation is not only a passive recipient of obligations, but also the bearer of rights against third parties. They may demand that others respect their normative role and refrain from unduly interfering with it or appropriating its functions.[14] This is precisely why status is an attribute not only of the weaker party, but typically of the stronger party as well.

What is more controversial is whether the rationale for the need to recognise statuses publicly extends to the exclusive use of titles when no actual function is appropriated. This seems problematic, particularly when it is claimed by the stronger party. In the third case I examined in Chapter 4, medical doctors claimed the right to exclude nurses from using their title. And this is against the background that nurses assist with, rather than undermine, the responsibilities of doctors towards patients. Social titles, moreover, are typically regarded as a *positional* social good. Their value lies in the fact that others lack it. It appears that the claim to have one's role recognised through the exclusive use of a title is one about social *rank* and cannot qualify as a moral entitlement.

Sometimes, however, it seems obvious that the stronger party has the moral right to be publicly recognised as the holder of the role to the exclusion of others. It would strike us as wrong if we collectively failed to recognise parenthood, say by using the same title ('carer') for all the different people who look after children. Similarly, there would be something inappropriate in the appropriation of the title 'parent' by a nursery worker or a babysitter. The idea here is that children must be able to distinguish the level of responsibility of their parents from that of nursery workers or babysitters. Exclusive titles are a way to signal to children the substantial degree of control that parents exercise over their lives and, in turn, the moral responsibilities that this control triggers. This is, again, for both instrumental and non-instrumental reasons. Ensuring that social titles track distinctive role-statuses is a way to give notice to the weaker party of the distinct vulnerabilities and dependencies they face in different social interactions. It enables them to demand the right level of respect in their various interactions. But it has expressive value as well. If carers and babysitters appropriate the title 'parent', it would diffuse the significance of the asymmetrical relation between parents and children and the imperative to balance it.

One might object that we should not generalise too quickly from the case of children and parents. In the case of parenthood, few people seek to acquire the role mainly to get the social esteem that comes from being called mum or dad. By contrast, doctors may seek the exclusive use of a title mainly in order to enjoy rank-status. Yet it seems to me that patients too must be able to know which standing interactions pose a threat to them when they fall ill. They must be able to understand that medical doctors have a set of responsibilities towards them

[14] Bentham included in his list of offences against status the wrong of 'usurping' someone's status, which is analogous to what I call status appropriation.

precisely because doctors are in a position to take advantage of their illness. The role of nurses is sufficiently close to that of doctors to exhibit the same range and types of threat to patients' vulnerability. The doctors' claim therefore appears to be exclusively about rank-status lacking any moral merits. But how about the case of a massage therapist with a doctorate who wants to be called a doctor? The concern here starts to be less about the rank-status of doctors and more about the role-status of patients. In principle, status can justify the type of claim medical doctors make without relying on the problematic notion of rank.[15] This is because the duty of public recognition of status relations entails a duty to allocate social titles in a way that matches, as far as possible, the asymmetrical interaction of the relevant role.

A clear case of the need to recognise the status of the stronger party is that of the judicial office. Judges must be protected from undue interferences with their responsibilities towards litigants, specially against the government. These responsibilities include duties of impartiality and treating litigants as equals. The common depiction of justice holding a sword and a scale, and the paraphernalia that judges typically wear are important ways in which we socially acknowledge the moral responsibilities that pertain to the role-status of the judge.[16] In Chapter 8, I will argue that the pre-nominal title 'Justice' is also a morally justified way to express social recognition of the judicial office. It tells the judge that litigants have significant social vulnerabilities, which ground moral duties towards them, as well as rights against interference towards third parties, such as government. This is why, for instance, it is a human rights violation for the government to remove a judge from office for party-political reasons. The notion of the dignity of the judge is meant to capture, not the judge's rank-status, but their role-status. Waldron is therefore wrong to analyse the dignity of a judge as a ranking notion and then seek to extend it to all humans.[17] The judge's dignity, just like human dignity, is ultimately based on Pufendorf's *dignatio* (inherent worth) not *dignitas* (rank-status). The judge ought to ensure that the asymmetrical relation they have with litigants is balanced, and the value of equality is projected—and protected—within that relation.[18] Waldron's assumption that the dignity of the judge is a ranking idea is another example of the failure to distinguish between role-status and rank-status.

[15] It is important to observe that title appropriations, when they do constitute a status wrong, wrong both status parties, and primarily the weaker one, whose vulnerable position triggers egalitarian demands. By contrast, claims of rank-status are made typically by the stronger party alone.

[16] I offer an egalitarian analysis of the scales of justice in George Letsas, 'Balancing as a Legal Method: What It Is and How (Not) to Do It', in C. Bezemek, M. Potacs, and A. Somek (eds), *The Vienna Lectures on Legal Philosophy*, Vol. 3 (Oxford: Hart, 2023).

[17] Jeremy Waldron, *Dignity, Rank and Rights* (Oxford: Oxford University Press, 2012), p. 29.

[18] Stephen Darwall also points out the incompatibility between moral egalitarianism, as found in Pufendorf and Kant, and ranking notions of dignity. See Stephen Darwall, 'The Social and the Sociable', 42(1) *Philosophical Topics* (2014), pp. 201–217.

5.6 Citizenship as a Status

The citizen/official relation can be concretised in different ways, depending on the specifics of the interaction. For example, a citizen can acquire the status of a litigant or a defendant, interacting with an official who is a judge. Or one can acquire the status of a prisoner, interacting with an official who is a police officer or a prison guard. Though the package of rights and duties that is attached to these statuses is different, reflecting the more precise vulnerabilities, the broader basis of these statuses is the same, namely the availability of the state's collective force against the weaker party.

The status-based vulnerability of the citizen vis-à-vis the government, caused by the availability of collective state force, helps to understand better Ronald Dworkin's non-positivist theory of law. Dworkin argued that the point of law is to justify the use of collective force by the government against citizens and that the content of legal rights and duties should be construed in the light of that point.[19] This appeared puzzling to many: why should we interpret legal materials creatively to improve them morally? But Dworkin combined the argument from coercion with two further claims: first, that political obligation is associative, connected to the role of being a citizen; and second, that the value of equality governs this association. These are all the hallmarks of the general model of role-status, as I have developed it here. First, Dworkin's use of the idea of associative obligations indicates the presence of a social relation; second, his emphasis on the value equality suggests that the relation is asymmetrical, posing a threat to equality; and third, his emphasis on coercion is meant to explain the nature of this asymmetry, namely the possibility of collective force used against persons.

Initially, Dworkin's reliance on associative obligation, as an analysis of the grounds of legal obligation, was widely misunderstood as a claim about the ethical significance of identifying with a nation, or a political community.[20] Admittedly, Dworkin was not clear about how we should understand the 'role' of being a citizen. It was Nicos Stavropoulos who developed, and defended, the view that state coercion is what changes the moral grounds of legal obligation.[21] Though Stavropoulos does not unpack coercion as a vulnerability, nor rely on the notion of status, he explains that, on Dworkin's model, it is the impact that legal officials have when they enforce rights and duties that makes a moral difference. The fact that citizens are vulnerable to the use of force by public officials,

[19] Ronald Dworkin, *Law's Empire* (Cambridge: Belknap Press, 1986), p. 93.

[20] Joseph Raz interprets the argument from associative obligations in this way in Joseph Raz, 'Revisiting the Service Conception of Authority', 90 *Minnesota Law Review* (2006), pp. 1003–1044. See Chapter 6 for a discussion of the connection between roles and identification.

[21] See Nicos Stavropoulos, 'The Relevance of Coercion: Some Preliminaries', 22(3) *Ratio Juris* (2009), pp. 339–358.

including at the request of other citizens, creates a social relation of asymmetry and, in turn, creates status-based rights and obligations on both citizens and public officials.

Crucially, it is not the fact that state authorities issue directives, and citizens may benefit from following them, or are prone to do so, that constitutes the asymmetry. The status of citizenship, and correspondingly of an official, is a way to recognise this asymmetry as a social threat to equality. It tells the citizen 'you may be subject to the force of state officials but you are nevertheless their equal'. And it tells the state official: 'you may be able to direct force against other citizens, but you are nevertheless their equal'. Being a state official does not make one a superior, a *ruler*. Nor does being an ordinary person make one inferior, a *subject*.

Leslie Green once objected that legal obligation cannot be associative because it is incompatible with a state's claim to political authority. That claim, for Green, is a claim about obedience, and—unlike associative obligations—one *obeys* a state (i.e. subjects their will to the will of the state).[22] Associates, by contrast, do not obey each other. In his reply, Dworkin rejected the obedience-based explanation and emphasised the egalitarian dimension of citizenship:

> My entire argument, however, aims to show that an obligation of obedience to collectively enacted laws is derivative from the more basic attitudes, which are not themselves attitudes of obedience, that hold among the citizens of a true community. The association I describe, to which obligations of different kinds attach, is an association of individuals in political community, not an association to which the state, which I insist is only a useful personification, is a party.[23]

I read Dworkin to be saying that being a state official does not place one *above* the citizen. The role of the official is to ensure that citizens treat each other equally when they exercise their legal rights and duties. Though the official, unlike the citizen, can use state coercion, its use ought to be constrained by the demands of moral equality. Seeing Dworkin's theory as an instance of a general model of role-status makes it a less peculiar theory of law than it was initially thought. Appeal to the role of the citizen is a shorthand for an asymmetrical social relation that poses a threat to equality. The value of the Rule of Law is a relation-specific instantiation of the value of social equality. In Chapter 7, I will provide a more detailed defence of the non-positivist claim that certain social roles are not created by institutions, through authoritative rules or collective beliefs.

[22] Leslie Green, 'Associative Obligations and the State', in Justin Burley (ed.), *Dworkin and His Critics* (London: Blackwell, 2004), ch. 14.

[23] Ronald Dworkin, 'Replies', in Justin Burley (ed.), *Dworkin and His Critics* (London: Blackwell, 2004).

5.7 Parties May Not Determine Freely the Terms of Their Relation

There is one thing that Maine got right. Status entails a restriction on one's contractual freedom. But, as I will explain in more detail in the next chapter, he misunderstood the nature of that restriction. The restriction does not relate to whether the law imposes on a person a legal relation against their will. It is not about restrictions with respect to legal entry. Rather, the restriction relates to whether parties within an asymmetrical relation are free to determine the terms of their relation, whether or not they have entered freely into that relation. Citizens cannot waive their right not to be tortured. Children cannot waive their right to primary education. Similarly, landlords cannot contract out of their duty to provide and maintain a safe and habitable property for tenants. Tenants cannot contract out of their right not to be evicted arbitrarily. Mortgagees cannot contract out of their right not to be subject to extortionate interest rates or penalties.

It is a mark of a status-based relation, whether consensual or not, that parties are not free to determine at will the terms and conditions of their relations. The main reason for this should be clear by now: the stronger party must not exploit their position to take advantage of the weaker party's vulnerabilities and dependencies. There are things that the weaker party cannot be held to, even if they agree. I may sign a contract that says that my employer may monitor my private life, or that my landlord may walk into my home any time they want, or evict me with 24-hour's notice. These undertakings have no moral value, and they should have no legal value either. Moreover, any terms that govern status relations must be interpreted in the light of the need to balance their inherent asymmetry. Just as legislation must be interpreted with a view to balancing the relation between citizens and government, likewise employment contracts must be interpreted with a view to balancing the relation between employers and employees. Ditto for tenancy agreements, patient care contracts, and student contracts. It is the role of courts to invalidate, or interpret away, terms that violate status.

At the same time, I should stress that not all contractual relations are asymmetrical. For a great number of contracts, parties enter into them from a symmetrical position. If you are into investment, you would be familiar with the terms 'a buyer's market' and 'a seller's market'. Sometimes there is an oversupply of products, favouring those who seek to buy. And sometimes demand outstrips supply, favouring those who seek to sell. There is nothing about being a buyer or a seller in that market that marks it out as an asymmetrical relation. Investors and traders move back and forth between buying and selling. Those who don't do this for a living are indifferent to whether it is a seller's market or a buyer's market. For these contracts, the principle of freedom of contract calls most of the shots: they are generally to be interpreted according to the will of the parties and the specific aims that they sought to pursue.

Consider, by contrast, housing. All of us need a roof above our head. This need is not contingent on particular societies, or cultures.[24] How housing is produced and distributed is a matter of collective arrangement, governed by property rules. A small minority of people own their home outright, with no need to pay for a mortgage or rent. But for most people, having a roof above their head depends on their ability to pay their rent or mortgage. This makes the position of tenants and mortgagees vulnerable. A spike in rent or interest rates is likely to make them homeless. Tenancy agreements and mortgage contracts must be interpreted to protect the position of the weaker party.

5.8 How Many Role-Statuses Are There?

It is an interpretive question which social relations that implicate fundamental interests are sufficiently stable and enduring, and display a sufficient degree of asymmetry, to trigger the status requirements of equality. I am here concerned with the general phenomenon, not its various instantiations. The law can only serve as a rough guide since there are bound to be mismatches between the moral and the legal dimension of status. The three modalities by which one may offend one's role-status (failure to recognise, interference, and appropriation) are sufficient to establish that status offences constitute a distinct phenomenon. We may call them primary status offences, as they are not fully reducible to the moral principles that justify the downstream rights and duties of the parties. But status offences also encompass the downstream wrongs that the weaker party risks suffering (which we may call secondary), because the duty to take collective action to prevent them is also grounded on the value of equality.

It is beyond the scope of this book to provide a comprehensive list of role-statuses. My aim is to present a general model of status, which can be adapted to specific cases. The following relations can be offered as useful paradigms:

- Citizen/Official
- Child/Parent
- Employee/Employer
- Patient/Doctor
- Student/Teacher
- Tenant/Landlord

[24] That is not to say that survival is not possible without housing. There are isolated tribes that live in nature and have no permanent dwellings. We might say that shelter is essential for survival, as protection against the elements of weather, whereas housing is essential for pursuing other important interests of well-being.

- Mortgagee/Lender
- Consumer/Manufacturer
- Litigant/Lawyer
- Insolvent/Creditor

This list is not meant to be exhaustive. Within these broad relations, there are many variations to one's status. A person can occupy the status of a carer or a guardian, rather than a parent. A person can be a refugee or an undocumented migrant, rather than a citizen. Within employment status too, there can be many variations, depending on the precise nature of the vulnerabilities and dependencies. Domestic or sex workers, for instance, may require a different package of reciprocal rights and duties. Note also that status relations cut across the formal divide between private and public law. Family law, long considered a special non-contractual case, is a clear case of status. And public/administrative law, in so far as it governs the asymmetrical relation between citizens and public officials, is also one of status.

Status, as a moral concept, tackles social threats to our standing as moral equals that pertain to non-contingent and standing relations. This is why citizenship, family, housing, employment, education, and health are central cases. But the specific threats posed within those relations can evolve and vary from time to time and place to place. We should be open to the possibility that new statuses have to be recognised and old ones to be reintroduced or reconfigured. I may have neglected some obvious cases or included borderline ones. As mentioned already, which social relations are status-based is an interpretive question. The account is meant to be broad and help persons in any asymmetrical relation, as well as lawyers and activists, to fight for moral equality. With this goal in mind, here is a general formulation of role-status:

> **Role-status:** An enduring asymmetrical social relation, whether consensual or not, that implicates objective interests of well-being and in which one of the parties suffers from significant vulnerabilities or dependencies. Status morality imposes: (a) the moral duty, legally enforceable, to balance the relation by vesting the parties with prophylactic rights and duties, whose aim is to protect the weaker party (b) the moral duty to shield the weaker party's self-esteem and to project the value of equality by recognising socially (and legally) the two parties *qua* status-holders.

6
FOUR OBJECTIONS

6.1 Introduction

In this chapter, I collect and address objections that can be raised against the account of status I put forward in the previous chapter. I have identified four. The first objection, which I will call the *fiduciary view*, acknowledges that status is about asymmetrical relations but takes a different view about the nature of this asymmetry: it holds that the asymmetry is necessarily of a fiduciary nature, whereby a person acts as a trustee, being under a duty to further the ends of another and restrict their own. The other two objections, by contrast, reject the thesis that status is about asymmetrical relations. What I will call the *deflationary view* holds that status is purely a taxonomical notion, a morally neutral way to describe a set of institutional rights and duties that the law has grouped together for convenience. The third objection, which draws on Henry Maine's well-known account, and which I will call the *non-volitional view*, holds that what is central to status is not asymmetry but absence of volition. In what follows, I aim to show that these competing accounts are either over-inclusive or under-inclusive. The fourth objection, which draws on Niko Kolodny's recent book, is that my account of status is too narrow because it captures only a small part of a bigger social problem: how to eradicate relations of inferiority.

6.2 The Fiduciary View

To my knowledge, Arthur Ripstein has provided the only account in the literature that recognises status as a distinct category of moral offences since Bentham. Ripstein argues that status covers cases where people pursue their ends interdependently but, unlike contract, non-consensually. An interaction is non-consensual either because a person is unable to give consent (say children) or because their consent—though competently given—is problematic due to the nature of the relation (say, students consenting to run errands for their teacher).[1] On Ripstein's account, certain relations based on contract are nevertheless status relations. Following Kant,[2] he draws the following distinction between status-based

[1] Arthur Ripstein, *Force and Freedom* (Cambridge: Harvard University Press, 2009), pp. 73–74.
[2] It is not an accident that Kant, like Bentham, was very familiar with Roman law, within which the notion of status was central.

Status in Law and Morality. George Letsas, Oxford University Press. © George Letsas 2026.
DOI: 10.1093/9780198936725.003.0006

and non-status-based contracts: in a purely contractual case, I give you a right over the use of my services so that you can pursue your own ends (and you do the same). In a status contract, by contrast, I am required to pursue your ends and, within the confines of our relation, set my own ends aside.

An example might help to illustrate Ripstein's view. Suppose you agree to paint my house for a fee. I now have a right to use your services to make my property prettier and you have a right to use my money to make yourself wealthier. Each is pursuing one's own ends and neither is burdened with the task of furthering the other's ends. The pursuit of ends is interdependent, but not shared. It is not my end to make you wealthier, but a side effect of wanting to have my house painted. In status relations, by contrast, I have no right to use your services in pursuit of my ends but must instead act to safeguard your ends. I may not request my students to paint my house because, as a teacher, I must treat them in a way that advances *their* ends, not mine. This is so even though the teacher/student relation begins contractually and even if the students were to agree to my request. As a teacher, my students' education is an end I share, not a side effect of my seeking to earn an income, and my power to direct their action cannot be used for non-educational purposes.

Ripstein's account is substantially wider than Kant's, who only recognised three status relations: parent/children, spouses, and master/servant. It tracks all relations in which one of the parties have, for whatever reason, fiduciary obligations to further the ends of others, while at the same time restricting the pursuit of their own ends. The basis for the fiduciary obligation may be as simple as the fact that someone agreed to be a trustee. Or it may be because one is a parent or a teacher. This is the sense in which, for Ripstein, all status relations are asymmetrical: one is in a situation where one cannot act solely in pursuit of one's own ends. The baseline of comparison is the purely contractual case where one is free to pursue one's own ends without constraints from the ends of others. Ripstein's account, like Kant's, is juridical in nature, seeking to identify normative relations that have a fiduciary element.[3]

I think Ripstein is right in locating the concept of status in the asymmetrical nature of certain relations. But I disagree with his conception of asymmetry. It picks out any relation where, in juridical terms, one serves as a fiduciary for another. It covers, for instance, bailment and trusts. But this seems to me over-inclusive. A wealthy individual may set up a trust for their family or leave their expensive car with a free valet service (bailment). On Ripstein's account, the relationship

[3] On fiduciary obligations as status obligations in general see Paul B. Miller, 'The Idea of Status in Fiduciary Law', in Paul B. Miller and Andrew S. Gold, *Contract, Status and Fiduciary Law* (Oxford: Oxford University Press, 2016); Paul B. Miller, 'The Morality of Fiduciary Law' 62 *William & Mary Law Review* (2021), pp. 1349–1395; James Edelman, 'The Role of Status in the Law of Obligations: Common Callings, Implied Terms and Lessons for Fiduciary Duties', in Andrew S. Gold and Paul B. Miller (eds), *Philosophical Foundations of Fiduciary Law* (Oxford: Oxford University Press, 2014).

between trustees and beneficiaries or between bailees and bailors is necessarily one of status, simply because trustees and bailees must hold and manage assets for the benefit of others, setting the pursuit of their own ends aside. Beneficiaries are vulnerable on this view because they are not able to consent to how trustees will manage the assets held for their benefit. Their vulnerability does not precede the trust, but rather is the result of it. Absent the interaction, there need be nothing vulnerable about beneficiaries or bailors. They may be socially and economically powerful and, on average, more so than trustees and bailees.

My account of vulnerability is different, however. The first difference concerns cases that, on both accounts, are status relations. Consider the case of employees. On my account, they are vulnerable vis-à-vis the employer due to several background social, economic, and ethical factors. These increase the likelihood that employees will fall victim to various injustices, such as exploitation, abuse, or unfair dismissal. The status of an employee is a way to mitigate these vulnerabilities and to restore a relation of moral equality between the parties. It does so by imposing mandatory terms (such as safe and decent working conditions) and by limiting the scope of what parties can validly agree upon contractually, such as waivers of the employee's right to privacy at work. Status makes the employer the guardian of the employee's interests, by vesting the relation with a set of reciprocal moral rights and duties.

Ripstein's explanation of why the employment relation is one of status, by contrast, is quite different. On his view, the vulnerability pertains to the employer, not the employee. The employer is vulnerable because it is part of the nature of the relation that employees are required to advance not their own ends, but the employer's. In doing so, they act in ways to which the employer is not able to consent. They might make representations to third parties that bind the employer or cause damage for which the employer will be vicariously liable. On Ripstein's conception of asymmetry, it is the employee, not the employer, who is the fiduciary of the other party's ends. The order of normative explanation is reversed.

The second difference between Ripstein's account and mine is that I do not consider a bailment or a trust to be a status relation. The fiduciary element in those relations is purely the result of a contract between parties that are situated symmetrically.[4] Unlike employees, bailors and beneficiaries do not suffer from any background vulnerabilities. To put this point differently: the concepts of an employee or a patient have an inherent social dimension, picking out systemic vulnerabilities or dependencies that a group of people face as a matter of social fact. By contrast,

[4] For the similarities between contractual and fiduciary obligations see Gregory Klass, 'What If Fiduciary Obligations Are Like Contractual Ones?', in Paul B. Miller and Andrew S. Gold, *Contract, Status and Fiduciary Law* (Oxford: Oxford University Press, 2016). For the differences, see Daniel Markovits, 'Sharing Ex Ante and Sharing Ex Post: The Non-Contractual Basis of Fiduciary Obligations', in Andrew S. Gold and Paul B. Miller (eds), *Philosophical Foundations of Fiduciary Law* (Oxford: Oxford University Press, 2014).

the concept of a bailor is not tied to social facts in this way. It is simply a taxonomical concept that we use to refer to a particular kind of contract. On my account, it is only those background social facts that explain why a party is weaker and why the stronger party acquires status-based obligations.

Someone attracted to Ripstein's account might object in one of two ways.[5] First, one might point to powerful employees who suffer from none of the dependencies or vulnerabilities I mentioned earlier. Celebrity TV hosts, for example, have bigger pockets than most TV stations can fill and are swamped with job offers. But, the objection goes, they still count as employees and are entitled to employment status. Second, it might be objected that the extent to which employers can impose unfair terms is contingent on and not constitutive of what employment is. In an ideal world, employees would not be vulnerable to accepting unfair terms.

With respect to the first objection, we must draw a distinction between the legal and the moral status of an employee. The former may be a poor approximation of the latter, as the Uber drivers example shows. The law typically allocates rights and duties based on the attributes that most people have in a certain position, rather than everybody. It caters for the average employee, not Oprah Winfrey. The fact that powerful employees might avail themselves of employment protection does not necessarily entail that, absent the law, they are entitled to that protection. It does not entail that they have the status of an employee in a moral sense. Insofar as a pure case of a non-vulnerable worker is conceivable, then the mere fact that they are under the direction of their employer seems to me insufficient to entitle them to employment status, understood as an additional set of rights and duties. Put differently, it would not be arbitrary for the law to exclude powerful celebrities from employment status, subject to conditions.

The second objection seeks to challenge that employees' social and economic vulnerabilities are constitutive of the employment relation. It is true that in a society of angels, people would not seek to exploit the vulnerabilities and dependencies of others yet would still need to employ others. But we should be careful about this hypothetical. If, and when, the background conditions that make employees vulnerable disappear, it would not follow that there would be no contracted labour. What would follow is that most, or all, employment contracts would in essence become contracts for services. Workers would no longer require the protective rights that employment status assigns since they would not be at risk of injustice. In Kantian terms, labour would move from a status relation to a purely contractual relation. I am sceptical, however, that any realistic scheme of labour economy can eliminate the vulnerabilities of workers. This is mainly because some of them are caused by factors that cannot be affected through legal and economic

[5] I am extremely grateful to Arthur Ripstein for discussion on these points. The formulation of these objections is mine, not his.

interventions. In the case of several role-statuses, such as patients, the relevant vulnerabilities track innate human dispositions.

Could Ripstein's account be modified to accommodate the sociological basis of the various vulnerabilities and dependencies? One might argue, for instance, that both the employer and the employee are vulnerable, but for different reasons. The employer is vulnerable because they cannot consent to how employees will further the ends of the business affairs, whereas the employee is vulnerable because they have limited bargaining power. The first vulnerability is the result of the employment contract, whereas the second precedes it. I set aside the question of whether this hybrid view can be attributed to Ripstein. He says very little about vulnerabilities that precede the relation, and whether they can take the plurality of forms that I discussed earlier (economic, political, cultural, biological, etc). Moreover, tying vulnerability to background sociological factors makes status hostage to empirical factors in a way that seems foreign to a Kantian moral framework.[6]

The main problem I find with this hybrid view is that it runs together two very different moral phenomena. The vulnerability of bailors and trust beneficiaries is juridical, the result of a contractual agreement; the vulnerability of patients, employees, students and refugees is of a sociopolitical or biological nature. This difference has a normative upshot. The latter vulnerabilities are more significant politically. It is not merely a matter of having the right set of legal rights and duties in place. We collectively can have an impact on social vulnerabilities. We can exacerbate or mitigate them. Our tax scheme or scheme of welfare conditionality may make employees even more vulnerable to exploitation. The government's immigration rules may make students on a visa even more vulnerable to exclusion. A privatised healthcare system may make patients even more vulnerable to abuse. We collectively must monitor constantly how these background factors change and affect the asymmetry of the relation. This explains why status relations are high up on the agenda of social justice. Labour exploitation, child and patient abuse, student harassment, exclusion of persons with disabilities, and the refugee crisis are all central issues in public affairs and political theory. By contrast, there is no political concern about the rights of bailors or trust beneficiaries.

I do not mean to deny that both juridical and social asymmetries may be presented as falling under a general concern about equality within relations. In that sense, the hybrid view of status wrongs is perfectly coherent, whether or not it can be attributed to Ripstein. But we already have the concept of fiduciary obligations to account for relations with juridical asymmetries. It seems to me that the

[6] Kant included spousal relations in his short list of statuses, which include the right to consent to sex. Elsewhere, however, he took the view that sexual relations are governed by animalistic instincts that cannot be squared with the purposive nature of human freedom. As Ripstein himself observes in a footnote, this gesture towards the background biological vulnerabilities of spousal relations poses a problem for Kant's view. See, Ripstein, *Force and Freedom*, p. 74, fn. 22.

emphasis on the sociopolitical dimension of background vulnerabilities not only singles out a distinct moral phenomenon, but also fits better the history of the concept of status as a moral idea. As discussed earlier, political theorists took status to be central in describing the transition from the ancient world to the modern world. The more restrictive account I put forward can better explain why status has this political significance.

6.3 Austin's Deflationary View

The deflationary view holds that status is identical with a set of rights and duties. For any fixed set of rights, duties, powers and the like, to have the relevant status *just is* to possess this set. Consider the following set: the duty to manage a university and direct its mission, the privilege to preside over university events and ceremonies, the power to sign off degrees, and so on. Having these normative attributes is what it means to be a provost. Status, on this view, serves as a shorthand for a given set of rights and duties.

The view is deflationary because it entails that any set of rights and duties grouped together can be a status. A human being, a citizen, a promisor, a tortfeasor, a dean, a manager—all can serve as shorthand for a set of rights and duties. It follows that each area of morality can be presented as status-based and, therefore, status is not a distinct sub-domain of morality. The category explodes to encompassing everything. John Austin, who held the deflationary view, was led to a similar conclusion about status in law:

> After the best consideration which I have been able to give to the subject, and after extensive examination of the opinions of others, I still find no mark by which a status or condition can be distinguished from any other collection of rights and duties.[7]

I have no quarrel with this use of status as shorthand for a given set of rights and duties. It is common, particularly within institutional contexts. 'What is your status within the organisation?', we often ask. But we should attend here to a distinction between a given set of rights and duties and the normative ground of that set. Knowing that the status of a provost consists in a set of rights and duties does not tell us anything about what, if anything, justifies having this set. The normative grounds could be very many: one may have signed a contract; or someone needs to be in charge to coordinate management and one just happens to occupy that position; or one simply has a certain ability (leadership skills). Alternatively,

[7] John Austin, *Lectures in Jurisprudence: Or The Philosophy of Positive Law* (New York: Henry Holt, 1875), p. 348.

it might be that nothing justifies the relevant set. The deflationary view tracks sets, not grounds.

My account of status, by contrast, tracks a particular normative ground for a set of rights and duties, namely relational equality within asymmetrical social interactions. The same is true of Kant's and Bentham's account. Bentham listed offences against status alongside the familiar categories, still accepted today, of offences against *the person*, against *property*, and against *reputation*. In line with the understanding of the term in Roman law, he defined status as the 'legal relation one bears to the persons who are about him' and divided it in two circles: domestic and civil. He went on to distinguish between the 'investitive' event that bestows status on a person and the rights and duties that the law attaches to it. Bentham's distinction is important because it suggests that status is not the artificial creation of the law or a way to classify obligations. Status, Bentham claimed, is 'an ideal base', 'about which are ranged rights and duties and sometimes incapacities'.[8]

It is common, for instance, to invoke one's role-status elliptically by way of exerting moral pressure. When someone tells me that I must not date a student of mine because I am their teacher, they do more than remind me of the set of obligations attached to lecturers by university management. They provide me with a reason why I must not. By contrast, the deflationary use of status is descriptive, making no assumptions about what, if anything, justifies the relevant set. Talking about the status of slave catchers in colonial America is simply a way to report an institutional fact.

Those who use status in a taxonomical sense are not therefore conceptually confused. They use the taxonomical notion of status, rather than the justificatory one. On the other hand, I do not think that these two uses of status, justificatory and taxonomical, are mere homonyms. The explanation I want to offer here is similar to the analysis of rank-status. The taxonomical concept supervenes on the more basic notion of role-status. The law started to use status with a view to capturing the asymmetrical social interaction that triggered a unique set of rights and duties. But the law does not usually make explicit the normative grounds for packaging a set of rights and duties together. As a result, the term was corrupted over time to refer to an institutionally recognised set of rights and duties, regardless of its ground. This ambiguity explains why John Austin was so utterly perplexed by status. On the one hand, he thought that it was the most difficult problem in the science of jurisprudence. On the other hand, he argued that it is simply a taxonomical concept that the law uses for the sake of convenience. He could not explain, however, why it is

[8] The suggestion that status is a non-legal quality inherent in a person infuriated John Austin, who thought that Bentham had betrayed two of the basic tenets of utilitarian philosophy: empiricism and legal positivism. Austin thought that talk of 'investitive' qualities was occult and mysterious, the kind of rubbish metaphysics that Bentham was seeking to debunk. For discussion, see Waldron, 'Does Equal Moral Status Add Anything to Right Reason?', https://papers.ssrn.com/sol3/papers.cfm?abstract_id=1898689.

convenient for the law to present the rights and duties of parents and children as a status, but not those of promisors and promisees or buyers and sellers. The taxonomical use of status has survived to some extent, but it is peripheral and not in competition with the justificatory understanding of status, which is my focus here.

6.4 Maine's Non-volitional View

Later attempts to capture the nature of status as a moral idea focused on a particular normative ground for holding a set of rights and duties, or, more accurately, its absence. In the mid-nineteenth century, Henry Maine defined status as that legal position which, unlike contract, holds irrespective of one's volition.[9]

Maine argued that the replacement of status relations with contractual ones marked a progressive transition from ancient law to modern law. The ancients typically restricted freedom to create legal obligations voluntarily, through contractual agreements. Consider Roman law. Romans burdened the head of a household (*pater familias*) with a wide set of obligations and responsibilities for all members of the extended family and the family estate. Dependent family members, in turn, lacked legal capacities to exercise rights in their own name and their legal relations were derivative from the power of the head of the household (*patria potestas*). Labour was mainly done by slaves, who could not legally contract to sell their labour in exchange for wages or choose not to work. Women were in a state of perpetual tutelage, being under the legal authority of the nearest male relative. Maine sought to document a substantive legal transition: modern law gradually stopped imposing these types of legal incapacity on categories of people based on accidents of birth. It does not take gender or kinship as the basis for restricting legal capacities or expanding legal responsibilities and recognises wide contractual and proprietary freedoms for everyone. Labour nowadays may only be contracted, never forced.

Maine's category of status is primarily descriptive, a way to capture a subset of legal norms that were later abolished as unjust. The mere absence of volition, however, fails both as a distinguishing feature of historic legal statuses and as an explanation of why they were unjust. Many legal duties apply irrespective of one's volition yet do not constitute a legal status in Maine's terms. Tort duties not to injure others or to compensate them when one does hold irrespective of one's volition and are morally justified. Moreover, many legal statuses that have survived to this day are morally unproblematic, such as infancy or bankruptcy. It is not the case that mere absence of volition is *sufficient* to make a legal status unjust. It was morally arbitrary to deprive a category of persons of contractual and proprietary freedoms because of their gender (tutelage) or kinship (slavery). But it is not

[9] Henry Sumner Maine, *Ancient Law* (Oxford: Oxford University Press, 1861).

morally arbitrary to do the same when one is born with severe mental incapacities or while one is a minor.

It might be suggested, alternatively, that non-voluntariness is a *necessary* condition for a legal status to count as unjust.[10] But this criterion is both over- and under-inclusive. First, it fails to capture all historic forms of slavery, which was not always a permanent state. It was possible for a free person to fall into slavery (e.g. following a lost war) or for slaves to achieve freedom (manumission). Second, the criterion includes permanent exemptions to contractual and proprietary freedom which are arguably morally permissible. Citizenship burdens one with lifelong legal duties and responsibilities irrespective of one's will. Non-nationals, for example, may be precluded from buying land in specific parts of the country. Individuals do not normally have a legal right to migrate to foreign states. Even if we should now think of statehood as morally problematic, the status of citizenship does not appear to be on a par with slavery or tutelage. Several citizenship-based restrictions which start at birth and last for life seem perfectly justifiable. Perhaps it can be suggested that, as a matter of *morality*, no one's moral profile should be fixed permanently, irrespective of their volition. But this too is over-inclusive; some moral statuses, such as one's filial duties, are arguably fixed at birth for life.[11]

Maine's view suffers from a further weakness which is worth highlighting. It picks out a set of legal norms (e.g. slavery, tutelage, villeinage) which constitute an injustice based, in part, on their non-volitional character. This renders the concept of status a necessarily pejorative term. It is an attribute attached to a class of persons in a discriminatory and unjustifiable way. But this fails to account for cases where status is used in laudatory, rather than pejorative, terms. Recall that by demanding the recognition of the status of an employee, Uber drivers treat the concept of status as a positive moral attribute. The relevant moral offence is disrespecting their status, rather than forcing one on them irrespective of their will. Few people think that the idea of employment status is morally objectionable or that the very idea of morally justified statuses is an oxymoron.

Early readers of Maine were conceptual imperialists, seeking to preserve the term 'status' for the relevant injustices of ancient law. They viewed it as the antithesis of modern-day contracts, the two being mutually exclusive. The great labour law scholar, Otto Kahn-Freund, objected vehemently to the use of the term 'status of employment' on the basis that it flouts Maine's definition.[12] The worry

[10] Waldron argues that historic legal statuses were inherently unjust insofar as they were *sortal*, fixing 'a person's permanent situation and destiny as far as the law is concerned', one that was not acquired, or lost depending on actions, or circumstances. See Jeremy Waldron, *Dignity, Rank and Rights* (Oxford: Oxford University Press, 2012), p. 59.

[11] See the argument in Niko Kolodny, 'Which Relations Justify Partiality? The Case of Parents and Children', 38(1) *Philosophy and Public Affairs* (2010), pp. 37–75.

[12] See Otto Kahn-Freund, 'A Note on Status and Contract in British Labour Law', 30 *Modern Law Review* (1967), pp. 635–644. For a more recent criticism along the same lines, see Katharina Isabel Schmidt, 'Henry Maine's "Modern Law": From Status to Contract and Back Again?', 65(1) *American Journal of Comparative Law* (2017), pp. 145–186.

was that if both slavery and employment are statuses, then the significance of the transition between ancient law and modern law would be lost. But, as shown by the claim of Uber drivers, this conceptual imperialism failed. We do not need to be conceptual imperialists about status to be able to understand that the abolition of slavery and its replacement with employment contracts constituted major social progress.[13] Even though the battleground of social justice shifted from the inequalities of feudalism to the inequalities of unrestricted free markets, the notion of status survived. Our modern struggle against social inequality found something in the concept of status worth preserving and reorientated it to the new threats posed to moral equality by unrestricted free markets. Any adequate philosophical theory of status must account not only for the ancient use of the term, but also for its modern one.

6.5 Kolodny's Argument from Inferiority

Around the same time as I published an early formulation of the main argument of this book,[14] Niko Kolodny published a very important book on social hierarchy.[15] His account is original and ambitious, seeking to unpack the very idea of moral equality as the absence of relations of inferiority to others. There is much that is common ground between his account and mine, and I have drawn much inspiration from his focus on social hierarchy as a central problem in political philosophy. As is common in philosophy, people tackle an idea at the same time, from different angles. Here, I aim to focus on the differences between us.[16]

The starting difference is that, unlike Kolodny, my focus is narrower: I aim to show that the concept of status is a central idea in moral philosophy. More specifically, I focus on role-statuses as enduring and non-contingent social relations that ought to be regulated by law. Kolodny, by contrast, makes the stronger claim that

[13] It is further evidence of the limits of the non-volitional view that generations of legal scholars modified Maine's account to make it applicable within contractual relations. The influential school of the relational theory of contract relied on the notion of status to capture regulatory restrictions on freedom of contract, which coincided with the rise of the welfare state and the retreat from the libertarianism of unrestricted free markets. The thought was that even in domains where people rightfully exercise contractual freedoms, there are objective limits to what they can agree. Status here is not deployed to capture *absence* of volition but *presence* of volition, whose significance must nevertheless be seen in the light the asymmetrical nature of the relation. On the relational theory of contract law, see Ian R. Macneil, 'Values in Contract: Internal and External', 78 *Northwestern University Law Review* (1983–84), pp. 340–418; Manfred Rehbinder, 'Status, Contract and the Welfare State', 23 *Stanford Law Review* (1971), pp. 941–955.

[14] George Letsas, 'Offences Against Status', 43(2) *Oxford Journal of Legal Studies* (2023), pp. 322–349.

[15] Niko Kolodny, *The Pecking Order: Social Hierarchy as a Philosophical Problem* (Cambridge: Harvard University Press, 2023).

[16] This section draws on a comment I wrote on *The Pecking Order* for a book symposium forthcoming in the journal *Jurisprudence* (2026), with replies by Kolodny. I have not had the benefit of Kolodny's response to my comment, when I wrote this section.

all claims of equality are claims against inferiority. I am not wedded to this claim, and it is not part of the argument made in Chapter 4. Moreover, there are several serious wrongs, such as race and gender discrimination, that permeate social practices, cutting across role-statuses and impacting not only certain enduring social relations but episodic interactions too. Combating discrimination is clearly an egalitarian concern but it is not one that the idea of status seeks to capture.

To motivate his account, Kolodny begins by arguing that we cannot account for what is wrong about relations of inferiority in terms of either cost to one's interests or a violation of one's rights. He then moves on to argue, positively, that relations of inferiority are a distinct kind of political wrong of which bondage, or caste systems, stand as paradigm cases. The relevant wrong is unified by the presence of the following three necessary conditions.

First, relations of inferiority involve some *genuine interactions or relations*. It must be the case that a person enters another's sphere of liberty in some causal sense, say by affecting their interests or by taking part in a joint project, such as membership in a political community. Kolodny helpfully unpacks this condition negatively, by giving examples of where there is no interaction: for instance, when two people have lived centuries apart, or when one enjoys goods in the privacy of their home that another person does not.

Second, relations of inferiority involve *a genuine ranking*, where one is above and the other is below. The reader here does not get much by way of elaborating on this spatial metaphor. I will return later to what ranking might possibly mean and whether ranking is an apt description of various asymmetrical relations.

And third, relations of inferiority hold between *natural persons*, rather than between natural persons and artificial entities, or between natural persons and natural objects or events.

When analysing further what interactions count as relations of inferiority, Kolodny offers us a pluralist picture, where various types of asymmetries obtain. There are roughly three cases. First, cases where there is asymmetry of power to impact each other's interests. If I can impact your interests more severely that you can impact mine, and I can do so more easily than you, then you are inferior to me. Second, cases where there is an asymmetry of the *de facto* authority to command actions from others. If I can order you to do things and you are likely to obey me (but not the other way around), then you are inferior to me. And third, cases where there are unmerited disparities of regard.

Of course, not all relations of inferiority, captured by the above three cases, are morally objectionable. Kolodny adds a proviso: there are cases where inferiority is 'tempered'—that is, where there are good reasons to have relations of inferiority. This is either because the tempering factors override *pro tanto* objections to inferiority, or because they extinguish them altogether. Examples here include professors telling students what assignments to write, and flight attendants telling passengers what to do on the plane.

The dialectic of Kolodny's argument is what we might call an *inferiority-first* approach. First, we identify descriptively a relation where there is, as a matter of social fact, an asymmetry of sorts that constitutes a relation of inferiority. Second, the existence of such a relation triggers normatively a *pro tanto* valid complaint by the inferior party and a demand for a justification. And third, we ask—again normatively—whether the relevant relation involves tempering factors that might all things considered make it justified.

Consider the example of the teacher/student relation. We note, first, that there is a social practice whereby teachers get to tell students what materials to study and what assignments to write but students do not get to do the same to teachers. This marks it out as a relation of inferiority, such that the student is justified to complain: why am I inferior here? We then ask about tempering factors: teachers' power over students is limited by subject matter (concerning only knowledge and educational matters), time and place, and other factors. We also look at empirical constraints, such as checks on the teachers' power over students (say by school authorities, or legislation), which prevent them abusing their power. We might then conclude that the relation of inferiority between teachers and students is all things considered justified. By contrast, no such tempering factors obtain in the case of the master/slave relation.

I agree with Kolodny that we should be pluralists about social hierarchy. One subtle difference between his account and mine is that I do not start from the premise that status relations are hierarchical and then ask whether its hierarchies can be mitigated. Instead, I claim that role-status presents a special case of social hierarchy because of its unique characteristics. First, these relations involve vulnerabilities and dependencies that are *non-contingent*. They are part of the human condition: everyone is a child before becoming an adult; everyone relies on others for gaining knowledge about the world; and everyone will fall ill during their life and require care and treatment by others. These are not vulnerabilities and dependencies that we can, or even should want to, eliminate through political action.[17]

Second, as we shall see in Chapter 7, these dependencies and vulnerabilities are not necessarily created by social practices or institutions. Children depend on others for food and shelter. Students depend on others to acquire knowledge. Patients depend on others to get treatment. These dependencies exist even in the state of nature, where institutions have not (yet) regulated parenthood, education, or the medical profession. When institutions emerge, they do not create these dependencies or vulnerabilities but merely seek to regulate them. This point is crucial

[17] We may want to eliminate diseases, but that is not the same as eliminating the role of the doctor. The biological fragility of the human body will always require some form of medical treatment, even if cures are available for every disease. Likewise, we may want to eliminate the need to work in order to gain a living wage, but this will not eliminate the many reasons we have to work *for* and *with* others.

because it shows that the hierarchical relation between the doctor and the patient is not in essence the product of an institutional authority *given* to the doctor by the state. It is not an asymmetry of institutional power. If I injure myself in the state of nature, and a passer-by is an expert at healing wounds, then we will occupy the 'proto-roles' of doctor and patient respectively, unmediated by any authority.

Role-statuses are not therefore necessarily part of a system of social stratification. They are unlike say the army, or a caste system, where every individual in the relevant group is ranked on a scale from the top (the General or the Brahmins), to the bottom (the Lieutenant or the Dalits). To be sure, political structures can exacerbate the vulnerabilities and dependencies within role-status relations. The law may fail to regulate doctors or give them power to interfere with patients' bodily integrity without their informed consent, as was the case for centuries. Kolodny brings to the fore the various ways in which political institutions create and reproduce hierarchies. But not all social hierarchies are created politically. Some track base-level interactions that precede political association.

A difference between my account and Kolodny's is that I do not take asymmetries in status relations to be explained in terms of authority. Doctors' superior position does not consist merely in the social fact that patients are likely to follow their instructions or that doctors can impact the interests of patients but not the other way around. The asymmetry within the doctor/patient relation is not a matter of authority, be it *de facto*[18] or formal, but of the vulnerabilities present in being a patient. It is part of the nature of the relation.

Third, role-statuses pick out hierarchies that are not to do with disparities of societal esteem or regard. Now, it is generally true that the stronger party in a role-status is typically highly regarded. Doctors and teachers enjoy more social esteem than patients and students. From a rank-status perspective, one would rather belong to the former group than the latter. But it's not doctors' social esteem that puts them in a position of superiority vis-à-vis patients. Rather, it is a bunch of other facts: that they know more about medicine than the patient, that they can perform treatments that patients are unable to perform on themselves, that patients typically feel ashamed and embarrassed about their ill-body, and so on and so forth. It is these background facts that constitute the asymmetry of the relevant relation, rather than the purely descriptive fact that patients are likely to obey doctors' instructions.

To be sure, as with the case of institutional power, disparities of societal esteem may exacerbate the vulnerabilities that characterise role-status relations. A patient may be excessively deferential to a famous doctor about their treatment. A student may run errands for their famous professor. But these asymmetries are super-imposed on asymmetries that precede the distribution, formal or informal,

[18] I understand *de facto* power to be a purely descriptive notion, picking out either the capacity to impact other people's interests, or the empirical likelihood that one will do so.

of social esteem. This is evidenced further in the fact that we cannot rank the role-holders in those relations comparatively. The student is not ranked against the patient, nor is the patient ranked against a child. Ditto for parents, teachers, and doctors. It makes little sense to ask: who ranks lower, a patient or a student? Or, conversely, who ranks higher, a teacher or a parent? To be sure, there is an inferior/superior divide within the same role-status. But this is not because the doctor is ranked higher than the patient. Ranking is an intentional action of placing others on a metric. That's not what is happening in the doctor/patient relation.

In sum, role-status seems to escape a characterisation as either a pure case of authority (institutional or *de facto*), or a case of disparity of esteem. It escapes the former because inferior parties have genuine moral reasons to be in the relation, and this relation is not the product of an institutional setting. And it escapes the latter because the superior position of the stronger party is not a function of their high social esteem.

The invitation I wish to extend to Kolodny is to recognise that certain forms of social hierarchy, what I call *role-statuses*, are a special case. They are not generated by either disparities of esteem or disparities of power (be they *institutional* or *de facto*). The common feature in all these relations is that the stronger party (parent, doctor, teacher, employer, landlord) is morally required to serve as the guardian of the weaker party's interests.

Why is it important to recognise this type of social hierarchy as a special case within a pluralistic framework like the one Kolodny offers? One reason, apart from analytic clarity, is that the way we should tackle these hierarchies is different. We combat unmerited disparities of social esteem individually, by making sure that we do not reproduce them in our public speech or let them influence our personal decisions. And we combat them politically, by robust anti-discrimination laws that protect unfavourable groups from being excluded from vital services and opportunities. We combat them, in other words, with a view to *eradicating* them or *mitigating* them. The same applies to unjust hierarchies created by political institutions. We have abolished slavery, caste systems, and tutelage. Where such relations persist informally, as in the case of modern slavery, we use the criminal law to prosecute perpetrators. When we fail, despite knowledge and ability, we are collectively responsible. But the aim is still the eradication or mitigation of these relations of inferiority.

By contrast, that's not the case with role-status hierarchies. The aim is not eradication or mitigation, but making sure that the parties don't violate their *role obligations*. We should make sure that the stronger party (the doctor or the teacher) acts like a guardian, rather than a master. The aim is to flip law's traditional approach: governments used to side with the interests of the stronger party. But now, they should side with the weaker party. Or at least, this is what I argue in this book. Apart from legal regulation, there is expressive value in publicly recognising that these are hierarchical relations. We must socially acknowledge the role of employees, refugees, tenants, and patients, as roles that come with role-rights against the relevant addressees, who have corresponding role obligations. But the main point is this: role-statuses are relations that we should not aim to eradicate *even though* they are asymmetrical. This is because they relate to stable, non-contingent aspects of the human condition. This seems to me to be a crucial difference compared to other forms of social hierarchy.

I am not sure how much of what I have said here so far threatens Kolodny's approach. I should hope that there is little or no tension. But I can see two areas where the idea of role-status might create problems for his account. The first relates to whether all relations of inferiority are *ranking* relations. Ranking can be seen as just another way to describe relations of inferiority; alternatively, it can be seen as what *makes* a relation one of inferiority/superiority. For example, it is social ranking that placed Brahmins above Dalits. Ranking, in turn, is typically understood as a form of collective intentionally, whereby we make it the case, either through a combination of patterns of behaviour and collective mental states, or through institutional action, that some groups are superior to others. But the problem here is that inferiority within role-status relations (e.g. teacher/student) is *not* a function of social ranking thus understood. Ranking can exacerbate it, but it does not create it.

If Kolodny is wedded to the above understanding of ranking, as a form of collective intentionality or institutional action, then his account could not accommodate role-statuses as I define them. Perhaps he would want to characterise role-statuses differently and dispute my account. But if he accepts that account, it seems unlikely that he would want to exclude them, given that many role-statuses figure as examples in *The Pecking Order*. So, in response he might go one of two ways. He might say that he does not understand ranking in a way that limits it to an act of collective intentionality, but in a broader way, as a synonym for a relation of superiority/inferiority or asymmetry. Ranking could just mean having superiors and inferiors. Though that reply would ensure that role-statuses are kept within his account, it does not address the point I sought to emphasise earlier, namely that caste systems are ranking relations in a very different sense to the doctor/patient relation. The point was that it is not in virtue of collective intentionality, or institutional action, that doctors are superior to patients. And we need some vocabulary to capture the difference between role-statuses and say, caste systems. It seems to me more accurate to say that caste systems are marked by relations of inferiority due to social ranking, whereas the doctor/patient relation does so due to different facts. Be that as it may, what is important is to acknowledge the distinction between these two kinds of social hierarchy, whatever terminology we use.

Alternatively, Kolodny might abandon the claim that all relations of inferiority are relations of genuine ranking. This option seems to me preferrable given the fact that role-statuses are stable and non-political forms of social hierarchy that we shouldn't aim to eradicate. And there is an additional reason I want to offer here.

It is important to observe that despite the asymmetries we find within role-status relations, there is still a sense in which we are nevertheless each other's equals. My doctor is not above me, in the way one group is above another in caste systems. One way in which this egalitarianism manifests itself is that role-statuses have a *two-way dynamic*. Doctors too fall ill and become patients. Parents grow old and become dependent on their children. Teachers take up courses in new areas. This two-way dynamic, together with the fact that role-statuses pertain to stable, non-objectionable, features of the human condition suggest that they are not inherently *in*egalitarian. Saying that they constitute a form of ranking, therefore, might distort their underlying nature. We gain in precision if we acknowledge that not all forms of social hierarchy are to do with ranking. To put the point differently: being ranked with a view to assigning institutional rights is inherently objectionable, whereas occupying a role-status is not. Being the weaker party within a role-status relation should not, from the get-go, be seen as an affront to social and political equality.

The second area of potential friction is connected to the first and has to do with what Kolodny calls tempering factors. Not all relations of social hierarchy are morally objectionable, all things considered. But they do trigger initially a valid *pro tanto* objection by the weaker party. Kolodny leaves it open whether tempering factors override objections against inferiority or extinguish them altogether. But this approach does not quite capture role-statuses. According to my account, the patient should not object to the relation of being the weaker party vis-à-vis the doctor. Rather, the patient, just like the student or the employee, should accept the relevant weakness as a stable and non-objectionable feature of the human condition. What they should object to, is for the stronger party to *abuse* their position and to be treated by them *as if* they are inferior. They should object, in Bentham's terms, to the stronger party acting like a master, rather than a guardian. Even if it turns out that doctors systematically abuse patients, due to the absence of tempering factors, they should still not call for the abolition of this hierarchical relation. They should simply insist that doctors comply with their role obligations.

This might seem like a subtle difference. But my point is that status relations, though asymmetrical, are not by nature objectionable. I do not know if Kolodny will challenge this point. He might, for instance, reply that patients, students, and employees should object not only to the potential abuse, but to the asymmetry of the relation as such, calling it one of inferiority. This would entail that in an ideal world we shouldn't have patients, students, or employees because these are all relations of inferiority. And perhaps one day, with suitable technological advancements made possible by artificial intelligence, we will get rid of doctors, teachers, and employers. But in our current, non-ideal world, we can and should settle for putting in place tempering factors. Or so Kolodny might reply.

I am not sure what we should say about that possible reply. In the previous chapter I made the point that there is no neutral baseline with respect to these interests of well-being: if we abolish these asymmetrical relations, we will not make the underlying vulnerabilities disappear. We are most likely to replace these asymmetrical relations with new ones. Moreover, the two-way dynamic of role-statuses is something we should consider when assessing whether the asymmetry within certain relations is inherently objectionable. At a higher level of abstraction, and taking into account all role-statuses, we might realise that an adequate degree of symmetry across persons obtains. It may then turn out to be morally indifferent that students are vulnerable vis-à-vis teachers. Students will one day be teachers and teachers have been students, just like doctors will be patients. And almost all of us at one point or another in our lives, will be a carer, a landlord, an employer, or a teacher. We will bounce up and down these role-status hierarchies. What we need to get right is the adequate legal regulation and social recognition of these asymmetrical relations.

7
ROLE OBLIGATIONS REVISITED

7.1 Introduction

What is the ontology of role-statuses? I have been using the idea of role to capture social relations that pose a threat to moral equality. Just like status, roles are understood to come with a set of rights and obligations. The standard way we use it in our moral practices is by saying that *qua* . . . [fill in the role], one has to do X and Y. Yet the idea of role obligations has somewhat of a bad name in moral philosophy. They are commonly associated with the Hegelian view that all moral obligations are embedded in roles that are created and defined by social or legal norms. A role-based morality seems problematic at the get-go. Surely there are no moral rights one has *qua* a slavecatcher or an SS guard. In this chapter I aim to show that certain roles, what I call role-statuses, are not the product of social or legal norms. They are inherently moral.

Ever since Dworkin defended a non-positivist account of legal obligation, it has appeared puzzling to many how contingent norms, enacted by fallible institutions, can have an inherent moral dimension. For legal positivists, the content of legal rights and duties is determined by social facts alone. The same puzzle applies to social roles: how can the role of a doctor come with a set of objective moral rights and duties? Is Pufendorf simply wrong to argue that statuses are moral entities? Surely, being a witch doctor, a shaman, a spiritual healer, or a eugenics doctor does not come with any set of real moral entitlements. The role of a doctor can be good or can be bad—it is all contingent on social facts. The standard view is to treat both law and roles as a social kind: something we humans create through our intentions, beliefs, and practices. The social constructionist approach, however, though intuitively plausible at first, cannot explain salient aspects of our moral practices. Roles that relate to asymmetrical social relations, I will argue, are moralised entities: they serve as a justificatory ground for equality-based rights and duties.

By making space for a general model of role-statuses, as moralised roles, we can also, I hope, make some progress in general jurisprudence. Legal rights are better viewed as role-specific rights, those attached to the status of being a citizen.[1] Thus

[1] Dworkin expressed preference for the term 'associative obligations' over the term 'role obligations', noting however that they refer to the same idea. See Ronald Dworkin, *Law's Empire* (Cambridge: Belknap Press, 1986), pp. 195–196. But he never provided a general explanation of role morality. I here aim to fill this gap. He might, of course, have rejected the general account of role obligations that I offer

Status in Law and Morality. George Letsas, Oxford University Press. © George Letsas 2026.
DOI: 10.1093/9780198936725.003.0007

understood, they are subject to the constraints of status morality, including the requirement to interpret the terms of the relevant relation in non-contractual[2] terms, with a view to balancing its asymmetry.

7.2 Role Morality

Before becoming a doctor, Chris Hutchinson played college football for the Michigan Wolverines. In 1992, he was named Defensive Line Man of the year, team captain, and Most Valuable Player. After graduating, he suffered complications from a tetanus shot and, soon after, retired from football to qualify as a doctor. During the first peak of the pandemic, he worked as an emergency room doctor in Detroit. Here is how he described working ten-hour shifts back-to-back:

> It's just what you do. You've got to do it. It's part of the job. I've got to do my job. I can't not come to work. Somebody's got to do this, and this is my role here. Put your mask on and have at it. Is it fun? Absolutely not, but somebody has to do it.[3]

The grip of morality on us is often intertwined with the social roles we occupy. There are things one ought to do *qua* doctor, teacher, or judge. Characteristic of role obligations is that they motivate agents to perform an action simply because it is their role, as Chris Hutchinson's remarks show. However, the notion that roles ground obligations can be puzzling upon closer examination. It implies that roles are self-justifying qualities (*qua*), grounding a set of moral obligations. The trouble is that we do not normally appeal to such qualities when we seek to justify an obligation. My moral obligation to help the victim of an accident is not derived from some role I occupy, say *qua* a passer-by. It is based on general moral principles regarding universal human interests in life and bodily integrity, and it holds irrespective of one's social role. Appeal to one's social role to justify action seems to suggest a peculiar kind of moral justification.

The question is whether certain social roles, such as being a doctor or a judge, are themselves morally significant. What I mean by this is whether certain social roles are moralised concepts. Non-moralised concepts, such as 'killing', can be

here, or dispute that his conception of law is a role-based one, as I understand it. We will never know. I have analysed further the connection between law's normativity and the role of citizenship in George Letsas, 'How to Argue for Law's Full-Blooded Normativity', in David Plunket et al. (eds), *Dimensions of Normativity: New Essays on Metaethics and Jurisprudence* (Oxford: Oxford University Press, 2019).

[2] The idea that there is social contract between government and citizens is one of the oldest in political philosophy. We should here note the analogy between interpreting contracts according to the specific intention of the parties and interpreting legislation according to the specific intention of its drafters.

[3] https://eu.detroitnews.com/story/sports/college/university-michigan/2020/03/25/this-my-job-er- doctor-ex-wolverine-chris-hutchinson-front-lines-covid-19-battle/5077980002/

applied on purely factual grounds without any moral judgment. By contrast, moralised concepts, such as 'murder', involve the application of a judgment regarding a person's moral responsibility, where the concept plays a special role in that judgment.[4] So, we might think that in his remarks, Hutchinson did not provide a justification for his sacrifice, since he did not cite some general moral principle. We might treat his statement as a descriptive reference to institutional facts regarding what was demanded of doctors during the pandemic. Alternatively, we might consider Hutchinson's appeal to his role to serve as a type of moral justification, one that is not dependent on empirical facts about what was required of him. We would then have expected him to express the exact same attitude even if the relevant authorities had not required of doctors to be at the forefront of fighting the pandemic. In this latter case, the role of a doctor is treated as a moralised concept, as a shorthand for a type of moral judgment.

Of course, it is far from clear what it means to say that certain social roles are moralised and what, if anything, is special about the moral judgment they are used to express. It is the aim of this chapter to shed light on this claim. 'Role' is a modern dramaturgical metaphor. At its most abstract level, it refers to a pattern of social interaction that is governed by a set of obligations. The genealogy of this philosophical idea is rich and complex.[5] The existing philosophical literature on role obligations has discussed the connection between roles and moral obligation in a different sense to the one I seek to elucidate here. An older tradition, influenced by Hegelian and stoic philosophy, supported internalism. Internalism considers roles as both social kinds and self-justifying entities.[6] It holds that certain obligations are grounded on roles, rather than on general moral principles. In Michael Hardimon's apt phrase, normativity simply 'flows' from the role.[7] Stronger versions

[4] For example, 'murder' picks out a special case of moral responsibility for killing, since not all killing is wrongful and not all wrongful killing is murder. It thus serves as a shorthand for a particular category of wrongful killing. See Gerald Dworkin, 'Compulsion and Moral Concepts', 78 *Ethics* (1968), pp. 227–233.

[5] The dramaturgical metaphor is widely used in sociology following the foundational work of Erving Goffman, in his *The Presentation of Self in Everyday Life* (Penguin Books, 1959). Older terms of the same notion employ the word 'station', as seen in the work of the British idealists. See F. H. Bradley, *Ethical Studies* (Oxford: Clarendon Press, 1988), p. 163: 'We have found ourselves, when we have found our station and its duties, our function as an organ in the social organism'. Most contemporary accounts of role obligations take the work of the German and British idealists as their starting point. See e.g. David Lubban, *Lawyers and Justice: An Ethical Study* (Princeton: Princeton University Press, 1988). But the notion of role obligations, under different labels, goes at least as far back as the Stoics. See Julia Annas, 'My Station and Its Duties: Ideals and the Social Embeddedness of Virtue', 102 *Proceedings of the Aristotelian Society* (2002), pp. 109–123.

[6] See G. W. F. Hegel, *Elements of the Philosophy of Right*, edited by Allen W. Wood (Cambridge, Cambridge University Press, 1991), p. 193: 'In an ethical community, it is easy to say what someone must do and what the duties are which he has to fulfil in order to be virtuous. He must simply do what is prescribed, expressly stated, and known to him within his situation.'

[7] See Michael Hardimon, 'Role Obligations', 91 *Journal of Philosophy* (1994), pp. 333–363. Hardimon's view that roles are institutional structures and that normativity 'flows from the role' is a rare contemporary expression of the Hegelian approach. His account has been the leading point of reference in recent decades.

of internalism have even held that the whole of morality emanates from roles.[8] However, a more recent tradition, influenced by rationalism, defends externalism.[9] Externalists posit that since roles are socially constructed, no aspect of a social role can be inherently self-justifying. Their normativity depends on contingent factors, such as whether the relevant community has done a good job drafting the obligations assigned to the role, or whether one has freely agreed to hold it. According to externalism, holding a social role does not necessarily entail any moral duty and, in this sense, there is no such thing as role morality.

The polarised nature of these two traditions has to some extent downplayed the significance of role obligations in moral philosophy.[10] Role morality is seen as either self-justifying, which seems implausible, or superfluous. After the Enlightenment, externalism prevailed, and the normativity of roles came to be seen in a confined sense: roles can only provide reasons contingently, either through contracting into them, or through self-identification.[11] We might presume, for example, that Hutchinson has an employment contract with the hospital and identifies strongly with his role and then seek to explain his remarks in that way.

However, this confined account of the normativity of roles leaves many aspects of our moral practices unexplained. Role-holders might refuse to comply with institutional requirements, invoking their role as a justification. Doctors, for instance, might refuse to engage in popular and government-mandated eugenics programmes on the basis that it would be an aberration of their role, as some doctors did in Nazi Germany. Role-holders might feel bound by their role even when they are jaded and no longer identify with it, as several doctors did after the Covid-19 pandemic. Third parties might hold role-holders to a higher standard than what their contract says, or what society at large expects of them. For example, many people think that allowing doctors to become salespersons for the drug manufacturing industry, as the current practice is in many countries, is in breach of their obligations *qua* doctors. As I will explain, these phenomena would make little sense if these social roles were non-moralised concepts. More importantly, insofar

[8] Cf. the Stoic philosopher Epictetus: 'Consider "who you are" and then each of your roles, when reflected upon, will indicate the duties that apply to you . . . [a]nd if you breach your duties, then we will say to you: "You have forgotten who you are and what your role is"', in Robert Dobbin (ed.), *Epictetus: Discourses and Selected Writings* (London: Penguin, 2008), para II.10, p. 96.

[9] See John A. Simmons, 'External Justifications and Institutional Roles', 93 *Journal of Philosophy* (1996), pp. 28–36; John A. Simmons. 'Associative Political Obligations', 106 *Ethics* (1996), pp. 247–273.

[10] Role morality has enjoyed little philosophical currency in the last century or so. See, however, Dorothy Emmet, *Rules, Roles and Relations* (London: Macmillan, 1966).

[11] This is one way in which many philosophers have sought to explain rationally our common-sense morality about roles. According to this explanation, no role is inherently normative, or moralised. Rather, roles are infused with normativity when holders develop certain attitudes towards their role. See Stefan Sciaraffa, 'Identification, Meaning and the Normativity of Social Roles', 19 *European Journal of Philosophy* (2009), pp. 107–128; Anne Baril, 'The Ethical Importance of Roles', 50 *Journal of Value Inquiry* (2016), pp. 721–734; Tim Dare, 'Robust Role-Obligation: How Do Roles Make a Moral Difference?', 50 *Journal of Value Inquiry* (2016), pp. 703–719.

as these phenomena exhibit some special normative upshots, it would be fruitful to explore which social roles are moralised and why.

How should an argument defending the moralised nature of certain social roles proceed? It is necessary first to examine the ontology of social roles. Almost every account in the literature accepts that roles are social kinds, in that they are constituted by social practices, institutions, beliefs, expectations and the like.[12] This drives a wedge between the ontology of roles and normative questions about their obligatoriness. Since it is this dichotomy that a moralised conception of certain roles challenges, I begin with a brief account of the orthodox ontological view that treats roles as self-referential social kinds. I move on to show, in Section 7.4, that certain social roles do not behave like social kinds: they involve a judgment about the role-holder's responsibilities, irrespective of facts about collective intentionality. I then proceed to the positive part of the argument (Section 7.5) which provides an argument for why certain social roles, what I call role-statuses, are moralised. Inherently normative roles, I argue, refer to a pattern of social interaction with weaker parties, who suffer from dependencies or vulnerabilities. These bilateral roles grew out of 'proto-roles'—that is, pre-institutional interactions where one party acquired *de facto* control of significant interests of another. What is special about them is that they pick out the moral responsibility that attaches to the stronger party in this pattern of social interaction, in virtue of its inherent asymmetry. The most significant feature of these roles is that we can hold the role-holder accountable to a higher standard than their voluntary undertaking, or what is generally expected of them by the community, and regardless of the degree of self-identification. This, I will argue, is the most important difference between moralised roles (role-statuses) and other, purely institutional social roles.

Before I begin, a few clarifications regarding the scope of the argument in this chapter might be helpful to the reader. First, I am interested in the way in which certain social roles create obligations, understood as directed categorical requirements, rather than mere *pro tanto* reasons. Clearly, there are several bases on which one may have a weak reason, prudential or otherwise, to take up a role and carry it out. For example, a person with high musical aptitude, or whose parents have a deep appreciation of music, can be said to have a reason to become a musician. Self-identification too, provides reasons to perform a role. I want to focus, instead, on more stringent requirements than these types of reasons—that is, on obligations that can be demanded of the role-holder by others.[13] This focus better fits the practice of role morality, though I have no space to defend this claim here.

[12] See Hardimon, 'Role Obligations'; Simmons. 'Associative Political Obligations', pp. 247–273; Sciaraffa, 'Identification, Meaning and the Normativity of Social Roles', p. 109. Hardimon defines institutions as 'ongoing, self-reproducing structures', with a 'public system of rules', including rules defining offices and positions.

[13] I bracket here questions about whether obligations are an instance of very weighty or conclusive reasons, whether they are defeasible, and many related questions which track broader debates between deontology and consequentialism, since they do not directly affect my argument.

Second, it might seem obvious to some that not all roles are social kinds. For example, the ontology of intimate roles, such as being a friend, or a parent, seems far less dependent, if at all, on societal beliefs and practices. As Pufendorf pointed out, family and labour roles precede the establishment of political institutions. However, my main aim is to make space for the view that certain heavily institutionalised roles, such as being a doctor, are moralised and this requires showing that even these roles are not social kinds.

Finally, I should clarify that I do not aim to adjudicate the debate between externalism and internalism, but rather to explore a neglected possibility. Like most '-isms' I treat them as broad traditions in moral philosophy, largely mapping onto rationalist and non-rationalist accounts of morality respectively. Unlike Hegelian and stoic accounts, the moralised account I offer is committed to rationalism and holds only for certain roles. In this sense my account is an externalist one. Unlike externalists, however, I believe that moral justification is internal to these roles and in that sense my account finds some merit in the older, internalist tradition.[14]

7.3 Roles as Social Kinds

The philosophical view that roles are social kinds got significant traction from a worry about bad metaphysics. The alternative view, namely that roles are abstract qualities one possesses (such that you must take an action *qua* a role-holder), struck some philosophers as an implausible ontological view. John Austin called role qualities 'occult and fictitious', the kind of rubbish metaphysics of which we should rid moral philosophy.[15] As we saw earlier, Austin thought that to have a role *just is* to be the holder of an aggregate of institutionally created rights and obligations.[16] This thought is based on a picture of roles as social kinds: they consist in facts about institutional practices that assign the role and define its content. We may call Austin's view an identity thesis about the relation between roles[17] and obligations. The identity thesis holds that roles just are packages of institutional rights and obligations, not merely correlated with rights and obligations.[18]

[14] Though my position can be seen as a middle one between internalism and externalism, it should be available to externalists who do not think that all roles are social kinds. But it is not available to internalists who think that some, or even all, social roles are self-justifying.

[15] See John Austin, *Lectures on Jurisprudence: Or The Philosophy of Positive Law* (New York: Henry Colt, 1875), p. 355. Austin was reacting against Jeremy Bentham's account, which treated roles as inherent qualities that form an ideal base around which obligations are grounded.

[16] Austin, *Lectures on Jurisprudence*, p. 357. For discussion of Austin's identity thesis see C. K. Allen, *Legal Duties and Other Essays in Jurisprudence* (Oxford: Clarendon Press, 1931), ch. 2.

[17] Austin used the term 'status' rather than 'role'. Some distinguish between status and role on the basis that not all statuses are roles. See Hardimon, 'Role Obligations', pp. 333–363. I here use the two terms interchangeably, following the way status is understood in law, i.e. as a set of normative powers.

[18] The identity thesis later became dominant. When the anthropologist Ralph Linton introduced the concept of role to sociology, he defined it as 'simply a collection of rights and duties'. See Ralph Linton, *The Study of Man: An Introduction* (New York: D. Appleton Century, 1936), p. 113.

Because no role is separate from a specified package of rights and obligations (it is that package), roles cannot be used to justify obligations, and so internalism must be false.

Most contemporary accounts follow Austin in treating roles as institutional kinds. Perhaps the most influential account of social kinds in recent decades, offered by John Searle,[19] takes roles to be a central case. I shall use Searle's ontological model as my focal point, with a view to exploring the implications it has for the normativity of roles.[20] In doing so, I am interested in paving the way for the idea of moralised social roles, rather than mounting a critique of existing theories of social ontology.[21]

Searle's account holds that social kinds are dependent on facts involving collective intentionality, such as beliefs, attitudes, desires, intentions, and so on. We construct social kinds by agreeing collectively to impose a point or purpose on brute physical phenomena. Objects that possess certain properties (e.g. have a flat surface, a back and four legs) are chairs whose purpose is to be used as a seat.[22] In the case of institutional kinds, Searle calls these purposes 'status-functions'. We have collectively agreed that certain objects count as money, certain activities count as war, certain actions and utterances count as marriage, and so on. For example, what it means for a ten-dollar note in my wallet to count as money, is to be collectively recognised as a medium of exchange. The upshot of Searle's account is that, though money is something we construct subjectively, and does not exist objectively, it is nevertheless an objective fact about the world that I have ten dollars in my wallet. Since facts about collective intentionality have an objective manifestation, social kinds can be given a naturalistic explanation even though they are human constructs. There is nothing occult about them.

Applied to roles, Searle's account is a version of Austin's identity thesis. A role exists when we have collectively agreed that people who meet certain conditions (e.g. have had training and passed certain exams) acquire a status (e.g. Medical Doctor) with certain functions (e.g. to treat common medical conditions). Searle

[19] John Searle, *The Construction of Social Reality* (Free Press, 1995).

[20] It is worth emphasising at the outset that Searle's model is not concerned with the justifiability of social kinds and is silent on the possibility of roles that are not social kinds.

[21] I am not concerned here with the popular, but vague, idea that the world is socially constructed. One can be a social constructionist about features of the social world including fundamental notions such as personal identity, truth, and social reality itself. Clearly, Searle's model will be of limited use as a general social constructionist model, nor does it aspire to be. For this point, see Ian Hacking, *The Social Construction of What?* (Cambridge: Harvard University Press, 1999); Sally Haslanger, *Resisting Reality: Social Construction and Social Critique* (Oxford: Oxford University Press, 2012). I also here set aside social roles which are wrongly considered to be natural kinds, such as roles to do with race or gender. For an account of such 'covert' social kinds, see Ron Mallon, 'Social Construction and Achieving Reference', 217 *Nous* (2017), pp. 113–131. For a recent, general account of social ontology, see, Brian Epstein, *The Ant Trap: Rebuilding the Foundations of the Social Sciences* (Oxford: Oxford University Press, 2015).

[22] Searle treats this phenomenon as an instance of a special kind of rules, which he calls 'constitutive', and which have the logical form 'X counts as Y in context C'.

notes, rightly, that the collective imposition of a function on persons differs crucially from the imposition of a function on artefacts. In the case of artefacts, like chairs, the function is causal—that is, the object's properties (shape and height) are such that they enable it physically to be used as a seat. By contrast, in the case of institutional roles the function is normative: doctors have powers (to prescribe medication), responsibilities (to provide urgent treatment), permissions (to ask and store sensitive medical information), and so on. We do not use a chair in the same way we use a doctor. Since, on Searle's view, the collective imposition of a function on physical phenomena is what it means for a social kind to exist, the status of a doctor is not separate from the related obligations. Rather, the above package of normative powers constitutes the role of the doctor.[23]

It is crucial to this ontological model that roles exist in part because they are believed to exist. They have a mind-to-world directionality: the meaning we attribute to the role determines which persons and functions it picks out. The model treats roles as different to other nouns that can be predicated on humans, such as a transphobe. Someone can be a transphobe even if nobody in society has beliefs about transphobia.[24] Though transphobia is ontologically dependent on human attitudes towards transgender people, it is not dependent on attitudes about the category of transphobia itself. Transphobia has a world-to-mind directionality. By contrast, if we had not collectively assigned under the category 'doctors' certain normative functions on people who possess medical knowledge, then the role of a doctor would never have existed. Social recognition of the kind 'doctor' is a necessary condition for its existence, but not so for the kind 'transphobe'.

Searle notes further that, unlike artificial kinds, the functions of institutional roles cannot be performed solely in virtue of a person's physical properties and depend on continuous human cooperation.[25] Someone who possesses medical knowledge can put it to some physical uses, such as giving first aid. But they would not be able to, say, issue a prescription or make a referral. They can only do so if they are regarded collectively by others as having these normative powers. According to the model, to have the normative powers of a doctor is to be recognised by others as having them. To be more precise: the content of the normative powers of a doctor is identical to the content of the relevant mental states of collective intentionality towards the role. This is a point worth emphasising. It is not the case that a social

[23] In Searle, *Construction of Social Reality*, Searle discusses honorific and symbolic roles, where there seems to be an imposition of status but without any assignment of normative powers. He concludes that these are special cases of normative powers, where certain honorific ways of referring to the status holder are licensed or become obligatory.

[24] For an argument that some social kinds can be mind-dependent without being self-referential, see Muhammad Ali Khalidi, 'Three Kinds of Social Kinds', 90 *Philosophy and Phenomenological Research* (2015), pp. 96–112.

[25] Some physical properties may be necessary for the object, or the person to perform the function. Money the size of a mountain would fail causally to serve as money. For this point and related criticism, see Khalidi, 'Three Kinds of Social Kinds'.

role may have functions whose content diverges from the propositional content of the relevant locus of collective intentionality. It could not turn out that doctors have the power to issue search warrants if few, or nobody, thought so.

By reducing the role's normative functions to facts about collective acceptance, the model of social kinds escapes Austin's worries about occult qualities. It's not a mystery why, as a doctor, one has the obligation to respect patient autonomy: it is simply because we have collectively agreed to impose this function on doctors. However, this reductionism has direct implications for the normativity of roles. Institutional kinds are seen as an efficacious tool to advance human goals. But human goals at given times may be inherently evil. The role of the SS guards in Nazi concentration camps was to execute the Nazi Genocide programme. Performance of such roles constitutes an egregious violation of the values of human dignity and equality. Precisely because the model of social kinds treats roles as the product of collective intentionality, their link to morality is contingent. Roles, thus understood, cannot be self-justifying: their normativity depends on standards external to the institutional practices that created them.

It is this point that externalist accounts of role obligations take as a given. Simmons defines externalism as the view that 'we are morally obligated to perform our institutionally assigned "obligations" only when this is required by a moral rule (or principle) that is not itself a rule of the institution in question'. A role may, or may not, consist in obligations that are validated by external, non-institutional, moral norms. When it does, the ground of the obligations is not the role, but the external moral norm. The link of role obligations to morality is not necessary, but contingent.

The identity thesis, however, imposes the following constraints on the normativity of roles. First, we cannot be in massive error about what obligations role holders have. It could not turn out, for instance, that doctors may issue search warrants. The content and scope of a role's normative powers is exhausted by the relevant mental facts of collective intentionality.

A second implication is that the only kind of disagreement that is possible about the scope and content of social kinds is factual disagreement over what is collectively accepted. Someone who disagrees about whether doctors may issue search warrants simply does not know enough about the powers that we have collectively agreed to give doctors. Once all doctor-related facts of collective intentionality are known to that person, then disagreement should be settled. Recall that to have a role just is to be subject to a set of obligations that consist in facts about collective intentionality. Those constitutive facts exhaust the ontology of roles. Put differently, disagreement about role obligations—understood as social kinds—cannot be evaluative, like the disagreement about what equality, or democracy requires. At best, we can only disagree about what social roles we collectively should have.[26]

[26] Khalidi argues that, for certain social kinds, there can be general agreement on the type (for example what counts as war) without there being an agreement that a particular token counts as war. See

Third, it cannot be the case that there are social roles whose existence we ignore, and which are waiting to be discovered. For example, we did not discover the role of the 'influencer', after social media emerged; we created it. Roles on the ontological model under consideration are human inventions, a complex social process by which we impose normative functions on physical persons.

Fourth, according to the identity thesis to have a role just is to have certain obligations. And according to externalism, role obligations cannot be self-justifying. It follows, if we combine the two theses, that the true normative ground of an obligation cannot be the fact that one occupies a social role. Suppose you are appointed to the administrative role of a Moots Officer by your Department, which involves organising moot competitions for the students and providing training. If I ask you why you are morally obligated to carry out the tasks assigned to you, it is not an available response to say, 'because this is my role'. Such a response would be question-begging, implying that your role was self-justifying.

To sum-up the discussion so far: the ontological model of social kinds treats roles as the collective imposition of certain normative functions on a person or a group of persons, with a view to advancing certain human goals. The link between roles and real moral obligations is contingent. Their content is exhausted by the propositional content of collective mental states. One cannot discover roles unbeknownst to us, nor can we collectively be in error about what they are.

7.4 Three Normative Phenomena

In this section, I present three normative phenomena which force us to depart from the ontological model of social kinds, at least for certain roles. The first is that we can make sense of pre-institutional roles, whose existence does not depend on any collective intentionality towards the role. The second is that we sometimes invoke roles to condemn institutional regulation, whereas sometimes we condemn institutional roles altogether. And the third is that we can be in error about what an institutional role requires, even when all facts about collective intentionality are known. I do not take these phenomena to challenge the account of social kind presented in the previous section. Rather, I take them to suggest that certain roles do not behave as social kinds.

Khalidi, 'Three Kinds of Social Kinds'. *Pace* Searle, he thinks that a particular set of hostilities can be war even if it is not considered as such by most or by anyone. It is not clear, however, whether his position can be reconciled with the view that war is a social kind, created by facts of collective intentionality. If there are no such facts with respect to a borderline case of hostilities, then it would be neither true nor false that it constituted war. I take Khalidi's argument to suggest, instead, that war is not a social kind all the way down.

7.4.1 Pre-institutional Roles

Suppose you live on a desert island, long before the development of any institutional practices and collective intentions involving the adjudication of disputes.[27] You are the sole inhabitant, though your island is in the middle of a natural fish passage where many islanders from further away come to fish. Food is hard to source, and everyone relies on fishing to survive. One day, two fishers (let's call them Alex and Robin) are after a large shoal of fish. The shoal lands on a sea platform that you have built and only you can access. If you try to reach the platform from one side, however, the fish will be released back into the water towards Alex's boat. And if you try to reach the platform from the other side, it will be released in the opposite direction and get caught in Robin's net. It is not possible for you to get the fish for yourself. Robin and Alex each pleads that you should release the fish towards their side. They urge you to act before the fish goes bad. Alex claims to deserve the catch because she had been chasing it for days. Robin claims that he should have it because, but for the platform, it would have ended up in his net. Neither party accepts that you have any legitimacy to decide the dispute. But they have no way of undoing whatever you decide. After listening carefully to their arguments, you award the fish to Robin on the basis that Alex uses dynamite, which risks extinguishing all the surrounding marine life. This, let us suppose, is the most reasonable decision to reach.

Now suppose that incidents like the one just described become regular. Passing fishers competing for the scarce resource get into frequent disputes, as fish get washed up on your platform. You engage seriously with every dispute by intervening, trying to do what is morally right by the parties. Unbeknownst to the passing fishers (they are different each time), you become accustomed to this task. You develop procedures for listening to their arguments (e.g. you wait to hear both parties before deciding) and seek to follow the rationale of your previous decisions. You take pride in the activity and think of it as an important part of your life.

It is plausible to think here that, despite the absence of collective intentionality, you have acquired the role of a judge. You have *de facto* the power to adjudicate the disputes, and, in virtue of that position, you are bound by a set of obligations with which we are familiar from the institutional office of the judge, such as the duty to hear both sides and to be impartial. Unlike that office, however, your position consists in a complex set of circumstances in which you unwillingly found yourself: you are in a unique position to adjudicate these disputes, you have no stake in the outcome, and you can carry out this task regularly and consistently. Taken together, they form the building blocks of what we may call the proto-role of a judge. Absent one of these blocks, we would not say that you have taken the role. For

[27] For a similar way of testing whether some part of morality (such as promising) is purely conventional, see T. M. Scanlon, *What We Owe to Each Other* (Cambridge: Harvard University Press, 1998).

example, if your involvement was one-off, then your adjudicative function would be episodic and hardly qualify as a role.

I will discuss possible objections to the claim that the circumstances just described are sufficient to qualify as a judicial role later in the chapter. Right now, I would like to elaborate on the less controversial claim that the person in the hypothetical would be bound by obligations that are at least similar to the institutional office of a judge.

This proto-role is bilateral, having addressees whose interests are systematically affected by the actions of the agent holding it. These *de facto* litigants face the risk of starvation while they are vulnerable to whimsical decisions or arbitrary changes of their rationale. They do not have the choice of opting out and submitting their dispute to someone else. There is an inherent asymmetry here between the agent controlling the platform and the fishers. The obligations of this proto-role are based on the need to balance this unequal relation at the moral level and protect the dependent parties against arbitrary exercise of power. Note, moreover, that we need not assume here that each fisher knows that other fishers are equally vulnerable to your decisions, or that fishers have formed mutually interlocking expectations that you be the legitimate judge of their disputes. No element of collective intentionality is required in order to justify the resulting obligations.

Several features of this proto-role of a judge depart from the identity thesis. First, the role here is not identical with the set of obligations attached to it. This is because the role and its obligations (they are the same according to the model of social kinds) are not created by some institution, through the process of collective intentionality. Instead, the role consists in certain non-institutional circumstances that give the agent the capacity to affect interests of dependent parties. The role, in turn, understood as a set of non-normative circumstances is what triggers certain moral demands and grounds a set of adjudicative obligations, rather than being identical with it.

Second, the relation of grounding that holds between the role and the resulting obligations departs from traditional externalist accounts. Recall that externalism identifies role obligations by reference to institutional facts, and then asks whether some external moral standard requires compliance to the role thus defined. On the standard externalist account, these are 'obligations' in inverted commas: it is a contingent matter whether they bind morally. In the hypothetical, by contrast, the obligations are genuinely normative, since they come into existence in virtue of the circumstances surrounding the role-holder and the role-addressees. No appeal to some further moral fact, like consent, is required. The normative work of general moral principles has already been done.

Finally, the hypothetical challenges the strict separation of the metaphysics of roles from normative questions. The ontology of the role is also sensitive to normative truths. Suppose that if you were to award the fish to Robin, you would get half of it, saving yourself from starvation. Morality would arguably permit you to save your own life, over that of strangers. This would entail, however, that you would no longer be in a position of impartiality vis-à-vis the parties. Rather than having to judge who has the stronger normative claim, you would have reason to find for Robin. The inherent lack of impartiality in your circumstances would disqualify you as a judge. 'You can't call yourself a judge', Alex would rightly object. This is because we take impartiality to be essential to the role of the judge, not just something we may, or may not, choose to assign collectively as one of its obligations.

7.4.2 Roles with Inbuilt Justificatory Force

Consider an institutionally created role you might hold, like that of the Moots Officer within a Department. Suppose that the Department formally assigns to you tasks that effectively amount to bribing the officials of the moot competitions to favour your students. Under the model of social kinds, bribing would become part of your role obligations. Suppose further that, as one should, you refuse to carry out this task. What responses would be available to you to justify non-compliance? Appeal to some general moral standard like the unfairness of corruption would be most people's reaction. What would not be a pertinent response would be to appeal to your role as a Moots Officer alone, claiming that bribing offends that role.

The model of social kinds explains why the above response would be impertinent. There is nothing to the role of the Moots Officer, over and above the set of obligations that the Department has collectively agreed. The only possible offence against the role would be to fail to carry out its collectively agreed functions. It would not be possible to invoke the role itself as a justification for refusing to bribe because, according to the identity thesis, the role is those obligations. Likewise, the Department would not be able to appeal to the role alone as a ground for criticising non-compliance, because according to standard externalists accounts the Moots Officer's obligations are not self-justifying. And in this case external moral norms recommend non-compliance.

Other roles are different, however, and this is perhaps easier to see starting with intimate roles. Suppose that the government proposed to ban parents from raising their own children, with a view to correcting educational inequalities. What responses would be available to parents? They could appeal to general moral considerations, such as that the ban will harm children. But, unlike the role of the Moots Officer, they could also react by invoking their parental role simpliciter. It offends the role of a parent, they could say, to be denied the freedom to raise one's own kids.[28] Such a reaction would be intelligible and pertinent, even if society were to

[28] The fact that parenting practices can bestow unfair advantages on one's children has been the subject of extensive discussion within the egalitarian literature. For the argument that some parenting practices, such as reading bedtime stories, are constitutive of the familial relationship see Harry Brighouse and Adam Swift, 'Legitimate Parental Partiality', 37 *Philosophy and Public Affairs* (2009), pp. 43–80.

agree collectively that the role of parenthood from now own will be assigned to state authorities. The same can be observed in the case of heavily institutionalised roles, such as doctors. The enlisting of doctors in the Nazi eugenics and euthanasia programme was not only morally abhorrent, but also an aberration of their role. Doctors who refused to comply with this evil programme could meaningfully invoke their role as a justification.

There are two related features that I seek to emphasise with these examples. The first is that not all roles behave the same when morally objectionable tasks are imposed collectively on the role-holder. Sometimes we react by condemning the role in its entirety, in the name of some general moral obligation. We say that the role of slave-catchers in the United States during colonial times was morally abhorrent and should never have existed. The role of a slave-catcher is entirely a social kind. We would not say that the tasks expected of slave-catchers offended their role. The same holds for the administrative role of the Moots Officer. By contrast, in cases such as doctors and parents, we react by condemning the specific tasks as offending the nature of the role. This suggests that for at least certain roles it is not entirely up to us, collectively, to determine their obligations as is the case with social kinds.

The second feature is that certain roles can be invoked elliptically as a justification. They have what we might call inbuilt justificatory force.[29] With respect to these roles, we typically use expressions such as 'Do you call yourself a parent?', 'that's not how judges behave', or 'a friend would never do a thing like that'. We do so with a view to holding people morally responsible.[30] That is not to say that the role itself is the normative ground of the putative obligation. Rather, the point is that the role here serves as shorthand for a moral explanation and that competent moral agents are able to perceive it as such.[31]

7.4.3 Disagreement and Massive Error

Recall that under the model of social kinds, it is not possible to have an evaluative disagreement over what the obligations of a given role are. There are plenty

[29] Christine Korsgaard argues that in enforcing role obligations no 'ought' is needed because 'normativity is built right into the role'. See Christine Korsgaard, *The Sources of Normativity* (Cambridge: Cambridge University Press, 1996). Similarly, Hardimon (1994) characterizes obligations of role as moral requirements 'whose normative force flows from the role'. I think, however, that this is only true of moralised social roles.

[30] Of course, we might use some of these expressions about other roles too. The question 'do you call yourself a banker?' might be used as a complaint by a bank manager towards an employee. But in such cases the expression is simply an elliptical way to appeal to the fact that one has voluntarily undertaken to perform a role, or has identified with it. Absent this fact, however, the expression would make little sense. Nobody thought to ask that question of the bankers who caused the 2008 subprime mortgage crisis.

[31] It is this elliptical justificatory function that encouraged the internalist view that roles are self-justifying.

of cases, however, where evaluative disagreement about the obligations of a role is common. Consider the role of an academic. It is currently part of the role of UK-based academics to ensure that students find their educational experience satisfying, to conduct research that has measurable impact outside academia, and to take part in immigration enforcement against students on a visa.[32] In my experience, there is little opposition towards these tasks among the British public, let alone outrage. Most academics find them unproblematic, part of the modern-day role of an academic. Still, it is open to disagreement on the basis that it is not the role of an academic to engage in immigration control of one's students or to treat them as consumers.[33]

In support of this argument, one may invoke several considerations: that the role of an academic is to pursue the intrinsic good of knowledge free from any interference by the government, to facilitate the pursuit of knowledge, regardless of how satisfying students find the process, and to treat students as equals without discriminating between them. Suppose states shut down all universities and create new ones, stipulating that from now on the sole role of academics is to provide value-for-money degrees, matching societal preferences. Such a development would not affect the force of the above arguments. Why so? Once more, we can see here that the role of a teacher relates to certain non-institutional circumstances that place students in a position of dependency. The relation between lecturers and students is characterised by an asymmetry of knowledge which, in turn, makes students dependent in several ways. Students' self-esteem depends on the judgment of their lecturers. They must be able to trust that the information imparted to them is accurate and that they make progress in their learning. This puts them at risk of exploitation, as lecturers may manipulate this trust for personal gain. This risk exists even outside of an institutional context. Much more of course needs to be said about the ethics of teaching. My point here is that the disagreement about the role of an academic targets not a set of institutional facts that everyone knows but the nature of the underlying relation and the moral duties that it triggers.

If the role of an academic were a social kind, it would be difficult to explain the above disagreement. We would have to portray the recent controversies about UK academia as disagreement over what the role of an academic should be. But this would be inaccurate. When I refuse to comply with university ordinances requiring me to exercise immigration control over my students, I take myself to be acting exactly as my current role requires, not the role I wish existed in some ideal world. The fact that most people do not agree with this position hardly affects its intelligibility. Yet massive error is not possible for social kinds, since they do not

[32] UK universities have been included in governmental policies aiming at creating a 'hostile environment' towards migrants. See Melanie Griffiths and Colin Yeo, 'The UK's Hostile Environment: Deputising Immigration Control', 41 (4) *Critical Social Policy* (2021), pp. 521–544.

[33] For criticism of the UK government's approach to higher education see Stefan Collini, *Speaking of Universities* (London: Verso, 2017).

have natural boundaries—that is, boundaries that exist independently of our concepts and attitudes towards them.[34] A person may be in error about what those facts are. If all roles were social kinds, it could not be the case that most of us are mistaken about what a given role requires.[35]

7.5 The Idea of Inherently Normative Roles

The previous section identified three normative phenomena where roles diverge from the ontological model of social kinds. Certain roles can exist and be invoked to justify a set of rights and obligations, without involving any collective intentionality. They can survive the institutional imposition of evil functions and their invocation suffices to exert meaningful moral criticism. They also admit of radical evaluative disagreement about what they require, even when all facts about collective intentionality are known. Taken together, these arguments show that certain roles do not behave like social kinds, flouting Austin's identity thesis. Instead, they are invoked to express a moral judgment about the responsibility of the role-holder, over and above facts about collective intentionality. They function as moralised concepts. But why?

I want to return here to the sea-platform case and the notion of a proto-role. At a first stage, we can imagine that several institutional roles with which we are nowadays familiar across cultures, such as doctors, judges, or teachers, began as proto-roles, like the one in the sea platform example. Consider the role of a doctor. There would have been a time when some person exercised the *de facto* power to treat others' ill-health. Either due to skills and abilities, or due to background factual conditions, that person started to exercise this power regularly, even over people who had little or no choice but to submit to it. For example, a person living on a dangerous path might have started treating regularly those injured trying to cross it, and gradually taken up the proto-role of a doctor. On the other side of the interaction, the injured locals who regularly needed the treatment, having no other option, became that doctor's 'proto-patients', perhaps also seeking advice about their injury after they were treated.

At a second stage, collective practices and institutions started to emerge, and gradually sought to regulate these existing roles, in the mode of collective intentionality. They did so by specifying or adding to the obligations already triggered by the nature of the interaction. But the reference of these types of roles was already

[34] For this argument, see Amie L. Thomasson, 'Realism and Human Kinds', 67 *Philosophy and Phenomenological Research* (2003), pp. 579–609.

[35] I here draw on Dworkin who also appeals to disagreement in order to argue against the positivist view that the determinants of legal content consist in social facts alone. See Dworkin, *Law's Empire*. Dworkin's argument was confined to law, and I extend it here to institutional practices that relate to proto-roles.

fixed at the initial stage, when parties engaged in an asymmetrical interaction, one that necessarily triggers a set of moral rights and obligations between the weaker and the stronger party. The reference was to whatever obligations substantively apply to people in these sorts of interactions.[36] Hence, when role-holders were later expected to engage in immoral tasks (such as doctors required to engage in eugenics), or perform at a level lower than the obligations owed to role-addressees, people could invoke their role as a shorthand for the moral obligations that in fact apply to the stronger party in the relevant interaction.

Not all roles are like that, however. Searle's model of collective intentionality can adequately explain mundane institutional roles, like the role of a Moots Officer, or culture-specific roles like the role of a porter or a concierge of a residential building. There are no pre-institutional settings in which the holders of such roles would have exercise *de facto* power over vulnerable parties. Likewise, the ontological model of social kinds can explain the artificial roles we find in games and sports. Absent facts about collective intentionality there would not be a goalkeeper in football, or a batsman in cricket. These roles are up to us, collectively, to define. Since it is only certain roles that depart from the model of social kinds, I propose that we should distinguish between two kinds of roles: purely institutional roles and what I shall call inherently normative roles.

Purely institutional roles are constructed through a process of collective intentionality, with a view to advance instrumentally certain human goals. These are self-referential in that they pick out whatever obligations and functions we happen to assign to them. Such roles, such as that of the Moots Officer, do not refer to standing social interactions with morally salient characteristics. Crucially, they become binding through voluntary undertakings, such as promise or contract. They typically form part of a large organisational structure which is devoted to the pursuit of a valuable goal and within which many other roles exist. The division of labour between the various organisational roles is largely arbitrary and different ways of carving them up would work just as well.

Inherently normative roles, by contrast, were not created by collective intentionality. Certain circumstances put agents in the position of exercising *de facto* powers over vulnerable agents, such as to adjudicate their disputes (judge), to educate them (teacher), or to care for them (parent). The capacity to affect dependent or vulnerable parties imposed on these agents a set of obligations, which in turn fixed rigidly the reference of these proto-roles. Institutions, after they emerged, did not create these roles by fiat but simply sought to regulate them. The roles retained their inherently normative character because they refer to whatever obligations indeed apply to agents in that set of circumstances. Consider this contrast: there is

[36] I here draw on Saul Kripke's idea of rigid designators and related causal theories of grounding. See Saul Kripke, *Naming and Necessity* (Cambridge: Harvard University Press, 1980), pp. 54–56. For discussion see Joseph Laporte, 'Rigidity and Kind', 97 *Philosophical Studies* (2000), pp. 293–316.

a possible world in which the role of a goalkeeper in soccer is primarily to score goals, rather than save them. But there is no possible world in which the role of a doctor is primarily to end lives, rather than save them. That is why requiring doctors to engage in eugenics appears to us an aberration of their role, and not just morally wrong. To be sure, we can think of doctors who have no patients or who have suspended their practice. But these are borderline cases where it is epistemically unclear whether the relevant capacity will materialise in the future.

If all roles were social kinds, it would be difficult to explain why we often associate normative aspects to roles in ways that seem inherent to them. According to the model of social kinds, roles are collectively imposed 'obligations' whose normativity is external. To invoke a role is simply to invoke the tasks we have collectively assigned on a group of persons. In some cases, however, we invoke the role as a normative standard to condemn those tasks. If all there was to roles was collective intentionality, we would always invoke external normative standards to condemn role-tasks that we find objectionable. The fact that we sometimes do not but, instead, invoke the role itself in order to condemn the institutional practice, suggests that we are appealing to a role whose ontology is independent of institutional facts.

The argument, however, is incomplete without showing what special function is served by moralised roles. Recall that for a concept to be moralised it must both be used to express a moral judgment about someone's responsibility and play a special role in that judgment. It is not clear, however, what special function is served by telling someone that *qua* a doctor, they ought to refuse to act as a salesperson for the drugs industry. If the function is merely to refer to the general moral principles that protect patients against exploitation, then the role of a doctor would serve no special purpose from a moral point of view. It would simply be an elegant way to point out that doctors are subject to moral obligations towards their patients. The judgment could be equally, and perhaps better, expressed by saying that it is wrong to exploit other people's vulnerability with a view to profiting financially, irrespective of whether one holds some social role. For example, a passer-by ought not to extort money from a victim of an accident to call an ambulance. Moreover, is it not clear that the general moral principles which ground the role obligations of doctors not to exploit patients form some distinct subdomain of morality. In fact, on certain relational egalitarian views, the whole of morality is concerned with eliminating the arbitrary exercise of power between people, whatever the relevant interaction.

I want to propose that the special function of moralised roles lies elsewhere. Consider the level of responsibility attached to moralised roles, when contrasted with purely institutionalised roles. In the latter case, the level of responsibility of the role-holder towards others is fixed transactionally, in conjunction with widely shared expectations of what some role involves. A musician is only bound to perform what was agreed with the concert organisers and is generally expected in a music performance. A concierge is only bound to perform tasks that are collectively expected of them (e.g. sign for deliveries) and are specified in their employment contract. Likewise, a Moots Officer has no obligations over and above what went into the administrative job description. It would make no sense to hold these role-holders accountable to a level higher than what was agreed and what is generally expected of them.

By contrast, it makes perfect sense to question the level of responsibility that is currently assigned to doctors or lawyers, even if it matches what they agreed to when they contracted into the role. It is well documented, for instance that the current structures of the medical profession in the United States create monetary incentives for doctors to peddle drugs that might put patients' health at risk.[37] Likewise, lawyers have structural incentives to inflate artificially their billable hours in a way that works at the expense of litigants, particularly those who cannot afford high legal fees. It would be a moral mistake for doctors and lawyers to think in those cases that they are off the moral hook, simply because they operate within the parameters of what is required of them professionally, and what is expected of them socially. A doctor criticised for acting as a salesperson for the big pharmaceutical companies might try to defend themselves by saying: 'I am just doing my job here, breaking no rules; it's what I signed up for and what is expected of me'. But this response does not answer the moral criticism levelled against them. The criticism is that doctors must not exploit patients' vulnerabilities with a view to profiting financially, regardless of whether they will face sanctions (institutional or social) for doing so. By contrast, this type of response is available to the holder of a purely institutional role. A concierge can absolve themselves of any responsibility for the sudden death of a resident by invoking collective intentionality. They can say that *qua* a concierge it is not their role to check residents for health symptoms, even if they could do so. Collective intentionality fixes the limit of their responsibility. By alerting a resident to possible symptoms of a cardiac arrest, a concierge would be acting in a supererogatory manner, in the way that a doctor who refused to profit from pushing unnecessary drugs to patients would not.

The special function of moralised roles is therefore to signal to role-holders when their level of moral responsibility departs from the mode of collective intentionality that characterises purely institutional roles. Sometimes, as in the case of doctors, judges, and teachers, responsibility is fixed by the general moral principles governing the asymmetrical nature of the role-holder's interaction with other parties. It can therefore be higher than what they have voluntarily agreed, or what is expected of them socially. But it can also be lower, in that the institutional tasks assigned to a moralised role may undermine the moral duties of the role-holder, as we saw in the case of academics required to perform immigration enforcement.

[37] See Bradford H. Gray, *The Profit Motive and Patient Care* (Cambridge: Harvard University Press, 1991); Marc A. Rodwin, *Medicine, Money and Morals: Physicians' Conflict of Interest* (Oxford: Oxford University Press, 1993).

The purpose of moralised expressions such as 'but you are doctor! A doctor should never do a thing like that, even if it is allowed by the rules' is to hold role-holders responsible to the appropriate moral standard.

7.6 Statuses as Inherently Normative Roles

I have been using the idea of role-status as a way to capture the fact that people hold a set of rights and duties in virtue of some position they occupy. It is now time to connect the idea of status with that of role obligations. Statuses are roles with inherent normativity. They got off the ground because of an inherent asymmetry in some social interaction, which later solidified into an enduring social relation. As a result, these roles are used as a shorthand for the general obligation to restore a relation of moral equality between the role holder and the role-addressee.

It is the inherent normativity of certain roles, the ones I call role-statuses, that led Hegelians down a wrong path. It is not that social roles, understood as products of collective intentionality, have any moral salience. Nor is it that people tend to identify with them. Rather, it is that certain roles are moral entities in Pufendorf's sense: they ground rights and duties in virtue of the asymmetry of the relation that the role picks out.

It is worth stressing that the normative significance of role-statuses does not derive from the ethical significance of the relevant role. For there needn't be any ethical value in the relation between the role-holder and the role-addressee. To be sure, certain social roles involve associations that instantiate intrinsic ethical goods, such as family or friendship.[38] And other roles, which need not be moralised, facilitate the pursuit of valuable forms of life, such as being a musician or a gardener, through means of self-identification.[39] However, doctors and judges owe obligations to patients and litigants respectively, regardless of whether they identify with their role. A patient may demand, as of right, that a jaded doctor respect their autonomy and asks for informed consent to treatment. Doctors' duties to patients are not grounded on self-identification or personal attachment, even if the presence of these two elements boosts the motivational impetus to carry them out.

More importantly, unlike with intimate relationships or other valuable associations, one has no ethical reason to be some doctor's patient, or some judge's litigant. Health and litigation are mere parameters for pursuing one's conception of the good life. Though an ethically valuable bond may be forged between a patient and a doctor, particularly in cases of prolonged treatment, it is not the point of the

[38] For a defence of associative obligations in terms of relationship goods, see Jonathan Seglow, *Defending Associative Obligations* (London: Routledge, 2013). See also Baril, 'The Ethical Importance of Roles'.

[39] See Sciaraffa, 'Identification, Meaning and the Normativity of Social Roles'.

interaction to create such bonds. Parties, especially the patient, would prefer not to have had that interaction in the first place. I do not mean to deny that associative goods and self-identification have normative significance. They can, for instance, explain the reason one has to fight false accusations about a deceased relative. Such obligations cannot be grounded on some prospective impact on the interests of vulnerable others. But the normativity of associations and self-identification present a different phenomenon to the one I want to elucidate here. An important aspect of role morality is the demand by others that role holders comply with their duties, regardless of their motivational attitudes towards the role. It is that aspect of our practices that the idea of inherently normative roles seeks to explain. Having said that, we should expect that holders of inherently normative roles will identify with their role in the sense that they will appreciate the moral significance of the power they have over vulnerable parties. A committed teacher will take pride in the fact that they do not seek to exploit students for personal gain.

7.7 Objections

One might raise this objection: even if it is correct that social roles grew out of circumstances ('proto-roles') like the ones described in the sea platform hypothetical, as I claimed earlier, these have nothing to do with obligations of role. Acting like a judge is not the same as holding the role of a judge. One can only do the latter, the objection goes, if appointed formally by some institution.

We can certainly see the force of this objection. We are very much accustomed to institutions regulating extensively our social lives. Judicial and other similar roles are regulated heavily by laws, professional bodies, codes of ethics, and the like. But it is not an analytic truth that roles are necessarily institutional kinds. The attribution of the role of a judge in the hypothetical does not stretch the semantic boundaries of the concept. The concept predates the development of legal institutions and the traditional image of the judge with a robe and a gavel. For example, according to ancient Greek mythology, Zeus served as a judge for various disputes among the other gods. The Greeks thought it was intelligible that the judicial role existed before the gods created humans. The ancients, moreover, thought that the whole of morality was role-based, even though they had far fewer institutions than us. It is conceptually possible that role morality preceded the creation of institutions.

There is another reason to think there is no difference in kind between proto-roles and heavily institutionalised roles. The literature on role obligations emphasises that the existence of a package of rights and obligations is the most central conceptual feature of roles. The set of obligations which obtains in the sea-platform hypothetical is the same as that of the institutional office of a judge, as we know it from advanced legal systems: impartiality, duty to hear both sides, duty to provide reasons for one's decision, and so on. The case meets a necessary condition for the existence of the judicial role. So, the objection under consideration must be that this condition is necessary, yet not sufficient: social recognition of the role and its obligations is an additional necessary condition. This second condition, however, is much more contentious. It seems conceptually hard to imagine roles without a set of normative functions.[40] But it is not hard to imagine a judicial role that has not been institutionally created. Just because certain roles are nowadays heavily institutionalised does not mean that they cannot exist outside that context. It would beg the question to assume otherwise.

A second, related, objection is John Austin's one from occultness. What are roles if not the product of collective intentionality? To claim that some roles are moralised entities seems to suggest that there might be roles that we have not yet discovered, or are unbeknownst to most of us. However, we saw earlier that the ontology of inherently normative roles is not some mystical quality. It consists in complex factual circumstances where an agent acquires the capacity to affect vital interests of dependent or vulnerable parties. These circumstances are no less naturalistic than those surrounding the process of collective intentionality which creates purely institutional roles. The difference is that the relevant social facts are not picked out by collective mental states. They are, instead, singled out by the normative principles that apply to the relevant set of circumstances. We will immediately realise that the circumstances of treating a person's ill-health, or judging disputes that affect vital interests, are morally significant and trigger a complex set of obligations. And it is because of that realisation that collective processes of regulation will gradually develop, singling out the agents involved as institutional role-holders. It is therefore unlikely, if not impossible, that moralised roles will exist without any social recognition.[41] The crucial point is that the process of institutional regulation is an epiphenomenon: it does not create the relevant role. It is, however, worth pointing out that institutional regulation may in principle affect the content of the obligations of inherently normative roles. I have so far argued that it fails to do so when it imposes evil tasks, or tasks that fall short of the role-holder's responsibility. But when collective intentionality specifies the relevant role obligations in a way compatible with the underlying moral principles, then it can have a normative impact. This would be the case, for example, when doctors are institutionally required to follow a protocol that ensures that patients have given informed consent.

[40] I take this to be close to an analytic truth about roles, in the sense that little, if any, argument is needed to support it. As Searle notes, even honorific roles entail a set of privileges with respect to how others should refer to the role-holder. It is possible of course to be interested in social roles in non-normative terms, as a way to predict behaviour, like some sociologists do. See the discussion in B. J. Biddle, 'Recent Developments in Role Theory', 12 *Annual Review of Sociology* (1986), pp. 67–92. But even then, it is the obligatoriness of the role (real or perceived) which is used as a proxy for predicting behaviour.

[41] This explains, I think, the appeal of philosophical traditions that prioritise social ontology over moral questions about responsibility. As is often the case in philosophy, these traditions capture a significant truth about the relevant phenomena, even when they unduly extend the scope of their claim.

The protocol may introduce details regarding the form, time, and place of giving consent, which would not directly be grounded on the abstract duty not to exploit patients. A doctor could carry out that role obligation even without following the protocol. However, the fact that these more concrete duties are reasonable ways to carry out the abstract duties of the role holder, and to ensure coordination and consistency across different doctors, explains why they would also become morally binding on doctors.[42]

Finally, it might be objected that I have underplayed the significance of voluntary undertakings as the ground of role obligations. Doctors and judges typically sign employment contracts and take oaths. They are not forced to take up the role. And so one might insist that even if the content of their obligations is not entirely determined by what they have agreed, they cannot acquire role obligations absent that agreement. The objection, however, fails to distinguish between the following two questions. The first is whether it is morally permissible to force a person to occupy a role. The second is whether a person occupying that role has a set of obligations *qua* a role holder. The two questions are distinct. Consider the following example. A state may impose, through criminal sanctions, that a certain number of school graduates go to medical school and, upon graduating, work as doctors in the public sector. Clearly, it is morally wrong in this case to force people to take up a particular profession against their will, at least on the assumption that enough people will normally choose to train as doctors and perform this public service. But it does not follow that these doctors do not have the standard duties owed to patients, such as respect their autonomy, or ask for informed consent to treatment. This is because these duties are triggered by the power they exercise over vulnerable parties in the relevant interaction, even if the interaction is forced on their part. The situation would be different, however, if the role was a purely institutional one. Suppose, to use the same analogy, that the state forces me to train and work as a musician. Unlike the case of the doctor, I would have no role obligations, such as to practise music or perform in concerts. I would, at best, have only prudential reasons to do these things.

7.8 Conclusion

Though it is difficult to downplay the significance of social roles in our lives, it is not easy to identify how they affect our moral profile. A long tradition in moral philosophy, which has long ceased to be dominant, treated them as the axiomatic

[42] The process by which institutional action or societal expectations may qualify the obligations of inherently normative roles are of course more complex than that and I have no space to explore this issue here. Suffices to say that the normative impact of these social facts will be determined by the abstract moral duties of the role-holder, duties that exist independently of collective intentionality.

basis of morality. Later, more liberal, autonomy-based, treatments of role morality confined it to the value of self-identifying with roles or associations that have some ethical significance. Both these traditions have treated roles as the product of collective intentionality, created and sustained by a complex practice of beliefs, attitudes, rules, expectations, and the like.

In this chapter, I have tried to show that not all roles are socially created in this way. Some roles (such as being a doctor, a teacher, or a judge), what I have been calling in this book role-statuses, are moralised. They are not thick concepts in Bernard William's sense because they do not incorporate culturally specific information.[43] They got off the ground as proto-roles, when agents exercised *de facto* control over vulnerable or dependent parties, triggering a set of moral rights and duties. When this control became enduring, and non-contingent, institutions and social norms sought to regulate them; but they do not create them from scratch. When these roles are used by way of moral criticism, they depart from the model of collective intentionality that characterises other, purely institutional roles. The special function these inherently normative roles plays is to signal that the responsibility of the role-holder may diverge from what they have agreed to undertake, or what is socially expected of them. As argued in Chapter 5, these role-holders are not free to determine at will the terms of their relation.

[43] For the distinction between thin and thick concepts, see Bernard Williams, *Ethics and the Limits of Philosophy* (Cambridge: Harvard University Press, 1985). I am grateful to David Enoch for bringing the relevance of this distinction to my attention.

8
TITLES AND THE SOCIAL RECOGNITION OF STATUS

8.1 Introduction

In this chapter, I bring the account I developed to bear on how titles can be used to serve role-status and rank-status. Recall that both rank-status and role-status relate to social recognition. Rank-status is a descriptive notion, denoting a hierarchy of social esteem, created by societal beliefs about which personal characteristics merit esteem. Role-status, by contrast, is a normative notion that requires legal and social recognition of one's vulnerable position within certain relations. Titles, as an institutional good, can be used to recognise both rank-status and role-status. In this chapter I examine the practice of awarding honours through honorific titles, as well as the practice of using terms of address for certain professions (e.g. 'Dr' or 'Professor') and public offices (e.g. 'Justice' or 'Senator'). This chapter is mainly 'applied' moral and political philosophy, looking at the relevant practices in the UK and the United States. But the premises of the argument I seek to make are universal: there is no individual moral right to be publicly esteemed and the government should stay out of the business of interfering with the public ecology of societal esteem. By contrast, the government ought to create, recognise, and police the use of titles for role-holders within status relations.

8.2 The Main Question

If, like me, you have booked a flight through the British Airways website, you cannot fail to notice the long list of available titles from which to choose: Mr, Mrs, Miss, Ms, Mstr, Captain, Prof, Dr, Dame, Lady, Lord, The Rt Hon, Rabbi, Rev, Sir, Baroness, Baron, Viscount, and Viscountess. You might think this list is slightly over the top, particularly if you haven't been raised in the UK. But it is nothing compared to the list of choices provided by the luxury department store, Fortnum & Mason. Its list includes HE (His/Her Excellency), HRH (His/Her Royal Highness), Marquess, Marchioness, His/Her Hon Judge, and The Hon Mr/Mrs/Ms Justice. It also includes most ranks within the army (from Lieutenant all the way to General), as well as the church (from Priest to 'The Venerable'). EasyJet, by contrast, only offer Mr/Mrs/Ms/Miss, while Morrisons and Iceland just add 'Dr'.

Status in Law and Morality. George Letsas, Oxford University Press. © George Letsas 2026.
DOI: 10.1093/9780198936725.003.0008

Apart from an indication of the shopping habits of these esteemed individuals, the list reveals a few things about contemporary attitudes towards honour and respect. Unlike other countries,[1] Britain has not abolished hereditary nobility titles. Remarkably, 92 hereditary peers (i.e. dukes, earls, and marquesses) still sit in the House of Lords (the number was 750 until the Labour government's reform in 1999). But the UK honours system has evolved to recognise merit rather than birth lineage, such as an individual's service, achievement, or bravery.[2] It does so through the annual award of honours by the government, such as knighthoods, damehoods, OBEs (Officer of the Order of the British Empire), and MBEs (Member of the Order of the British Empire). Titles are also used for those holding public office on a non-hereditary basis, such as appointed members of the House of Lords (Lord/Lady),[3] elected members of the House of Commons (Rt Hon), ambassadors, the judiciary, and the army. Finally, titles are used—not just in the UK but in most countries—in the case of two professions, at least one of which is esteemed universally: medical doctors (Dr) and academics (Professor/Dr). By 'honorific' titles I mean to refer generically to all the above titles, even if—as I will try to show—some of them should not be understood as honorific in substance.

It should be uncontroversial that any state-sponsored recognition of noble lineage, let alone one that comes with legal privileges, is incompatible with our contemporary commitment to the value of human equality. But it is far from obvious how egalitarian societies should regulate the use of titles in other cases. Does individual merit, properly understood, warrant the use of a title? Should the holding of certain public offices (e.g. Member of Parliament, the judiciary, and ambassadors) or certain professions (e.g. doctors and academics) be adorned with a title? I am not asking whether an egalitarian society ought to recognise and reward merit, though this is certainly an important background issue. I want to ask, instead, whether whatever role merit plays in an egalitarian society, it ought to include the exclusive use of an accompanying title. We might agree that the best lawyers should be appointed to the bench, and the best scientists and athletes should be recognised for their service and achievements by the relevant associations and professional bodies. But this is not yet an argument in favour of imposing a duty on the rest of us to refer to these individuals as Lord, Lady, Dame, or Sir.

The question I aim to pursue might appear trivial, but it is not. Titles have a specific historical provenance. We have inherited them from pre-modern,

[1] Several countries have legislative or constitutional provisions that abolish or prohibit hereditary nobility titles, or nobility titles in general. Among them are Germany, Austria, Hungary, Greece, and the United States.

[2] This practice is hardly new in one respect. Since very early on, nobility titles would also be granted for various acts of service to the monarch, including raising funds. See Jonathan Dewald, *The European Nobility, 1400–1800* (Cambridge: Cambridge University Press, 1996).

[3] One should distinguish between titles and accompanying terms of address. Upon appointment to the House of Lords, one acquires the title of Baron/Baroness, but is addressed as Lord/Lady. Other titles (such as Professor) function pre-nominally as both titles and terms of address.

honour-based, monarchical cultures, founded on the morally objectionable notions of hierarchy and rank. Whether they can be redeployed to serve the values of an egalitarian society is not obvious. Titles have a distinct social ontology. They project the need for deference in social interactions. A damehood or a knighthood is not simply an honour conferred on a person, like a medal or a trophy. They come with the expectation that the title holder will be treated with deference in all their dealings with others, treated, that is, as more worthy of respect than others. Whether we have a moral reason—or even a duty—to do so, through using the respective honorific title, is what interests me here. My focus will be on the UK, but the account is meant to be general and applicable to any country that has an honour system of awarding titles.

Before I start, I should declare a conflict of interest. I use my academic titles and expect others, both students and third parties, to acknowledge them. I click on either 'Prof' or 'Dr' on the British Airways website and, like so many colleagues with a PhD, dread the confusion with a medical doctor (a 'real' doctor) in case of an emergency. Clearly, I am not the most unbiased person to write on this topic. The argument I will put forward will seek to defend the use of titles for judges, legislators, and medical doctors, but argue against honorific titles used for service or achievement. I will also be sceptical about whether professors should be using their title outside an academic context. As you might suspect, I do not hold a knighthood or other such honour, but several of my colleagues do, and I mean no offence to any of them. I simply aim to explore our collective moral responsibility for the existence of an honour system of titles, not that of individual title holders.

8.3 Titles as Positional Institutional Goods

We should first distinguish between honorific titles and non-honorific titles. Some titles are purely descriptive, denoting one's profession, employment, or position within an organization; they do not necessarily express high societal esteem towards the holder of the title. One may, for instance, have the job title of a management consultant, a nurse, or a bank trader, and take pride in it. At university, one may be a moots officer. Society, of course, will inevitably place a differential degree of esteem on everyone's profession, from high (say judge) to low (say rubbish collector), creating an informal ranking of esteem. This can be gauged anecdotally, through conversation, or through opinion polls. But it is not the primary aim of regular job titles to denote high societal esteem on the part of society. By contrast, the point of honorific titles is precisely to elevate the holder to a high rank of societal esteem. How exactly titles achieve this will be explored shortly. First, I want to draw attention to the fact that most honorific titles also serve as, or correspond with, terms of address. This syntactic particularity is far from normatively inert.

Consider the fictional case of Jo Doe. If Jo Doe qualifies as a medical doctor, they will not only possess the qualification of a doctor, but also, they will be addressed as 'Dr Doe' by others. If Dr Doe later becomes a professor of medicine, they will not only possess the title of a professor but will also be addressed as 'Professor Doe'.[4] If Professor Doe is subsequently appointed to the House of Lords, they will not only possess the title of a Baron or Baroness, but also be addressed as 'Lord Doe' or 'Lady Doe'. And finally, if Jo Doe is awarded a knighthood for their contribution to medical science, they will be addressed as 'Sir Jo' or 'Dame Jo'. They will also be able to combine titles when used pre-nominally (e.g. Professor Dame Jo Doe), and while in Germany, they will be able to sign as 'Prof. Dr Jo Doe' (not done in the UK).

But how do these pre-nominal titles communicate the presence of high societal esteem? Titles, particularly when accompanied by terms of address,[5] are an institutional way of creating a positional good.[6] A good is positional when the main, or the only, reason why people desire it, is the widely known fact that not everyone who desires it can have it. They are status symbols. For example, a lot of people buy land in prime location, paintings by famous artists, or more recently NFTs,[7] mainly because many people want them but only few can have them. The known scarcity of the good is a factor that boosts its desirability, often to the point of vanity where it is desired *only* because few or only one person (e.g. in the case of a famous painting) can have it.

The scarcity of positional goods can be biological (stunning looks), material (diamonds, or land in prime location), or institutional. Institutional positional goods, however, are distinctive because of the way in which intentionality is involved in the creation of the good. Institutions, such as the army or the university, create statuses and then typically rank them. Generals sit at the top, colonels in the middle, and lieutenants at the bottom. Similarly for Professors, Readers, and Lecturers. Institutional ranks are nowadays created and distributed—at least in theory—based on merit-based criteria, such as performance or experience. But this was not always the norm and certainly not with nobility titles granted by the institution of monarchy. What is crucial, however, is that even under merit-based criteria, an equally competent individual will not be able to hold the relevant rank without institutional recognition. The most experienced and competent

[4] About a decade or so ago, the UK academic ranking system (Lecturer/Senior Lecturer/Reader/Professor) started to move to the US one of Assistant Professor/Associate Professor/(Full) Professor. Some Assistant and Associate professors then started using their title as a term of address (e.g. 'Professor Doe, Assistant Professor of Medicine'). Unsurprisingly, this did not go down very well with those holding chairs. In the United States, by contrast, anyone teaching a class is addressed as professor.

[5] Not all honours serve as address terms. OBEs and MBEs do not, for instance. Similarly with Fellowships of the British Academy (FBA), or the Nobel Prize. These honours are used as post-nominals, e.g. 'Joe Doe, FBA', or 'Jo Doe, Nobel Laureate'.

[6] For the notion of a positional good, see the discussion in Chapter 4.

[7] Non-Fungible Tokens (NFTs) are digital works of art that are unique or of a limited number, being a token on a blockchain.

combatant can be a General only if recognised by the army as a General. Likewise, the best expert in a particular field of research can be a professor only if recognised by an established university as a professor. Only institutions can award titles and create corresponding hierarchies of esteem.[8]

We can shed more light on the institutional dimension of titles by looking at philosophical work on social ontology. Titles, and social statuses more broadly, are social kinds. They are neither natural entities, nor moral concepts. They can be seen as a particular instance of a social kind that John Searle calls *institutional kinds*.[9] As discussed in the previous chapter, Searle's account links statuses with functions. On his view, all social kinds are dependent on facts involving collective intentionality, such as beliefs, attitudes, desires, intentions, and so on. We construct social kinds by agreeing collectively to impose a point or purpose on brute physical objects, or on persons. Objects which meet certain conditions (e.g. have a flat surface, a back and four legs) are chairs whose purpose is to be used as a seat.[10] In the case of institutional kinds, Searle calls these purposes 'status-functions'. A status exists when institutions agree that people who meet certain conditions (e.g. have had training and passed certain exams) acquire a status (e.g. Medical Doctor) with certain functions (e.g. to treat common medical conditions). Searle believes that institutional statuses exist in part because they are *believed* to exist.

Searle moves on to note, rightly, that the collective imposition of a function on persons differs crucially from the imposition of a function on artefacts. In the case of artefacts, like chairs, the function is causal—that is, the object's properties (shape and height) are such that they enable it physically to be used as a seat. By contrast, in the case of institutional statuses the function is normative: Doctors have normative powers (to prescribe medication), responsibilities (to provide urgent treatment), permissions (to ask and store sensitive medical information) and so on. We do not use a chair in the same way we use a doctor. Since the collective imposition of a function on physical phenomena is what it means for a social kind to exist, the status of a doctor is not separate from the related obligations. Rather, the above package of normative powers *is* the status of the doctor.

I do not think that Searle's account, however, fully captures the nature of honorific titles, as distinct from professional and other statuses.[11] Honorific titles nowadays need not involve any functions attached to them. Someone can hold an honorific title (e.g. a Marquis), as many still do in Britain, without having any

[8] This is not to deny that communal beliefs can also create social hierarchies, through the use of laudatory or derogatory terms about specific groups, based on class, gender, race, or other criteria.

[9] John Searle, *The Construction of Social Reality* (Free Press, 1995).

[10] Searle treats this phenomenon as an instance of a special kind of rules, which he calls 'constitutive', and which have the logical form 'X counts as Y in context C'.

[11] In *The Construction of Social Reality*, Searle does discuss honorific and symbolic roles as a seemingly deviant case where there is an imposition of status but without any assignment of normative powers. He concludes that these are in fact special cases of normative powers, where certain honorific ways of referring to the status holder are licensed or become obligatory. I think he is right that honorific

role or responsibilities in virtue of holding that title. Historically however, from the Middle Ages to early modernity, social statuses came with normative functions. Society was divided in roughly three classes ('estates'), each having separate functions: clergy, farmers and merchants, and nobility. The main function of nobility initially was to fight wars and protect the kingdom. Knighthood wasn't merely a title; it was also a job description. Later, it involved the running of large estates and the employing of workers. And within these functions, came several legal privileges.[12]

Yet to be a nobleperson was more than to have a set of tasks, responsibilities, duties, legal privileges, and the like. These functions came with an additional layer of institutional and social norms, whose aim was to communicate publicly that the nobility status was higher in esteem than the other two estates, and the highest in society. These norms included titles and terms of address ('My Lord'), norms of etiquette (e.g. bowing when greeting), norms around attire (wigs), accent, paraphernalia, and so on. And these were heavily marked by their public character: nobles did not just enjoy institutional privileges and high social status; they had to be *seen* to do so in the public sphere, with pomp and circumstance. It is a mark of an honorific title that it is not only used as post-nominal qualification but also accompanied by a term of address. This is precisely because the holder's high esteem must be communicated publicly and, by so doing, create or reproduce a social hierarchy of esteem. By using honorific titles, monarchical institutions created a scarce good (the official recognition of esteem or honour[13]), decided which statuses should have it, and ensured that it is projected to the public (through terms of address). By doing so, they typically succeeded in making it the case that the public esteems that status accordingly.[14] To put it crudely, honorific titles (along with other similar norms) are a top-down way to create and reproduce hierarchies of social esteem. The hierarchy consists in structured relations between citizens within which some citizens are publicly perceived to be inferior to others.

It is worth emphasising here that honorific titles, even when awarded on the basis of merit, could not achieve their purpose if everyone was free to use them. If everyone were to be addressed as Sir and Dame, then the honour associated with receiving a knighthood would evaporate. When titles lose their positional character, they are no longer carriers of esteem. This is what happened when the

titles are meant to have this normative effect on how holders are addressed. But, as I will seek to explain, honorific statuses differ substantially from other institutional statuses.

[12] A nobleperson had the right to sue a commoner for defamation, but a commoner lacked such right. For discussion of the so-called scandalum magnatum see Jeremy Waldron, *Dignity, Rank and Rights* (Oxford: Oxford University Press, 2012).

[13] Honour is an ambiguous term, which can be used to denote a rigid code of ethics used customarily by a particular group (e.g. 'honour killings'). I use it here to mean esteem or, in Darwall's sense, appraisal respect.

[14] They do not always succeed of course, as the example of the French Revolution shows.

honorific terms 'Master' and 'Mistress' evolved gradually from expressing honour to denoting everyone's marital status (Mr and Mrs)[15] and are nowadays used mainly to mark the formality of an occasion rather than the relative esteem of a person. There are also some important differences between the positionality of honorific titles and the positionality of expensive goods, such as land in prime location or luxury cars. Both honorific titles and money are institutional kinds. But in the latter case, the relevant institutions (i.e. the Bank of England and the market) do not distribute money with a view to awarding an honour. Rich people are widely esteemed, particularly if they have earned their fortune rather than inherited it and have shown some skill in the process. But the primary aim of a market economy is to distribute wealth rather than honour, even if typically, the outcome of market transactions will make the winners the object of societal esteem. Being wealthy is not a title, nor is there a pre-nominal term of address for rich people.[16] I will return to the comparison between honour and wealth in the next section.

8.4 Honorific Titles and Their Relation to Hierarchy and Deference

The preceding analysis helps to explain why the social meaning of honorific titles is linked to objectionable attitudes of social deference or even servility. A Baron or a Baroness is not just someone who may have a set of functions attached to an esteemed status—for example, fighting wars in pre-modern times or sitting in the House of Lords nowadays. It is someone who must be addressed publicly as 'Lord' or 'Lady' with a view to projecting (and in part constituting) their higher societal rank of esteem relative to others. The public use of the title is meant to remind everybody that there is a running order of societal esteem and to consider their place within it. This should not be taken as a natural condition of human societies. Even if we accept Hobbes's view that humans have a natural disposition to seek glory, it does not follow that institutions should seek to manage and distribute it in an official, top-down way, let alone make it relevant to social interactions between people. People may have a vague sense of a ranking of esteem in their society without finding it relevant to the way they interact with others. Honorific titles, and especially pre-nominal terms of address, aim to make a ranking of esteem relevant to how people should interact in the public sphere. But relevant how? Well, I want to argue, by calling for deference on the part of those who rank lower. This is clearly the case when an honours system uses, as the UK one does, the nobility titles that we have inherited from inegalitarian, status-based monarchies. But I am

[15] This was the case for both men and women. See Amy Louise Erickson, 'Mistresses and Marriage, or a Short History of the Mrs', 78(1) *History Workshop Journal* (2014), pp. 39–57.

[16] Some businesses think they can achieve this by labelling their expensive products for 'VIPs', which mainly invites ridicule.

very much tempted to think that when there is social pressure to use any official honorific title, even a made-up one with no odious past, it necessarily communicates the need for social deference. I make no case of this stronger claim here, however, as it is not necessary for the argument.

The social deference that honorific titles trigger can be mild (e.g. one lets the esteemed person speak first or long, with no interruptions, nodding in agreement or holds the door for them), moderate (one offers to do more for them than what is the norm in the circumstances, or lets them jump the queue) or severe, reaching the point of servility (e.g. running errands for them or providing free services).

Note that I am not saying that every time a person addresses the holder of an honorific title, they *necessarily* feel or behave in that way. I am saying, instead, that it is the logic of honorific titles to create this hierarchy and to shape social interactions accordingly. In the typical case, they succeed even if a significant number of people may privately oppose the background hierarchy, or harbour contempt for the person holding the title. Recall, moreover, that the honorific titles in which I am interested do not denote the grounds for which the person was taken to merit the award. One may be awarded a knighthood for excelling in all kinds of activities or, in case of corruption or poor judgment, none.

I should also clarify that I am not making an argument against honorific titles on the basis that the practice has become corrupt and rarely places esteem where esteem should be placed. Clearly, there have been glaring cases of poor judgment and corruption in the UK. Consider the 'cash for honours scandal' of 2006 or Boris Johnson's resignation honours, just to name a couple of examples. My argument should stand even if the practice is not corrupt and the government does a fairly good job identifying meritorious recipients.

To summarise: honorific titles are a special instance of an institutional positional good for three reasons. First, their purpose is not simply to create a scarce institutional good but to manipulate the way in which society places esteem on different people and to effect publicly a social hierarchy of esteem. Second, unlike professional statuses, honorific titles can be detached from any functions that the person must carry out in virtue of holding it. The title 'Dr' is necessarily attached to the functions of a medic. But the titles 'Sir or Dame' and pre-nominal terms of address (Lord/Lady) can be awarded on a person irrespective of their status and its functions, or indeed irrespective of whether they have any. And third, honorific titles have a public dimension in that their point is to shape the way people interact socially, by calling for deference towards the holder of the title.

8.5 The Instrumental Argument: John Adams and Montesquieu

After the United States gained independence from Great Britain, Founding Father John Adams thought that the newly established office of the President needed to be made 'dignified and respectable' in the eyes of the nation. When a debate arose at the Senate about the title of the new office, Adams proposed that the US President be addressed as 'His Highness the President of the United States of America and Protector of the Rights of the Same'. The proposal was met with ridicule by fellow revolutionaries, who could not comprehend why Adams would seek to attach a title of European royalty to a republican office. Royal and nobility titles were after all largely hereditary, a central feature of the inegalitarian, status-based, monarchies of Europe. And the US Constitution, like so many other post-revolution constitutions in Europe, prohibited explicitly the granting of nobility titles.[17] Adams was accused of harbouring anti-republican tendencies and even betraying the ideals of the revolution.

Yet Adams's defence of titles was interesting and certainly not anti-republican in spirit.[18] He thought that republics face a two-fold difficulty. First, how to motivate citizens, particularly the most talented and competent ones, to hold public office and to serve the public good. And second, how to prevent the ill-effects of avarice, where citizens only care about money and wealth. As Montesquieu before him, Adams thought that the European tradition of nobility, and the related notions of honour and dignity, performed a valuable function, that of creating an elite and directing its actions towards the public good. It was part of the status of a knight, for example, to fight heroically in wars. The practice of nobility achieved this, on this hypothesis, by exploiting people's natural passion for distinction and status. One would not self-sacrifice for money or wealth. But one would do it if that is what the honour of holding a particular title requires.

Montesquieu, however, thought that honour was unique to monarchies. According to his typology of systems of government,[19] republics were founded on civic *virtue*, despotic regimes on *fear*, and monarchies on *honour*. This typology was based on the motives and attitudes of political actors, which Montesquieu thought play a pivotal role in sustaining the regime. In republics, which have a smaller population, citizens are motivated by their love of country and love of equality. They are not self-interested, nor do they have personal ambitions. In monarchies, these motives are replaced by a system of honour based on 'preeminences', 'ranks', and 'distinctions' where 'each person works for the common good, believing he works for his individual interests'.[20] By having an institutional honours system, monarchies could exploit people's self-interested motivation for glory to serve the common good. This, Montesquieu thought, was an astonishing

[17] See Article I, Section 9, Clause 8 (The Foreign Emoluments Clause): 'No Title of Nobility shall be granted by the United States.'

[18] I here draw heavily on Luke Mayville, *John Adams and the Fear of American Oligarchy* (Princeton: Princeton University Press, 2016).

[19] Montesquieu, *The Spirit of the Laws*, translated by A. M. Cohler, B. C. Miller, and H. S. Stone (New York: Cambridge University Press, 1989).

[20] Ibid., p. 27.

institutional mechanism: 'Is it not impressive that one can oblige men to do all the difficult actions and which require force, with no reward other than the renown of these actions?'[21]

I shall call this the *instrumental argument* for an honours system. It relies on the following premises. First, people have a natural disposition to desire to be esteemed by others and to seek praise and glory. Second, this desire can be harnessed institutionally, and be suppressed or exploited. Third, an honours system can adequately motivate citizens to serve the common good, by exploiting this disposition, and do so to the same extent as egalitarian attitudes like civic virtue. And fourth, it is permissible to use an honours system insofar as it promotes the common good.

Contrary to Montesquieu, however, John Adams thought that this argument should apply with greater force to large-scale republics. His worry was that in large-scale republics, unlike say Athens or Rome, it is hard to cultivate attitudes of civic virtue and to suppress self-interested motives; pursuit of self-interest is more likely to dominate citizens' motivating reasons. And if not reorientated towards the common good, self-interest will be directed towards money and wealth and inevitably corrupt the politics of the common good.

Does this sound familiar? It is tempting here to compare the contemporary state of politics in the United States and the UK and think that there might be something to John Adams's argument. British politics, one might think, has been bad in the last decade or so, but not as bad as US politics. President Trump may be the type of politician that Adams had in mind when he proposed a title as a way to cultivate civil virtue and suppress self-interested motives—to put it mildly. And perhaps the residual monarchical character of the British establishment has something to do with the relative resilience the British political system shows to populism. Perhaps the unelected Monarch and the unelected second chamber of the UK Constitution serve as a better 'check and balance' than the US Senate and the US Supreme Court. Perhaps the 'Right Honourable' members of the House of Commons are more likely to be resilient to populism and less likely to be corrupted by money than US politicians. Or perhaps, awarding a knighthood to an exceptional athlete, like Mo Farah, an immigrant who was trafficked illegally to the UK, helps to curb the public's xenophobic sentiments, and inspire other immigrants to pursue excellence. I can only speculate.

To be sure, this speculation rests on a idealised picture of British politics and an overly bleak picture of US politics. The hypothesis is empirical and difficult to test. We cannot know if the United States would never have the current President if the office was addressed as 'His Highness'. Perhaps this title would have attracted an even worse candidate. True, there is significant sociological research showing that desire for status is a powerful human disposition, and that, unlike desire for power

[21] Ibid.

or wealth, it never plateaus: the more one has the more one wants.[22] But the effect of people's desire for status in society and different types of institutional arrangements and modes of governance is much harder, if not impossible, to ascertain. I certainly do not intend to challenge the empirical premises of the instrumental argument here. Instead, let us assume that a system of honours can have the instrumental benefit that Montesquieu and Adams envisaged, and many more in addition. Perhaps, for instance, honours help sustain excellence in science, arts, and humanities, through competition, as Rousseau thought.[23] Assuming there are such benefits, I want to ask whether an honours system, as it exists in the UK and other countries, is compatible with the values of a modern-day liberal democracy. Can an egalitarian society 'mix-and-match'? Can its constitution be based on equal civil liberties and equal rights to political participation, yet create a ranking of societal esteem with a view to exploiting, for the common good, people's desire for status?

8.6 Is There a Moral Right to Be Publicly Esteemed?

I want to start by explaining further why I labelled the argument above instrumental. I have in mind here the familiar deontological contrast between instrumental and rights-based justifications for governmental action.[24] Government may adopt a policy, like subsidies or tax cuts, on the basis that it promotes the common good. No one, however, has an individual right that such a policy be adopted and there are usually other ways that the common good can be served. Rights-based considerations, by contrast, justify governmental action (or omission) on the basis that the failure to take the action would morally *wrong* a person. For instance, it would be wrong for a government to deport immigrants to a country in which they are likely to be subjected to torture (the principle of *non-refoulement*). The principle is not justified by its contribution to the common good but by the fact that it would constitute a directed moral wrong to a person. Moreover, rights-based considerations often conflict with the pursuit of the common good. It could be, for instance, that the principle of non-refoulement results in an increased risk to public safety and national security. But this would be insufficient to justify violating the right to non-refoulement. Instrumental justifications are therefore weaker, in that rights-based justifications always prevail in case of conflict. To use another familiar example from law: individuals have a right to be presumed innocent in the course of a criminal trial, even if substantially more criminal wrongdoers would be convicted without the presumption.

[22] Cecilia Ridgeway, *Status: Why Is It Everywhere? Why Does It Matter* (New York: Russell Sage Foundation, 2019).

[23] See Jean Jacques Rousseau, *Second Discourse on Inequality* (London: Penguin Books, 1984).

[24] I here draw on Dworkin's distinction between principle and policy. See Ronald Dworkin, 'Hard Cases', 88(6) *Harvard Law Review* (1975), pp. 1057–1109.

Now, before I argue that an honours system, even when based on merit, conflicts with rights-based considerations, I want to take some time to discuss why there is no such thing as a *moral right to a title*. This is not Montesquieu's argument,[25] but the culture of monarchies was certainly premised on the thought that nobility was 'entitled'[26] to enjoy their honours. And historically there has been a *legal* right to a title in various instantiations of the institution of monarchy. It was an offence, for instance, to impersonate a member of the nobility.[27] This idea, of course, seems preposterous to most of us nowadays and rightly so. One's birth lineage is a morally arbitrary feature and incapable of grounding any moral claims, let alone claims for preferential treatment or privilege. However, the UK's contemporary honours system now tracks merit and just not birth lineage. And so, one might argue that, if someone merits an honour, then that person has a moral right to it. For instance, one might argue that the winner of a league has a right to the championship title. Or that Mahatma Gandhi had a right to win the Nobel Prize for peace, for which he was nominated unsuccessfully five times. And everyone knows of course of a colleague who clearly merited to be promoted to a chair and was not. We often refer to such cases as an injustice, which indicates the presence of a wrong.

I think we should distinguish, however, between the right that certain positions, qualifications, or opportunities be awarded on the basis of merit and the right to an honour, such as an honorific title. Clearly, the former sense of a right involves broader questions about the nature of justice and the place of merit, or desert within it. Meritocrats hold that at least part of justice is desert-based and that a number of positions (e.g. jobs or university places), or resources (e.g. income) within a just state should be awarded on that basis. They differ substantially over the scope of application of merit-based criteria and what it means to allocate something on the basis of merit. Meritocratic arguments have been subject to powerful criticisms on various grounds[28] and it is not possible to do justice to this literature here. The extent to which any theory of justice will accommodate merit-based criteria depends on its general background commitments.

What I want to point out, instead, is that merit-based arguments for distribution involve goods that, under a given theory, it is legitimate for the government to distribute, such as income, wealth, education, or employment. A person may have

[25] Though Montesquieu did suggest that honours were only appropriate for (hereditary) nobility. It is not clear though whether this was because he thought nobility was socially conditioned to seek honour in way that other classes weren't.

[26] The etymological link between titles and entitlement is not, of course, accidental.

[27] In England, the Court of Chivalry was established in the seventeenth century with jurisdiction over matter of heraldry, including rank. In the case of *De La Ware v West* (1636) the defendant was fined £500 for impersonating a member of the nobility. See Richard Crust, *Charles I and the Aristocracy* (Cambridge, Cambridge University Press, 2013), ch. 3.

[28] See indicatively, John Rawls, *A Theory of Justice* (Cambridge, Harvard University Press, 1971); Elizabeth Anderson, 'What Is the Point of Equality', 109(2) *Ethics* (1999), pp. 287–337; Daniel Markovits, *The Meritocracy Trap* (Penguin Books, 2019); Michael Sandel, *The Tyranny of Merit* (New York: Farrar, Straus and Giroux, 2020).

a merit-based claim to be admitted to a very competitive medical school based on their grades, or exam performance. This, however, is not the same as the claim to be *esteemed or admired* for deserving that good. Government need not take any view as to how estimable it is to study medicine or become a doctor, compared to other, less competitive, degrees or indeed compared to not going to university. Or, government may publicly project *equal* esteem to all degrees, celebrating the achievement of everyone who completed secondary education. So even if there is a merit-based right to a resource or a good, it does not entail a right to be esteemed for deserving that good, unless esteem itself is a good that government may legitimately distribute.

Can esteem be the object of a right that the government may distribute? There are serious problems with this suggestion. From a first-personal perspective, esteem has emotive aspects which, like love or affection, cannot be demanded by others as of right. Nobody has a right that others *feel* admiration for them. At best, the putative right is the right to the *expression* of esteem, even if it is not sincerely felt. The more serious problem, however, is the one identified by Stephen Darwall in his well-known account of morality as second-personal standpoint and his distinction between recognition-respect and appraisal-respect. Darwall insists on the discrepancy between morality and status-determining attitudes like esteem, annoyance, or contempt.[29] He calls such attitudes 'third-personal' because they are not used as the basis for making demands on people; rather, they merely report the impression of merit, or demerit one has towards third parties. Morality, by contrast, involves what Darwall calls a 'second-personal' perspective, a practice of placing demands on one another. When someone violates our rights, we feel indignation at them and we are entitled to address them face-to-face ('second-personal')—for example, by blaming them or demanding that they stop the violation. On Darwall's view, morality involves a kind of relationship between people which consists in the authority, or standing, to make second-personal demands on others and to regulate one's behaviour in the light of those demands. By contrast, no such standing exists with respect to attitudes like esteem, admiration, or contempt towards third parties.[30] If I believe that my work attracts far less esteem than it deserves, I have no moral standing to call my peers to account. My lack of status as an academic does not constitute a moral relation between me and the rest of the

[29] Darwall calls societies organised around the idea of status 'orders of honor respect', and contrasts them with orders based on respecting others morally, as persons. In his *Honor, History, and Relationships: Essays in Second Personal Ethics II* (Oxford: Oxford University Press, 2013), p. 36, he writes: 'honor respect's object is not, though second-personal respect's object is, an essentially normative idea. The dignity of persons we acknowledge in second-personal respect is their being warranted objects of respect—as I analyze it, their having the authority to demand this respect, or as Rawls puts it, their being "self-originating sources of valid claims" (Rawls 1980: 546). Whether someone has status or rank, however, is simply a matter of whether he or she is in fact the recipient of the relevant honor respect.'

[30] Darwall, *Morality, Authority and Law: Essays in Second-Personal Ethics* (Oxford: Oxford University Press, 2013), p. 36.

academic community. By contrast, I do have standing to blame a colleague who stole my work, however bad it was.

Of course, institutions that award goods on the basis of merit, such as jobs, must rate the applicant's work. But it is their work that they are meant to be rating, not the esteem of the applicant. And they are meant to do so against specific criteria. The academic sector is particularly poor at grasping this point. Departments, even in top universities, sometimes award a chair to a person who is highly esteemed in the profession, but who has produced little work, or work of little value. Some universities ask for 'esteem indicators' in promotion applications or rate articles on the basis of the 'prestige' of the journals in which they were published. They should try to read the actual work instead. And we all have come across top-quality work by people who are not esteemed simply because very few people have read their work.

So the complaint 'why don't you rate me?' cannot be a moral complaint even if one deserves to be rated by others. It cannot be the object of a moral right. If, therefore, we have reasons to have an honours system whereby we collectively express publicly esteem for the people we rate, this cannot be because these people have a moral right to that esteem. Any justification for an honours system must be instrumental, of the kind offered by Montesquieu and Adams.

8.7 The Argument from the Public Ecology of Esteem

To recap: I have assumed that there might be public benefits to an honours system, and specifically the award of honorific titles. In the case of public offices, such as the Houses of Parliament and the judiciary, honorific titles might help to attract competent and talented individuals, or to disincentivise them from being corrupted by money. In Montesquieu's words, honours can oblige people to do phenomenal actions of sacrifice for the common good, just for 'the renown of these actions'. In the case of recognition of achievement or service, honours might help to promote excellence in science, arts, humanities, or sports. In the case of bravery, it might help to promote civic-mindedness or ethical behaviour more broadly. Though no individual has a *right* to these honours, we might collectively be better-off by having a practice to that effect.

Still, I think it is reasonable to worry about whether the award of honorific titles conflicts with individual rights and in particular the right to be treated as an equal. People might have in mind here the social dimension of the right to be treated as an equal, namely the right to equal standing in our social interactions. Under the heading of relational equality,[31] political philosophers have objected to

[31] See Samuel Scheffler, *Equality and Tradition, Questions of Value in Moral and Political Theory* (Oxford: Oxford University Press, 2010).

an 'administrative' conception of equality; one that is concerned solely with how the state distributes resources to individuals. They have emphasised instead the pertinence of equality in how people interact with one another, especially in their day-to-day interactions.

I think that the focus of relational egalitarians on how we interact socially with one another is rightly placed. As citizens, we must be able to look each other in the eye. Philip Pettit calls this the 'eyeball' test: 'people should be so resourced and protected in the basic choices of life—for short, the basic liberties—that they can look others in the eye without reason for fear or deference of the kind that a power of interference might inspire'.[32] Similarly, Waldron argues that, with the advent of human rights and equality, we were all elevated to the status of an earl or a duke and 'we look up to each other'.[33] For Waldron, our status as free and equal citizens, with the same human rights and civil liberties guaranteed by law, has made us all nobles, enjoying the dignity that in the past was only a privilege for the few.

Yet it is not easy to concretise what fundamental human equality requires in the social sphere. There are many people with whom one interacts daily and towards whom one will harbour a range of negative attitudes, from indifference to contempt. As argued before, there is no right to the public expression of esteem on the part of others and no duty to express equal esteem to everyone. Moreover, social interaction takes place against the background of several unequal distributions, such as with respect to income or wealth, many of which might be justifiable under a theory of distributive justice. For example, if I prioritise family life over work, there is nothing wrong about having less income than a hard-working academic who does the opposite and has gained substantial pay rises. It is fine if I run into them while boarding a plane and they are in first class, whereas I am in economy. And it is equally fine if they indicate subtly that they do not rate my work, acknowledging me with a fake smile as they turn left into the first class section of the plane. We can still be said to look each other in the eyes. But what if their ticket reads 'Sir Jo Doe'?

I think there is a difference there and I will seek to explain why. The key idea is that we should not only be concerned with inequality in the distribution of resources but also, as Kolodny emphasises in his book,[34] with *inferiority*. If nobility in monarchical society was premised on a particular management of societal esteem, then in an egalitarian society it is not enough to distribute goods and rights equally. We must also keep an eye on how social esteem operates in the public domain. But what is government meant to do in that domain? Seek to tamper with

[32] Philip Pettit, *Just Freedom: A Moral Compass for a Complex World* (New York: W. W. Norton, 2014), p. 16.

[33] Waldron, *Dignity, Rank and Rights*, p. 60.

[34] Niko Kolodny, *The Pecking Order: Social Hierarchy as a Philosophical Problem* (Cambridge: Harvard University Press, 2023).

the distribution of esteem and tell us who to esteem and whom not? Or let a thousand flowers bloom?

I think it is problematic to take the former approach. Consider honorific titles that are not attached to any office (e.g. the judiciary or Parliament) but are awarded annually by the government upon recommendations of the Honours Committee.[35] Recall the discussion in Section 8.2 about what honorific titles are. They are not merely a recognition of distinction. It is a way to create a top-down hierarchy of esteem and to make that hierarchy relevant to social interactions, through the use of terms of address. Honorific titles would not be a positional good if it was not the case that one has the right to use them in their social encounters (e.g. telephone calls, emails, bookings and purchases, public events, etc.) and expect others to acknowledge them and use them accordingly. Of course, there is no *legal* obligation to address someone as Sir or Dame. Nevertheless, there is a rigid social norm without which honorific titles would not be a positional good. And if honorific titles were not a positional good, then they would not be able to produce the instrumental benefits for the public good under Montesquieu's argument. In other words, honorific titles can only exist, and perform their instrumental function, if there is a social norm that puts pressure on people to use them. And the use of honorific titles carries a clear social meaning, calling for the expression of deference in social interactions. Finally, and this is crucial, honorific titles under the UK honours system are awarded by the government, rather than some private or charitable organisation dedicated to the advancement of a particular discipline. A knighthood is not an Oscar, or an induction to the Rock & Roll Hall of Fame. It is awarded in the name of the whole political community (i.e. in the name of us collectively). Its expressive message is that citizens ought to endorse the ranking of esteem adopted by the government and use it in their social interactions.

And herein lies the main moral objection to honorific titles, in my view. In an egalitarian society, government has no right to project a ranking of societal esteem in the way people interact with one another, let alone one which calls for deference. It is for each one of us to decide what, if any, level of esteem to express in our social interactions, and to seek to influence the public ecology of esteem accordingly. It is part of our fundamental right to freedom of thought and expression.[36] To be compelled, or even pushed, by government to express esteem violates this core liberal right. This entails, in turn, that there should be a public ecology of esteem: a bottom-up culture where esteem is distributed organically through the myriad individual choices we make as thinkers and speakers: from following or

[35] Some honours are still the prerogative of the King and of a resigning Prime Minister. The Committee submits recommendations for the monarch's New Year Honours List and the Birthday honours.

[36] For the normative link between thought and speech, and the wrongness of compelled speech, see Seana Shiffrin, *Speech Matters: On Lying, Morality and the Law* (Princeton: Princeton University Press, 2014).

liking someone's posts on social media, to attending their talks or gigs, buying their books or albums, or setting up a fan club.

That is not to say that a public ecology does not inevitably result in hierarchies and deference in social interactions. I may act in a deferential or even servile way if I meet my favourite author or musician. But this should be my choice, not one imposed on me by the government. In other words, the problem is not that esteem is inherently hierarchical or that it leads to deference or servility. The problem is that an honours system is a collective imposition of an official, top-down ranking of esteem which results in social deference for the wrong reasons. It imposed, admittedly in a non-coercive way but nevertheless rigidly, a group's ranking of esteem (the people who sit on the Honours Committee) on others. This imposition violates both equality (why should *anyone*'s ranking of esteem be imposed on others?) and individual rights (it is for each citizen to decide how much esteem and deference to express in their social interactions). Since this is a rights-based argument it should, if sound, prevail over any instrumental justification for an honours system. Even if awarding honorific titles produces instrumental benefits, it cannot trump each citizen's right to equality and freedom of thought and expression.

The previous section sought to establish that a distribution of societal esteem cannot be based on an individual moral right to be esteemed. I am now making the stronger argument that esteem is not the type of good that should be collectively distributed, at least not in the sense of expecting, demanding, or nudging people to comply *publicly* with an official ranking of esteem. I am assuming here that at least in large political communities, it is neither possible nor legitimate to eradicate citizens' disposition to rank each other on an esteem metric. I have no esteem for the Kardashians and for people who spent their whole day reading gossip magazines about them and I publicly express my contempt. And, no doubt, a whole lot of people have no esteem for what academics do. The solution is not that we should try collectively to suppress this disposition, or to project the message that the Kardashians are as estimable as say, John Rawls. Rather, in an egalitarian society, any public perception of the esteem that different people enjoy should be informal and develop in a bottom-up way, through everyone's decisions about when to express esteem and to whom. The public ecology of esteem, in other words, should be diffuse, dynamic, and unmediated by governmental action. As a result, it will vary from one sphere to another. A person may be highly esteemed at their sports club but enjoy low esteem at work, or in society more broadly.

I hope that the above argument helps to explain why we should find honorific titles objectionable. It is a way to unpack the worry that honorific titles prevent us from looking each other in the eye in the public sphere. I now want to turn to how the above argument plays out in the different categories of honorific titles: a) knighthoods and other honours for achievement or service; b) professional honorific titles, such as Dr and Professor; and c) honorific titles attached to public offices, such as judges (Lord Justice) and politicians.

8.8 Application

8.8.1 Honorific Titles Awarded for Achievement or Service

I should hasten to stress that the scope of my argument so far is rather narrow. It applies to honorific titles whose social meaning calls for deference, and which are awarded by the government for achievement. We should recall here the distinction between post-nominal honours awarded by institutions and associations dedicated to specific excellences, on one hand, and pre-nominal honorific titles awarded by the government, on the other. The first category includes honours such as being awarded the Nobel Prize by the Royal Swedish Academy of Sciences or being elected Fellow of the British Academy. These honours are not accompanied by honorific terms of address, and one is not expected to acknowledge them in social interactions. Their aim is not to shape the way citizens interact socially with one another, let alone call for deference. There is no 'FBA', or 'Nobel Prize' title option at Fortnum and Mason. It is therefore permissible, according to the argument so far, that academies or associations dedicated to a particular form of excellence award honours to individuals. The British Academy of Film and Television Arts (BAFTA) does not have the power to change how people address those who win its awards. Unlike the government, they have no power to award honorific titles. If I am not into cinema or television, I would not know how esteemed a BAFTA winner is, nor would I care. If I interact with them socially, and they do not carry an honorific title, I will express the amount of esteem that I deem to be appropriate.

One might object here that my argument hangs on a technicality—that is, on whether an honour comes with a pre-nominal title. But the argument is more complex than that. First, pre-nominal titles have a rigid social meaning, largely due to their historical provenance, which projects a social hierarchy between people. Second, pre-nominal honorific titles are awarded annually by the government (i.e. in the name of us all) and therefore constitute a collective endorsement of a hierarchy of esteem between citizens. Third, there are practised social norms, and hence social pressure, to use a person's honorific title in social interactions, even outside their professional activities. By contrast, there are no such norms with respect to awards or fellowships of sector-specific associations.

Another objection might be that I am making too much of the social norms around terms of address. Some people who hold knighthoods do not use their title in their social interactions or signature, nor do they expect others to use them. I have heard some title holders say that it makes them very uncomfortable. And no doubt there are people who could not care less about whether someone is knighted and would never address them as Sir or Dame. I am not denying that this is the case and I have no empirical evidence about how regularly the relevant etiquette norms are observed. My point is that honorific titles would not be able to serve as a positional good if they were not used in practice by both the holder and the public, perhaps against their deeply held beliefs. The fact that the UK honours system has persisted for a long period of time, and that most people accept the honour,[37] shows that the social norms have sufficient rigidity to make honorific titles a positional good. Even if we suppose, however, that the relevant social conventions are withering away, a state attempt to get people to conform to a convention that seeks to create a social hierarchy of esteem would still be in breach of the value of social equality, as it would risk instituting such hierarchy.

8.8.2 Honorific Titles Attached to Professions

Perhaps the most widely used title is that of a medical doctor. It is both a pre-nominal title and a term of address. It is primarily descriptive, denoting the functions of a person's professional role, rather than honorific. It is awarded by the relevant professional body upon completion of a degree and relevant practice. Its historical provenance is not tied to the institution of monarchy and nobility. Doctors have existed throughout human history and in radically different types of systems of government. So this case is outside the scope of the argument I made so far and its use appears far less objectionable that that of Dames and Baronesses. Still, we may question why the profession of a medical doctor should be adorned with a pre-nominal title in social interactions, whereas other professions are not. There are hundreds of occupations, some of them very important socially, that do not have a pre-nominal title. A nurse, for example, will not find a title on which to click on the British Airways website, let alone on Fortnum and Mason's.

And indeed, a great deal seems to hang on the title of a doctor. Consider the controversy around medical titles discussed in chapter 4. Various experts complain that so-called CAM ('Complementary and Alternative Medicine') therapies—such as homeopathy, nutritional therapies, acupuncture, and chiropractic treatment—are often placebos, not based on medical evidence.[38] And they are also concerned about the use of the title 'doctor' by healthcare practitioners who are not medical doctors.[39] The concern is partly motivated by the fact that the use of the title is

[37] Not everyone, of course. David Bowie turned down a knighthood in 2003.

[38] See R. B. Bausell, *Snake Oil Science: The Truth about Complementary and Alternative Medicine* (Oxford: Oxford University Press; 2007).

[39] See David Colquhoun, 'Doctor Who? Inappropriate Use of Titles by Some Alternative "Medicine" Practitioners', 121 (1278) *New Zealand Medical Journal* (2008), pp. 6–10.

often illicit, made by unscrupulous practitioners who aim to deceive the public about their medical qualifications and who pose a threat to patients' health.[40] But sometimes the concern is wider. In the United States, nursing schools nowadays offer a professional doctorate in nursing practice (a 'DNP'). This is not equivalent to a PhD, but it nevertheless confers on graduates the title 'doctor'. Nursing practitioners think it is important that holders of a DNP are able to use the title 'Doctor' in their nursing practice.[41] But medical doctors are worried that losing the exclusive use of the title 'doctor' within the healthcare sector will result in losing control over the profession, with nurses gaining powers to treat patients directly, without a referral by a medical doctor.[42] They believe that, because of their extensive training, they should be the sole gatekeepers of patients' entry to medical care.

One might interpret the medical doctors' concern as an attempt to maintain their superior status of esteem. If every healthcare practitioner has the title of a doctor, then the positionality of their title is radically diminished. A similar concern, I think, might be seen in the recent academic practice in the UK of awarding professorships to university staff on the basis other than research. Doctors (and professors), moreover, use their titles not only in a professional setting (i.e. in their interaction with patients), but also socially, in their interactions with everyone. A postperson will deliver a parcel to Dr Jo Doe and might be inclined to show social deference not shown to other recipients. So, we must be able to explain why this should be the case, particularly if only some professions enjoy this privilege.

I think, however, that the title of a doctor differs substantially from those awarded as honours. It tracks a status that has a distinctive function: to treat patients. The status is primarily relational, capturing the interaction between doctors and patients. It is moreover, an asymmetrical one in that patients are vulnerable vis-à-vis doctors. By assigning a status ('doctor') to the stronger party we collectively signal to the status-holder that they bear a special responsibility not to exploit the vulnerability of the weaker party. In addition, we signal to the weaker party (the patient) that the interaction with the stronger party poses a threat to their rights and that they bear this heightened moral responsibility. The heightened moral responsibility is built-into the status of the doctor.

This argument here is not that, by allowing doctors to use a unique title, there will be fewer instances of patient abuse, say because doctors will be better regulated, or better motivated to refrain from abusing their patients. I do not mean it in instrumental terms, in the way Montesquieu does. Rather it is that, given the asymmetrical nature of a standing social interaction between doctors and patients,

[40] See A. Gilbey, 'Use of Inappropriate Titles by New Zealand Practitioners of Acupuncture, Chiropractic, and Osteopathy', 121 (1278) *New Zealand Medical Journal* (2008), pp. 15–20.

[41] See Nancy Dirubbo, 'Words Matter', 31 *Journal of the American Association of Nurse Practitioners* (2019), pp. 280–281.

[42] Gardiner Harris, 'When the Nurse Wants to Be Called Doctor', *New York Times*, 1 October 2011, available at: https://www.nytimes.com/2011/10/02/health/policy/02docs.html

status is a way to project the value of human equality into the relation and assure the weaker party that their rights will be taken seriously.

Now, unfortunately for my own titles, this argument does not quite extend to non-medical doctors and professors. There is an asymmetrical relation there too, of course, between teachers and students. When used within an educational context, the titles of (non-medical) doctor and professor, can be seen as referring to the general status of a teacher. In that context, their use is therefore justified in the same way as a doctor's title is. But not everyone who teaches students is a (non-medical) doctor or a professor, and not every (non-medical) doctor or professor is a teacher. And unlike medical doctors, there is no rationale for professors to use their title outside an academic setting—say, when they take a plane. There are no legal philosophy emergencies on a plane.[43] There are, by contrast, medical emergencies, and being able to identify a nearby doctor serves a valuable goal, without compromising social equality. Admittedly, I struggle to see the rationale for why the postperson or the flight attendant should address me as Professor, as much as I may welcome it.

Of course, I do think that the pursuit of academic knowledge is an intrinsic good and that if many people who do not pursue knowledge are given professorships, then this undermines the pursuit of knowledge. Moreover, professorships are not awarded by the government in the name of the community, so the social meaning of the projected hierarchy is less rigid. Recall that my argument placed emphasis on government's involvement in creating an official hierarchy of social esteem, as a constitutive element of the wrong. Nor is the title 'professor' tied to inegalitarian societies based on nobility. So, I do not think that the value of social equality *condemns* the use of professorial titles, at least compared to knighthoods. And it is comforting that in a heavily materialistic and consumerist culture, academics are recognised in public discourse. But these considerations do not appear strong enough to justify a social norm whereby the titles of academics, but not other professions, are used as terms of address in social interactions outside the university.

Could Montesquieu's instrumental argument apply here? It is often said that in our profession we do not get paid well, or enough, but that at least we enjoy societal respect and the prestige of our title. The thought would be that this perk is a way to attract talented people to academia and away from becoming bankers or lawyers, and to sustain excellence in the pursuit of knowledge, which is a public good. And this can all be done 'on the cheap', so to speak ('great actions done just for the renown of these actions' in Montesquieu's terms).

I am sceptical, however, about the empirical assumptions of this argument and whether people's choice to become academics is the product of a judgment based

[43] A renowned philosopher uses this out-of-office message: 'I am away on sabbatical leave. If your query is urgent, you should contact someone other than a philosopher.'

on this calculation. More importantly, I am sceptical that the prestige of a title is the right motivation to become an academic and, for that matter, to hold public office. Clearly, the proper motivation for taking up an academic profession is a genuine interest in the pursuit of knowledge. And the same should be said about public officials: we should worry if their main motivation for holding public office is the status that comes with it. In this respect, status stands alongside money and power, as inappropriate motivations for holding public office. In fact, this worry should perhaps apply with greater force to status, if it is empirically the case that human thirst for status, unlike power or money, is insatiable.[44]

8.8.3 Public Officials

Honorific titles for public offices present a hybrid case. Unlike professional titles (such as Dr) they are awarded by the government, rather than a professional association. But unlike knighthoods, they pertain to a status with distinct functions, such as the functions of a judge. And that is a crucial point: like the status of a doctor, the status of a judge pertains to a bilateral asymmetrical relation, that between the court and the litigant. These bilateral relations (what I call in this book role-status) have weaker and stronger parties. They are asymmetrical in that the weaker party suffers from dependencies of vulnerabilities vis-à-vis the stronger party. Similarly, for the relation between Members of parliament (MPs) and constituents. Within the context of these interactions, the argument made in favour of doctors' titles also applies. The judge has a set of duties and responsibilities towards litigants in virtue of holding that role and it is morally significant to signal this set to both the weaker and the stronger party.

So, the government's involvement in the creation and use of judges' titles can be justified in that it is not aimed at placing societal esteem on them, but at signalling the heightened moral responsibilities of the judge. True, the term of address used in the UK is the generic term (Lord/Lady Justice) that we have inherited from the period of nobility and raises concerns about social hierarchy and deference. An appropriate modernising reform, like the one which renamed the judicial branch of the House of Lords to 'UK Supreme Court', would be to change the title to 'Justice Jo Doe', as is the practice in the United States.

The case of members of the legislature is like that of a judge. In the United States, members of the Senate and the House of Representatives are addressed as 'Senator Jo Doe' and 'Congressman/Congresswoman Jo Doe' respectively. Insofar as voters are in an asymmetrical relation with legislators (I think they obviously are), then these titles can be justified as a way to denote that relation.

44 A claim made by Cecilia Ridgeway in Ridgeway, *Status*.

In the UK, by contrast, Members of Parliament (MPs) do not have a title. The term 'The Honourable Member' is used only in the chamber of the House of Commons when MPs refer to one another. The convention is that MPs do not address each other by name, nor directly, but instead address the speaker and use the name of the MP's constituency to refer to each other (e.g. 'The Honourable Member for Holborn and St Pancras'). The convention is used to cultivate civil exchanges between MPs rather than encourage the public to refer the MPs in a way that expresses esteem. Outside the House of Commons, MPs do not use 'Rt Hon.' as a title. But if an MP becomes a member of the Cabinet, and thereby of the Privy Council, then they do acquire the title 'Right Honourable' (Rt Hon.) which they keep for life, even if they leave office. According to the argument put forward here this is problematic: both the minister and the MP hold offices that impact the interests of citizens. They are the stronger party in a role-status relation (official/citizen) and they should both have titles that register publicly this asymmetry.

By contrast, there is less justification for the practice of awarding nobility titles to peers in the House of Lords and referring to them as Lords and Ladies, even if there is a plausible justification for an unelected second chamber. Apart from the problematic connotations of these titles, peers in the House of Lords have no constituents. They are not elected, and they do not represent citizens. Though they do have the power to delay and improve legislation, they are nevertheless not in a direct relation with citizens.

There is, finally, one crucial upshot of my argument: holders of a public office may only use their title *while* in office. Since the title aims to signal the moral responsibilities owed to a weaker party in a relation, there is no rationale for using the title when one cannot impact the interests of the weaker party. This upshot is against part of the current practice: former Presidents of the United States, for instance, are addressed as 'President Jo Doe'. But the practice is less uniform about retired judges.

8.9 Conclusion

What's in a title? A lot, I have tried to show. Honorific titles are positional social goods created by the government with a view to expressing esteem publicly and thereby instituting a formal and top-down hierarchy of esteem. This hierarchy is not innocuous but corrupts the public ecology of esteem by calling for social deference based on arbitrary grounds. One of the oldest attempts to justify titles is the argument that this practice promotes the common good by motivating self-interested individuals to perform actions 'just for the renown of those actions'.

I have argued that this argument is instrumental and cannot be premised on an individual moral right to be esteemed, even if one deserves to be esteemed. Moreover, I questioned whether this is the right motivation to have for people who take up public office or pursue knowledge. I then sought to show that the instrumental argument fails because it conflicts with rights-based considerations and in particular the right to equal standing in social interactions. My argument was based on the claim that government has no business tampering with the public ecology of esteem by instituting an official, top-down, ranking of esteem. Each one of us has a right to try to shape the public ecology of esteem from the bottom-up, and a right that no one (particularly the government) imposes an official order of esteem in our social interactions. Though esteem inevitably creeps into our social interactions, rankings of esteem should be informal and diffuse, and be the aggregate product of people's ever changing views about who is estimable and who isn't. When this is the case, we can meaningfully say that *we look each other in the eyes* in the public domain.

The application of this account to the UK practice of using honorific titles has not produced clear results, as applied philosophy often does. I have defended the use of descriptive pre-nominal titles (such as 'Doctor Joe' and 'Justice Joe'), when stripped of associations with nobility, on the basis that they stress they heightened moral responsibilities of the functions of the status-holder, rather than place esteem. But I have argued against the governmental award of honorific knighthoods, which are not tied to any functions, as well as honours awarded to peers in the House of Lords. Reform of parliamentary titles is long overdue, but no doubt unlikely to come any time soon. Finally, the argument does not condemn the practice of awards by non-governmental organisations (e.g. by the British Academy, BAFTA, or the Academy of Motion Picture Arts and Sciences), when it is not accompanied by pre-nominal honorific titles. These awards perform valuable instrumental functions, without compromising social equality.

9
FROM CONTRACT TO STATUS—AN INCOMPLETE TRANSITION

I have argued in this book that, despite our natural status as moral equals, we all enter certain asymmetrical social relations around key components of our ethical lives: family, politics, labour, housing, health, and education. These relations pose a threat to equality for two reasons: first, because they harbour tendencies by the stronger party to exploit the weaknesses and vulnerabilities of the weaker party; and second, because the weaker party faces the risk of losing their self-esteem and, in turn, taking themselves to be socially inferior. Social recognition, a key dimension of the idea of status, is morally required to project the value of equality into these relations. Law has an essential role to play, not only by vesting the weaker party with prophylactic rights and duties but also by registering publicly that, despite having weaker and stronger parties, these social interactions remain relations between moral equals. Being a party to these relations is an important social role that is inherently normative, the basis for a set of moral rights and duties. Status is not an archaic and problematic idea, but an important moral notion. Few would argue that the status of an employee, or a minor, are not morally significant. But we have lost sight of the fact that they are instances of a general moral category with a long philosophical pedigree. Though status does not capture all problems of social inequality, it does single out a distinct and unified area of moral concern.

I should like to end by returning to Henry Maine's thesis that we have historically progressed from status to contract. As I sought to explain in this book, his thesis not only distorted the moral dimension of status but also contributed to treating various social relations as purely contractual. It eclipsed the relational character of status and the asymmetry that characterises it. It left Antonio, the character with whom this book started, thinking that, as an employee, it's his responsibility to own a vehicle; that losing his job was on him. It prioritised the notion of contractual freedom, obscuring the fact that many contractual relations, as well as several non-contractual, are inherently asymmetrical.

Contrary to Henry Maine's influential thesis, the transition that took place historically is a transition within role-status, rather than a transition from status to contract. The law used to side with the stronger party to status relations concerning labour, family, and housing. In the beginning of the twentieth century, it treated these relations as purely contractual, allowing the stronger party to dictate unfair terms in the name of freedom of contract. This was in no small part due

Status in Law and Morality. George Letsas, Oxford University Press. © George Letsas 2026.
DOI: 10.1093/9780198936725.003.0009

to the influence of Maine's thesis, and of the historical school of jurisprudence, upon judges and lawyers. But after the second half of the twentieth century, the law started to side with the weaker party (the employee, and the tenant). Nowadays, countries with progressive legislation impose statutory limitations to contractual freedom. Legal systems started to break free from the doctrinal spell of Maine's thesis that mandatory restrictions on contractual freedom signal a regressive move.

People who are sceptical about resurrecting the notion of status often have in mind the notion of *rank*-status, what Pufendorf called *dignitas* (as opposed to *dignatio*). They associate status with nobility, aristocracy, or—nowadays—celebrities. It does not help that Waldron's influential account of dignity, which seeks to defend the equal moral worth of people, also employs this ranking notion of status. But this approach, I have argued, is flawed, since it does not do justice to the legal and moral history of status, which was never about societal esteem. The more fundamental notion of status was always that of role-status, tracking social relations that pose a threat to social equality and that need to be recognised and regulated. It was *role*-status, not *rank*-status, that was taken to be the basis of legal rights and duties.

Still, the transition from contract back to status remains largely incomplete. Many statuses, like that of a tenant, are not adequately recognised and protected, contributing to homelessness.[1] Moreover, there are various new threats posed to the weaker parties within these role-statuses. The gig economy has created new ways of exploiting workers. The way the property market works in big cities (e.g. because of short-let online platforms) is reducing rapidly the availability of affordable housing, exacerbating the vulnerable position of tenants. Powerful corporations lobby governments to refrain from regulating commercial activities, securing a near monopoly, and imposing unfair terms on consumers—particularly with respect to the digital use of their personal data. The deterioration of the public healthcare system drives patients to the private sector, which typically charges high medical fees for unnecessary treatments.

Of course, there are other sources of resistance towards adequate protection of status, such as neoliberal political ideologies, or social conservatism. Governments often defend the lack of regulation, or deregulation, on the basis that it boosts the economy and, as a result, everyone benefits. But this argument is flawed, wrongly pitching the egalitarian moral duty to protect vulnerable parties against economic efficiency, as if efficiency is a genuine moral value.[2] We must not let contractual freedom call all the shots in the name of economic growth. To do so would be to offend the moral value of social equality which takes precedence over any concern

[1] For the many ways in which legal institutions are responsible for homelessness see Beth Watts-Combe and Lynne McCrorie, 'Structural Injustice, Homelessness and the Law', in Virginia Mantouvalou and Jonathan Wolff (eds), *Structural Injustice and the Law* (London: UCL Press, 2025).

[2] See Ronald Dworkin, 'Is Wealth a Value?', 9(2) *The Journal of Legal Studies* (1980), pp. 191–226.

about market efficiency or economic growth. Status as a moral idea, which this book defended, can help to boost the political argument for statutory intervention and more effective regulation. We must stress that, morally speaking, employees, tenants, and patients are entitled to legal protection *qua* status holders. These are not relations whose terms the stronger party may dictate at will.

The role-based conception of status, as I have presented here, can help to place these relations out of the realm of short-term, party-political changes and into the core principles of the relevant area of law, protected by courts. It is not an accident that, from a doctrinal viewpoint, fewer and fewer interactions fall within contract law proper, and have formed instead a special area of law, such as consumer law or medical law, where different principles apply.

A related reason why the transition from contract to status remains incomplete is that we have lost sight of the fact that status is primarily a moral relation, one that is governed by the value of equality. The statuses of an employee, or a tenant, are not artificial legal constructions. Unlike say, the statuses of a consignor or a carrier, they are not a legal shorthand for referring to a set of rights and duties that the law happens to assign at a given time and for a given activity. As Pufendorf saw centuries ago, statuses are primarily moral entities, granting their holders a set of rights and duties. Status, as a moral concept, is now largely neglected in law, having suffered a blow by the distortions of the historical school of jurisprudence. Yet appreciating the moral significance of status, and the way in which it serves as 'a moral field for persons to exist in', as Pufendorf puts it, is essential, if they are to be adequately regulated. Legal recognition of role-status protects a vital moral defence to which the weaker party is entitled: by protecting their equal self-esteem, weaker parties can insist on equal terms of social cooperation. We need to rehabilitate the notion of moral and legal status.

In legal practice, the gap left by insufficient statutory regulation of status relations has been partially filled by human rights litigation. Human rights courts have intervened to protect the statuses of children born out of marriage,[3] employees,[4] domestic workers,[5] and tenants.[6] Scholars have started to turn to the idea of vulnerability as a key dimension of human rights protection.[7] And human rights courts have been willing to examine complaints arising within private law disputes, on the basis that they—indirectly—engage the responsibility of the state, when state

[3] *Marckx v Belgium*, European Court of Human Rights, Judgment of 13 June 1979.

[4] *Barbulescu v Romania*, European Court of Human Rights, Judgment of 5 September 2017. For a human rights approach to the status of employment see Joe Atkinson, 'Employment Status and Human Rights: An Emerging Approach', 86(5) *Modern Law Review* (2023), pp. 1166–1196.

[5] *Siliadin v France*, European Court of Human Rights, Judgment of 26 July 2005.

[6] *Kasmi v Albania*, European Court of Human Rights, Judgment of 23 June 2020.

[7] See Corina Heri, *Responsive Human Rights: Vulnerability, Ill-treatment and the ECtHR* (Oxford: Hart, 2023).

courts interpret and apply private law.[8] This trend, in turn, has led scholars to speak of a process of 'constitutionalisation'[9] of private law, implying that the relevant relations were previously subject only to freedom of contract. These developments are no doubt positive. But we might be sceptical about whether human rights law, on its own, can offer adequate protection of status relations. We need much more than the intervention of human rights courts. I think this is so for several reasons.

First, there is a lingering prejudice against the idea that human rights law should also protect rights that arise, not simply in virtue of our humanity, but out of special private relations or transactions. The claim that human rights are rights we have *simply* in virtue of being human has been a recurrent theme in the philosophy of human rights.[10] It is offered as a criterion to demarcate human rights as a subset of moral and legal rights and to block expansive or 'overreaching' interpretations.[11] It rides on the back of conservative attacks on human rights courts, whose true target is individual rights themselves. And it puts pressure on judges to narrow the scope of human rights, using arbitrary doctrinal devices such as the margin of appreciation.[12]

To be sure, the philosophical distinction between natural rights and rights arising out of special relations is an old one, going back at least as far as Pufendorf. But there is no reason why this philosophical distinction should have any bearing on legal practice. If human rights law were to be restricted to natural rights, and exclude status-based rights, it would shrink to an unrecognisable degree. It would have to exclude rights one has in virtue of being an employee, a family member, a tenant, a patient, or even the stronger party to a status-relation, such as being a judge.[13] The view that our legal human rights should only encompass our natural rights does not fit the practice of human rights, nor should it do so.[14]

[8] This is known as the horizontal effect of human rights and as the doctrine of 'drittwirkung' in German Constitutional Law.

[9] See H.-W. Micklitz (ed.), *The Constitutionalisation of European Private Law* (Oxford: Oxford University Press, 2014).

[10] The theme has come back to prominence since the publication of James Griffin's book *On Human Rights* (Oxford: Oxford University Press, 2008) and the debate between political and moral conceptions of human rights to which it gave rise. See Adam Etinson (ed.), *Human Rights: Moral or Political?* (Oxford: Oxford University Press, 2018).

[11] The Universal Declaration of Human Rights (UDHR) is often criticised for making reference to the right to leisure and to 'periodic holidays with pay', which no human rights court has ever enforced.

[12] I have criticised this doctrine in George Letsas, 'Two Concepts of the Margin of Appreciation', 26(4) *Oxford Journal of Legal Studies* (2006), pp. 705–732; George Letsas, 'The Margin of Appreciation Revisited: A Reply to Follesdal', in Adam Etinson (ed.), *Human Rights: Moral or Political?* (Oxford: Oxford University Press, 2018).

[13] The rights of judges not to be arbitrarily dismissed by government have been protected by human rights courts. See *Oleksandr Volkov v Ukraine*, European Court of Human Rights, Judgment of 9 January 2013; *Baka v Hungary*, European Court of Human Rights, Judgment of 23 June 2016. Upholding these rights is perfectly justified under status morality, whereas it wouldn't be under the orthodox theory of human rights.

[14] I have argued that there is no 'one size fits all' theory of the practice of human rights in George Letsas, 'Dworkin on Human Rights', 6(2) *Jurisprudence* (2015), pp. 327–340.

More importantly, the distinction between natural rights and status-based rights is artificial from the point of view of the value of equality. As we saw, both our natural (human) status and our adventitious (role-based) statuses are governed by the value of equality. For instance, as far as the foundations of human rights are concerned, there is no doubt that labour rights are human rights,[15] even though they arise within the context of a private relation; not everyone is or will be an employee. Perhaps the law should prefer the term 'fundamental rights' as European Union law does,[16] severing the strict conceptual identification of this area of law only with natural rights—that is, rights we have 'simply' in virtue of being human. The putative test of rights we have '*simply* in virtue of being human' has failed spectacularly to account for human rights practice and its appeal is hopefully diminishing.

The second, related, reason why we might want more than human rights law to protect status is that the current wording of human rights treaties tends to focus on general rights rather than relation-specific rights. As a result, it does not project adequately the existence of an asymmetrical relation and the fact that there are rights and duties one has *qua* the weaker party (and correspondingly, *qua* the stronger party) in a relation. Though human rights treaties recognise the rights of citizens (and non-nationals) against government, it generally frames rights by identifying interests of well-being (e.g. to private life, expression, property), rather than the asymmetrical bilateral relations through which these interests are pursued. The fact that the stronger party (e.g. the employer, or the landlord) has relation-specific moral duties tends to go unnoticed. It is not just our relation with the government, and its courts, that is asymmetrical, but also our relations with actors with whom we interact non-episodically, and which impact significant aspects of our well-being.

Finally, as human rights courts themselves often point out using the idea of positive obligations,[17] the effective protection of vulnerable status-holders requires large-scale legislative interventions. Government may need to introduce criminal sanctions to protect domestic workers from conditions of slavery. It may need to invest resources to reduce how long it takes litigants to have their case decided by courts. It may need to introduce a proportionality assessment to the test of unfair dismissal within employment law. These things require statutory intervention by the legislature, for which human rights litigation can and should serve as an impetus. Often, existing legislation, seemingly innocuous, creates and exacerbates vulnerabilities within status relations.[18] Proper legal regulation of status requires a

[15] See Virginia Mantouvalou, 'Are Labour Rights Human Rights?', 3(2) *European Labour Law Journal* (2012), pp. 151–172.

[16] See the Charter of Fundamental Rights of the European Union.

[17] See Vladislava Stoyanova, *Positive Obligations under the European Convention on Human Rights* (Oxford: Oxford University Press, 2023).

[18] For the idea of state-mediating structural injustice, see Virginia Mantouvalou, *Structural Injustice and Workers' Rights* (Oxford: Oxford University Press, 2023). For an argument that protection of legal status can address structural injustice see George Letsas, 'Structural Injustice and the Law: A Philosophical Framework', in Virginia Mantouvalou and Jonathan Wolff (eds), *Structural Injustice and the Law* (2025).

stable and detailed statutory framework that signals publicly the importance of the relevant social relation and prevents *ex ante* the stronger party from abusing their position, rather than merely compensating the weaker party *ex post facto*.

It was beyond the scope of this book to examine normative gaps or inconsistencies in the legal doctrine of different jurisdictions, with respect to this or that status. This is work for another day, holding the theory firm and shifting one's focus to the 'facts on the ground'. My aim here was to provide a general philosophical theory of status. I can only hope that the role-based conception of status defended in this book will strengthen the political argument for social recognition and for more effective legal protection of employees, tenants, patients, students, consumers, prisoners, and anyone who finds themselves in an asymmetrical social relation. We cannot escape status. But we collectively can make sure that, in both law and morality, we each enjoy the status to which we are entitled.

Index

For the benefit of digital users, indexed terms that span two pages (e.g., 52–53) may, on occasion, appear on only one of those pages.